CATTLE KINGDOM

KINGDOM

Early Ranching in Alberta

To the memory of my father.

CATTLE KINGDOM

Early Ranching in Alberta

Edward Brado

VICTORIA • VANCOUVER • CALGARY

Orginally published by Douglas and McIntyre 1984
First Heritage House edition 2004. Reprinted 2009

Heritage House Publishing Company Ltd.
#108 – 17665 66A Avenue
Surrey, BC V3S 2A7
www.heritagehouse.ca

Library and Archives Canada Cataloguing in Publication
Brado, Edward.
    Cattle kingdom: early ranching in Alberta / Edward Brado.

Includes bibliographical references.
ISBN 978-1-894384-57-5

    1. Ranching—Alberta—History. 2. Northwest Territories—History—
1870–1905. I. Title.

FC3670.R3B72 2004   971.23'02   C2004-901706-3

Heritage House acknowledges the financial support for its publishing program from the
Government of Canada through the Book Publishing Industry Development Program
(BPIDP), Canada Council for the Arts, and the province of British Columbia through
the British Columbia Arts Council and the Book Publishing Tax Credit.

Printed in Canada

Acknowledgements

Many people have contributed significantly to this book. The original stimulus came from reading L.V. Kelly's 1913 account of the southern Alberta range, *The Range Men: The Story of the Ranchers and Indians of Alberta*. Kelly's book has been followed by more scholarly and balanced works, but it still conveys best the authentic flavour of the early west.

I owe a great debt to Grant MacEwan of Calgary and David Breen of the University of British Columbia for their extensive research and writing on southern Alberta. I thank Bert Sheppard of Longview for reading and advising me on portions of the manuscript; Harry Brayne and the late Charlie MacKinnon, both of Calgary, for their reminiscences; Jean Hoare and Marjorie Sharples, both of Claresholm, for material on the Oxley and Winder ranches respectively; Eloise and Chester Davis of Fort Macleod for background on their town, and Bryan and Hazel Shantz, formerly of Nanton, for their hospitality on my visits to southern Alberta.

Dorothy Blades of the Rocking P Ranch at Nanton and Hugh Dempsey of Calgary contributed their profound knowledge of the range, its people and customs, and as well read the full manuscript.

I appreciate the assistance of the staffs of the Glenbow-Alberta Institute Archives and Library of Calgary, the Public Archives of Canada in Ottawa, the Parkland Regional Library in Lacombe and the Historical Society of Montana Archives in Helena; of Ruth Bertelsen Fraser and Bob Amussen, my patient editors, and of Alda Brado, my mother.

The following have kindly granted me permission to quote from previously published works; Doubleday Inc. for *Where the Wagon Led* by R.D. Symons and *The Pioneer Years* by Barry Broadfoot; Constance Loree for *Before the Fences* by Fred Ings, and the Glenbow-Alberta Institute for *Letters from a Lady Rancher* by Monica Hopkins and *The Big White Hat* by W.J. Wilde.

And finally, a note on spellings and names. I have used the English spelling "ranche" where it was customarily used at the time, rather than the American "ranch". In 1892 the settlement at Fort Macleod was incorporated as a town, and in a gesture of independence and sophistication dropped the "Fort" to become Macleod. Fortunately, the citizens of Macleod, always conscious of their heritage, later restored the "Fort" to their town's name. For consistency, I have used Fort Macleod throughout the book, except where inappropriate. Until 1905 the shortgrass ranching country of present-day southeast Alberta lay within the District of Assiniboia of the North West Territories, and southwest Alberta within the District of Alberta. In 1905 the boundary between the new provinces of Alberta and Saskatchewan was shifted eastward to the 4th meridian.

Lacombe, Alberta
1984

CONTENTS

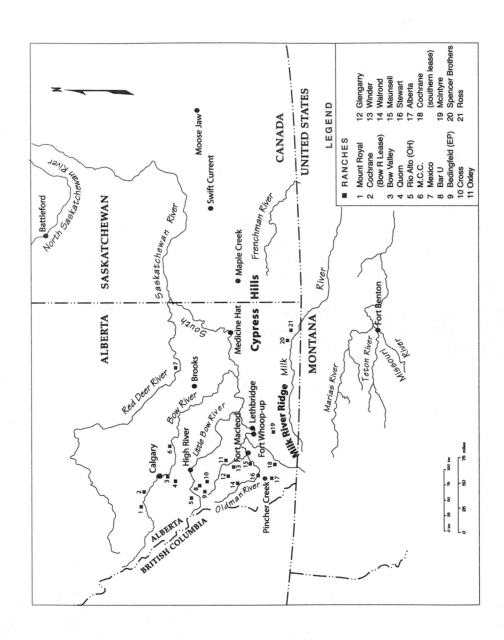

N

Battleford •
North Saskatchewan River

ALBERTA | SASKATCHEWAN

Red Deer River

Calgary •
High River •
■ 6 ■
■ 2
■ 3
■ 4
1 ■
5 ■ 8 ■
9 ■ 10
12 ■ 11
14 16
17
18 ■
Pincher Creek •

Bow River
Little Bow River

Brooks •

South

Saskatchewan River

Moose Jaw •

Swift Current •

Maple Creek •

Cypress Hills

Medicine Hat •

Fort Macleod •
Lethbridge •
Fort Whoop-up •
19 ■
20 ■
21 ■

Milk

Milk River Ridge

Oldman River

ALBERTA
BRITISH COLUMBIA

CANADA
UNITED STATES

MONTANA

River

Frenchman River

Marias River

Teton River

Missouri River

Fort Benton •

0 km 25 50 75 100 km
0   25   50   75 miles

LEGEND

■ RANCHES

1 Mount Royal
2 Cochrane
  (Bow R Lease)
3 Bow Valley
4 Quorn
5 Rio Alto (OH)
6 M.C.C.
7 Mexico
8 Bar U
9 Bedingfield (EP)
10 Cross
11 Oxley
12 Glengarry
13 Winder
14 Walrond
15 Maunsell
16 Stewart
17 Alberta
18 Cochrane
   (southern lease)
19 McIntyre
20 Spencer Brothers
21 Ross

Chapter One

THE AMERICAN TRADITION

In the mid-19th century the Great Plains of North America west of the 98th meridian were still shunned by agriculturists. This meridian marked the approximate limit of the eastern forest and the beginning of the grasslands, the boundary between areas of dependable rainfall and those of greater risk. To the east of the line the land was settled with prosperous farms and growing towns and cities; but to the west the land was largely empty of European settlers except for isolated pockets in California and Oregon and around such early mining centres as Denver in Colorado and Virginia City in Nevada.

The western plains were considered part of the Great American Desert, a region quite unsuitable for agriculture, at least as it was then practised. Eventually, of course, the desire for land and new technology would open up the plains region, but in the interim, between the disappearance of the buffalo and the rush of homesteaders, a new type of culture developed and bloomed briefly. This was the cattle kingdom, perhaps the most appropriate culture that white settlers ever produced on the North American plains.

The cattle kingdom had its origins in the period of Spanish and Mexican ascendancy in the southern part of North America. The Spanish missions in California herded cattle initially for dairy purposes, training the local Indians to manage and maintain the herds. Other herds came under the control of individual *rancheros*, or small landowners, who established a tradition of handling their cattle from horseback. Cattle were slaughtered for their hides and tallow; California did a brisk export trade in these products. Beef was not an important product at the time.

During the 1830s the herds, which had multiplied remarkably under the favourable conditions of the country, were systematically slaughtered, so that by the time of the great gold rush in the late 1840s, there were so few cattle left that it was necessary to bring livestock from the east. The California herds did not recover for many decades, but the brief period of cattle-raising left a legacy of terms and customs which were adopted by cattlemen in other parts of the continent, including western Canada.

While cattle were raised in large numbers in the eastern part of North America, they were not the primary interest of eastern farmers. By contrast, beef cattle were almost the sole interest of the ranchers in the west at the time of the cattle kingdom. Furthermore, the method of managing cattle in the west gave rise to what became the dominant characteristic of ranching, the use of horses for handling the animals, and all the social and cultural trappings that derived from this custom.

The true cradle of the cattle kingdom was southern Texas, an area bounded on the south by the coast of the Gulf of Mexico from Brownsville to Matagorda, the Rio Grande as far as Laredo, and San Antonio in the north. During the 17th, 18th, and 19th centuries the Spanish and Mexicans founded several small settlements and missions in the region and imported numbers of cattle, descendents of Andalusian calves brought to the island of Santo Domingo in the early 1500s. The Spanish were interested principally in domestic cattle, that is, cows and bulls: they did not castrate their young male calves to produce good beef steers.

The Spanish cattle thrived under the natural conditions of the region, particularly along the well-watered and sheltered valley of the Neuces River. Neither the Spanish nor the Mexicans exercised much control over their herds, with the result that many animals took to the bush. Soon large herds of half-wild, half-domestic cattle freely roamed the nearby plains. There was, of course, much natural selection among these cattle as scrub animals gradually died out. Over a long period of time, then, a distinct breed evolved: the famous Texas longhorn.

The longhorn, the product not only of natural selection among the wild Spanish cattle but also of some interbreeding with other imported strains, was a tough, rangy animal with a light body, long legs, and thin loins and rump. Perhaps its most noted characteristic was its horns, which could measure up to eight feet from tip to tip; it was sometimes remarked that the longhorn could be packed into its own horns. Colours ranged from dull yellow through red to black. These cattle were hardy animals, too. They could travel long distances with relatively little water, which made them ideal for the long drives to northern markets. They were fierce when angered and could move fast. This gave special importance to the close relationship between a cowboy and his horse; it could be fatal for a cowboy to be caught on foot near angry longhorns. The famous American adventurer and hunter Col. Richard Dodge wrote in 1877 that the "wild bull is 'on his muscle' at all times; and though he will generally get out of the way if unmolested, the slightest provocation will convert him into a most aggressive and dangerous enemy ... I admit some very decided frights, and on more than one occasion have felt exceedingly relieved when an aggressive young bull has gone off bellowing and shaking his head, his face and eyes full of No. 8 shot, and taking the herd with him."

In 1836 Texas passed from Mexico's control and became an independent republic. Many of the Mexican landowners simply abandoned their estates and herds.

The economy of Texas in the late 1830s was based on the production of grain and cotton; as in other parts of North America, cattle were largely incidental to most farming operations. But the herds in the wild continued to increase; there was plenty of grass, water, and space. By 1830 there was an estimated 100,000 head of cattle in the southeast corner of Texas; in 1850, about 330,000, and by 1860, about 3.5 million. These herds spread to the north and west, some becoming virtually pests to the settlers.

Some enterprising Texans, however, began to view all this meat on the hoof as more of an opportunity than a problem. They looked around for markets, rounded up some of the cattle on "cow hunts" and drove them overland or shipped them by flatboat to New Orleans. During the 1850s they discovered a demand for feeder cattle in Illinois and before long Texans were driving cattle north to markets in Independence, Missouri, and Kansas City, Missouri, where the longhorns were picked up by northern buyers. As a result of the California gold rush, there was a demand in California for beef to feed the gold miners, and though the drive across the continent was long, difficult and dangerous, several Texans made the journey with herds. These evolving markets, however, made little overall impact upon the vast herds which still ran wild in Texas.

The Civil War (1861–65) cut off these outlets to the west and north, and when the Union armies took the Mississippi River, even shipments to the Confederate forces from Texas were blocked. But the war also fostered the development of industrial giants in the northern cities with huge factories employing thousands of workers who needed food and wanted beef. As immigration expanded, and as railways with their thousands of labourers thrust west, the potential market for southern cattle grew. In the mid-1860s cattle bought in Texas for four dollars sold for forty dollars in northern markets, and soon buyers from the north and sellers from the south were looking for ways to satisfy the great northern markets. The northerners might find the longhorn meat "teasingly tough," but they still wanted it.

The years after the Civil War saw the beginning of the great trail drives north from Texas over 1500 miles of prairie, treacherous rivers, past Indians and outlaws. The immediate object for the drives was a railhead from which cattle might move to markets in the north and east. The destination for the early drives was Sedalia, Missouri, but the drovers and their herds met strong opposition from the farmers in this area who feared Texas fever, a lethal disease of the spleen in cattle; southern cattle carried microscopic ticks which transmitted the disease. While the longhorns were practically immune to Texas fever, it wrought havoc among the northern herds. Consequently, the Missouri and Kansas farmers pushed for quarantine regulations forbidding the entry of Texas cattle into eastern Kansas and southwest Missouri. In some cases they resisted the Texans with arms. Opposition on Sedalia was so fierce in 1866 that the driving season that year was considered an utter disaster. It became apparent to the drovers that the cattle trails to the north must move farther west.

At this point, Joseph G. McCoy, 29 years old and one of three enterprising brothers who operated a cattle business in Springfield, Illinois, entered the picture. After an examination of the situation and the opportunities it might present, McCoy negotiated a commitment from the Kansas Pacific Railway to pay him five dollars for every car of cattle loaded at a site he planned to choose. The railway was, of course, anxious to develop some eastbound traffic on its line to Kansas City; most railways in the west found plenty of freight westbound for the developing centres, but very little eastbound. McCoy then obtained a similar commitment from another company to carry cattle from Kansas City to Chicago.

After considering several towns for his purpose, McCoy finally settled on Abilene, Kansas, as the best location from which to ship cattle, even though it lay within the quarantine zone demanded by the farmers. The matter of the quarantine was overcome, however, with an endorsement from the governor of Kansas, who was convinced by McCoy of the economic benefits which would come to the area if he was allowed to proceed with his plans.

McCoy bought 250 acres near the little town of Abilene, at that time little more than a few sod shacks. He put up a large stockyard and later added several buildings, including a hotel for the cattlemen called the Drover's Cottage. He then dispatched a rider south to tell the cattlemen driving herds north of his facilities. By mid-August the first herd of longhorns arrived at Abilene and the town was in business—the first real cattle town in the west. (The term "cowtown" was a later, derogatory expression.) In 1867, 35,000 head of cattle reached Abilene. Of these, about 18,000 were shipped east by rail, some were trailed farther east, and the rest were put out on the surrounding plains where there was plenty of grass and water. In 1869, 75,000 head passed through Abilene; in 1870, 350,000, and in 1871, the peak year of Abilene's career as a cattle town, 700,000.

The development of Abilene marked the beginnings of the great cattle kingdom of the western plains. The significance of Abilene itself lay simply in its location where the north-south cattle trail intersected the east-west railway. The town's heyday as the dominant cattle town was relatively brief; the trails gradually shifted westward as the railways moved west and farmers and the quarantine line followed. This movement gave rise to other cattle towns—some lasting for only a single driving season—such as Wichita, Ellsworth, Dodge City, Ogallala, and Newton. Abilene, however, remained in the public's mind as the quintessential cattle town—wild, wide open, and given to excess. In fact, like most cattle towns, Abilene had a split personality: a wild and wicked town when the herds and cowboys arrived from the south, and a somewhat more respectable and subdued town the rest of the time.

The cattle towns basically served as centres where buyers could meet sellers. Buyers included ranchers from the northern ranges who wanted yearlings and two-year-olds as stocker cattle; farmers and feedlot operators from the middle west who looked for full-grown steers for final fattening, and representatives of the large packing houses who bought cattle for the eastern terminal markets and for slaughter.

Following the peak year of 1871, cattle prices declined steadily as business conditions in the United States deteriorated. A small corn crop in the midwest decreased demand for feeder cattle, and the first steers coming off the developing northern ranges at the same time that consumers were purchasing less beef depressed prices. Then the great financial panic of 1873, which brought about the collapse of the Northern Pacific Railroad, created a situation which forced many drovers from the south to sell their herds at distress prices. Eighteen seventy-three marked the nadir of the depression, however, and the cattle industry slowly began to recover and move towards its spectacular climax.

A number of developments in the mid and late 1870s set the stage for a dramatic expansion in the cattle business. One was the opening up of the northern ranges in Wyoming and Montana. There had long been a small cattle industry in the northwest along with the Old Oregon Trail and in the mountain valleys, an industry which was able to supply meat to the gold seekers during the rushes in Montana in the 1860s. But the ranchers in Montana needed markets beyond their local region if they were to survive and expand. They were anxious that the Northern Pacific Railroad complete its line west from Minnesota, and were disappointed when the company halted construction as a result of the 1873 crash. However, the Union Pacific, crossing Colorado and Utah to the south, boosted the country north of its line, realizing that expansion of the cattle industry there would provide additional traffic.

In Montana, then, there was expansion of the beef industry from two directions as cattle spilled onto the grassy plains from the mountain valleys, and cattlemen from the south pushed into the territory looking for additional range. There remained one firm obstacle to the cattlemen's occupation of the range—the Indians. The best grasslands in Montana were closed to the cattlemen, for practically all of eastern Montana was given over to Indian reserves and exclusive hunting grounds. Not only did the Indians prevent the ranchers from expanding into the grasslands, they presented a barrier to penetration by the railroads as well. Consequently, there was great pressure brought to bear by the ranchers to remove the Indians.

In the late 1870s the Indians of the northern plains found their country further threatened with the discovery of gold in the Black Hills of Dakota Territory and the subsequent rush of miners to that area. Demands by the gold seekers for protection brought in the United States Army. The ensuing and highly-publicized campaigns against the Indians drew much attention to the western United States with its potential for cattle-raising. By 1879 the Indian barrier had been effectively removed by government action and the Montana range lay open for the cattlemen.

The 1870s also saw the development of refrigeration, which allowed carcasses to be delivered to eastern American markets, and even to Europe, without spoiling. In 1875, 36,000 pounds of dressed beef were shipped to England; by 1881 this figure rose to 110,000 pounds annually. At the same time, live animals were still being shipped overseas, to be slaughtered when they landed in England.

The flood of cheap American beef in England pushed down prices there, much to the concern of the agricultural community, which began to feel very threatened.

The British had long been involved in various land companies and development projects in the American west, and there was still plenty of British money looking for suitable investment opportunities. By 1882 there was a veritable rush among Scottish and English capitalists to invest in American ranches. That year the British-owned Matador Ranching Company, one of the largest cattle companies on the plains, got underway. In 1883 a number of Scottish capitalists organized a company to purchase the operations of Alexander Swan in Nebraska and Wyoming and combined them with several other properties. The resulting Swan Land and Cattle Company controlled a range 130 miles long and from 42 to 100 miles wide, and a herd of 150,000 head. By the mid-1880s there was so much foreign investment in the western range industry that the United States Congress appointed a committee to investigate the situation. It found that almost 21 million acres of public lands were under the control of foreign companies. Indeed, it turned out that most of Wyoming was, in fact, controlled by British investors.

The most flamboyant of these foreign operators was undoubtedly Moreton Frewen, an Englishman who centred his interests along the Powder River in Wyoming. While on a hunting trip with his younger brother Richard, Frewen had seen the virtually empty Powder River valley and quickly made plans to develop and promote a cattle enterprise there on an enormous scale.

In 1879 he bought two thousand head of Shorthorns and the "76" brand from a rancher on the Sweetwater River. He then built a large two-storey house called The Castle on the west bank of the Powder. A master of promotion, Frewen gained enormous publicity in the press and entertained a steady stream of his aristocratic and moneyed friends from Britain and the United States. (In 1881 he married Clara Jerome, second daughter of New York financier Leonard Jerome; Frewen thereby became an uncle to Winston Churchill, whose mother was Clara's older sister.) His visitors were treated to continental cuisine (with fresh flowers rushed in by special train), taken on excursions to the mountains, and, as a finale, given a grand tour of the "76" range to see the cattle and be dazzled with the prospect of huge dividends.

In 1882 Frewen returned to London and launched a British-financed corporation which consolidated his holdings and furnished him with additional money for expansion. The company, capitalized at £300,000 ($1,500,000), took control of Frewen's inventory of livestock and property valued at $260,000. Frewen himself received $60,000 in cash and $200,000 in ordinary shares from the deal, as well as the position of manager of the new firm, the Powder River Cattle Company. The company's funds were deposited in a Wyoming bank and Frewen embarked upon an ambitious program of expansion including slaughterhouses, feedlots, and vastly increased numbers of cattle.

The pressure of increased herds on the range caused grazing conditions to deteriorate during the mid-1880s, and Frewen decided to move the "76" herds to a better range in the Alberta District. He entered into negotiations with the Dominion government for a 20-year lease, but found that he was unable to convince his board of directors in London of the value of such a move. He further argued with the directors over the payment of unearned dividends, steadfastly maintaining that any profits should be retained and reinvested in the ranch in order to meet possible future crises. The board, however, insisted upon dividends. As a result, Frewen resigned from the company in 1885, left Wyoming, and returned to England to concentrate on his own interests.

The rush for western lands and ranches was not confined to Scotland

and England. American investors in the east fell over themselves in their attempts to get in on the boom. In 1881 Gen. James S. Brisbin published a book called *The Beef Bonanza, or How to Get Rich on the Plains* in which he virtually promised success and wealth to those who worked hard. Brisbin described some of the companies and individuals who had done so well on the range, tempting even more people to invest in what he had described as an almost sure thing.

By this time the peculiar psychology of a boom held thousands of people in its grip, at least those living outside the range country. Newspapers and magazines reported huge profits—25 percent, 33 per cent, 50 per cent on invested capital—to be made. The Boston *Herald* told its readers in 1882 that

> with the present high prices of beef, and the cow literally jumping over the moon, western cattle men are reaping a rich harvest, and many of them will make almost independent fortunes this summer ... large transactions are made every day in which the buyer does not see a hoof of his purchase, and very likely does not actually use more than one-half the purchase money in the trade before he has sold and made an enormous margin in the deal.

Bill Nye, whose trenchant observations on the cattle industry appeared in the Laramie *Boomerang* and various other newspapers in the east and west, wrote in 1883 that "three years ago a guileless tenderfoot came into Wyoming, leading a single Texas steer and carrying a branding iron; now he is the opulent possessor of six hundred head of fine cattle—the ostensible progeny of that one steer." Surely a remarkable return on investment, to say nothing of an equally remarkable miracle.

One of the most prominent figures of the cattle kingdom was an extraordinary Scot, John Clay. The son of a farmer in the Scottish borderlands, Clay displayed such ability that he was appointed manager of a neighbouring estate at the age of 21. With the money earned from this position, Clay took a trip to the United States, mostly for pleasure, but he also intended to search out opportunities by which he could advance himself. While visiting in New York on his way home, he met George Brown, publisher of the Toronto *Globe,* one of the Fathers of Confederation and the owner of a large farm near Toronto called Bow Park. Brown, who was a Scottish immigrant, invited Clay to visit Bow Park, an invitation the young traveller accepted with alacrity.

About this time George Brown was planning to incorporate his farm as a private company and was looking for investors in Scotland in order to expand his Shorthorn cattle operation. A number of investors in Edinburgh put money into Brown's venture, among them the Nelson family of publishing fame. John Clay's father also invested about £10,000, and the younger Clay was hired as Brown's agent in Scotland to purchase and ship stock to Bow Park.

Brown's company began to run into difficulties soon afterward, so the investors sent John Clay to investigate and report back to them. As a result of Clay's recommendations, the shareholders relieved Brown of his position as manager of Bow Park and appointed Clay in his place. Since the future for Bow Park appeared grim, Clay would up its affairs and returned to Scotland.

About 1880, the British government appointed a Royal Commission on Agriculture to examine the American beef industry and its effects on British agriculture. John Clay was appointed as a sub-commissioner. Clay's travels and studies of the American range sparked his imagination, and when a Scottish syndicate bought a 115,000-acre ranch in California shortly afterward, he became involved in the cattle business as both investor and manager.

As the flood of Scottish investment in the range industry rose, Clay was made superintendent of the British-owned Western Ranches Ltd. operating in the Dakota Territory and he represented other investors as well. He later established his own commission business in Chicago and became president of the powerful Wyoming Stock Growers' Association.

Canadians also poured money into the booming cattle industry on the American plains during the early 1880s, at the same time that the Dominion government was encouraging investment in the Canadian North West. In 1882 a number of wealthy businessmen and well-connected politicians formed the Dominion Cattle Company. Many of these men were also involved in various Canadian cattle ventures. W.B. Ives, member of Parliament from the Eastern Townships of Quebec and son-in-law of the minister of agriculture, held about $14,500 of stock. (The Ottawa *Free Press* caustically noted that "Mr. Ives' exemplary 'patriotism' induced him to invest in a Texas ranche instead of one in our own Northwest ... ") Other shareholders included Sen. A.W. Ogilvie ($3,200), Sen. Matthew H. Cochrane—who was also a director—($5,000), and R.H. Pope, son of the minister of agriculture ($18,000). The Eastern Townships Bank was also interested in the Dominion Cattle Company to the tune of $190,000, and Hugh McKay of Montreal put in $84,000. Another important principal in the Dominion Cattle Company was J.P. Wiser, member of Parliament, whose distillery in eastern Ontario provided the foundation for his fortune. Wiser eventually became president of the company and owned two ranches in Kansas as well.

The Dominion Cattle Company received much attention in eastern Canada, and the Ottawa *Free Press* reported that "during the session of 1885,

almost every member of the House of Commons received a circular from
Mr. Ives' friends inviting him to [buy] stock in the company. The ranche was
represented as being of unlimited area, and the cattle roaming over it would
not remain still long enough to be counted. The dividends to be paid were
enormous, and hence many people jumped at such an opportunity for a safe
investment."

The Canadian syndicate purchased the entire stock and range rights of
J.M. Day, one of the largest ranchers in the Texas Panhandle. The Dominion
Cattle Company established the Box T as its brand, and ran its stock on about
1,750,000 acres in Lipscomb County and the Cherokee Strip (Indian Territory) to the east.

The physical basis for the cattle boom in the United States was free
grass, the seemingly limitless pasture of the public domain. Most of the large
ranchers neither owned nor leased the land on which they ran their cattle;
rather, they operated on the public domain only with the tacit approval of
the federal government. However, some cattlemen did purchase the land on
which they had put up their buildings and corrals. And while many investors in the cattle industry were led to believe that they had purchased "range
rights," these rights were wholly imaginary, for they existed only by custom
on otherwise unoccupied land and were not recognized by law. Theoretically,
the public domain was free to all, and a man claimed a share of it simply by
occupying the land with his herd.

Control of water on the arid plains meant control of the neighbouring
land. Many ranchers maintained control of vast sections of range by purchasing strips of land along rivers and streams, thereby effectively shutting out
other ranchers. Their range was considered to extend back from the water to
the divide between it and the next stream.

As pressures increased on the grasslands, some cattlemen began to fence
off their range. The development of barbed wire fencing and the subsequent
enclosing of lands by both settlers and ranchers contributed to innumerable
conflicts between the two groups. The settlers claimed that the cattlemen
fenced off land that was not theirs, which was indeed true, while the ranchers
complained that the settlers' fences inhibited the movement of their cattle,
which was also true. Even among the cattlemen there were conflicts as newcomers "trespassed" upon the ranges of the older, established ranches. The
situation was further complicated when sheepmen began to move herds into
Wyoming and Montana.

As the cattle boom entered its last phase, the purchase of stocker cattle
of almost any kind drove prices steadily upwards. Longhorns continued to
move out of Texas and Colorado where the ranges were becoming badly over-

grazed. By the early 1880s cattle began to move from the midwestern states to the western plains in a significant reversal of the traditional direction of cattle movement. The shipment of these eastern cattle ("pilgrim cattle") was beneficial in that it introduced better grades of animals than the longhorns to the northern ranges; but at the same time these cattle were more susceptible to bad weather and disease, especially pleuropneumonia. As they were also more expensive than the longhorns—about $35 compared with $24—they also represented a greater financial risk for the cattleman.

Investment companies bought out many of the old stockmen, some of whom continued to manage their ranches for the new owners while others retired from the range to the sidelines to watch developments. By 1884 ranges everywhere were becoming badly overcrowded. Tensions rose and tempers flared while water rights based on land ownership became more and more expensive.

In 1884 drought struck the southern ranges and prices began to weaken. Autumn of that year brought additional setbacks, as fierce storms ravaged the southern range. The situation was further exacerbated by an order of the federal government that thousands of cattle grazing on the lands of the Indian Territory (Oklahoma) had to be cleared out and the owners of these cattle had little choice but to push them on to already overcrowded ranges outside the Territory.

The summer of 1886 was hot and dry following a mild winter. Fires swept over the plains, destroying the grass, and cattlemen could find little good feed for their stock. While prices continued to decline, the cattlemen figured the drop was only temporary and held their stock back from shipment, waiting for prices to rise. Demand for stocker cattle had virtually disappeared however, and by the fall prices were $10 to $18 lower than the previous year. Many ranchers began to look around for good winter range on which to hold their herds, but found there was little available. The cattle were generally in a poor condition to face winter on the open range, and an air of apprehension hung over the plains.

In November violent snowstorms swept across the ranges. Cattlemen hoped and prayed that this was not a portent of things to come, but even if it was, they still expected that most animals would survive the winter, although in weakened condition. And indeed, a warm spell in mid-December brought a collective sense of relief—but only briefly. The break was followed by plummeting temperatures and storms which covered the range with ice and crusted snow. Weeks passed without a break in the bitter cold, and cattlemen and their investors prepared for the worst.

A warm wind finally blew across the plains in March and cattlemen rode out onto the range to assess the damage. The extent of the disaster was soon apparent. Cattle by the thousands lay dead on the range, piled in the coulees and along the water courses, and pressed against fences, barriers, or shelters. Those animals which managed to survive staggered about in pitiful condition, with frozen ears, tails and legs, and many so weak they could hardly move. Estimates of losses by individual outfits ranged from 15 to 80 percent of their herd. So shocking was the devastation that Granville Stuart, the patriarch of the Montana cattle industry, wrote that "a business that had been fascinating to me before, suddenly became distasteful. I never wanted to own again an animal that I could not feed and shelter."

The "Big Die-Up" of 1886–87 shook the cattle kingdom to its foundations. Many companies collapsed. The Swan Land and Cattle Company went into receivership within a year, and the Frewen brothers departed, prompting the Cheyenne *Daily Sun* in November 1887 to comment that "of all the English snobs of great pretensions, who flew so high and sunk so low, probably the Frewens are the chiefs … They conducted business … on a system … that has brought an important and legitimate business into discredit in the East." The great structure of promotion and speculation—and frequently fraud—began to topple. Even the Dominion Cattle Company had its problems when shareholders discovered that the dividends they had received were really paid out of capital rather than profit.

Prices for cattle remained low as thousands of head were shipped to market in order to settle accounts. At the same time sources of new capital dried up, resulting in a serious shortage of money needed to spur recovery, just as the industry headed into the prolonged and general depression of the later 1880s and 1890s.

The cattle industry on the plains had been undergoing some very significant changes before the Big Die-Up, but the disastrous winter certainly hastened them. Ranchers appalled by the sight of their starving cattle and staggering losses, started to put up more hay and feed for their weaker calves and other stock during the winter. They also began to manage their range more carefully, grazing cattle at different areas during the year in order to have good winter pasture in reserve. These new methods required more fencing, and the open range began to disappear, except in certain remote areas such as eastern Montana. The removal of thousands of cattle and the departure of many ranchers left the country open for settlers and homesteaders.

The conflict between the cattlemen and the farmers and small stockmen reached its dramatic climax in Wyoming, the state most dependent upon and dominated by the cattle industry. Even before the territory achieved statehood in 1890, Wyoming cattlemen had effectively controlled the government, exercising their power to a great extent through the Wyoming Stock Growers' Association (WSGC) and the Wyoming Livestock Commission.

An 1884 law, pushed through the Wyoming legislature by the stock growers' association, made all branding illegal between 15 February, before the calves were dropped, and the date of the association's general spring roundup, the only roundup permitted by law. One benefit of this statute was that it prevented the frequent gathering of cattle, which had a weakening effect on the stock. But as the association also had stringent controls over the admission of new members, small stockmen and other "undesirables" could easily be excluded from the general roundup. Furthermore, in the roundup, all stock with brands not accepted by the Stock Grower's Association were classified as mavericks (animals whose ownership was not known) and sold, the proceeds going into the association's coffers. An attempt to enact similar regulations in Montana failed; the governor there called such legislation a menace to personal liberty.

As settlers continued to move into Wyoming, agitation against the domination of the state's affairs by the association increased, some of the resistance taking the form of shooting stock and stealing, or "rustling," the cattle. Cattlemen retaliated through the Wyoming Livestock Commission which instructed its inspectors at all loading points to seize cattle shipped by suspected rustlers, sell them, and hold the funds from such sales. If the owners of the seized cattle offered a bill of sale as proof of ownership, the document was to be disregarded and the so-called owner told to travel to Cheyenne to present evidence to the commission that the cattle were indeed not stolen. Such arrogant actions and reversals of accepted principles of law only served to inflame public opinion against the big ranchers and cattle companies. The association did not define what it meant by rustlers, a term which they seemed to apply to just about everyone who did not support the organization.

So far as the members of the Wyoming Stock Growers' Association were concerned (and most were large cattle companies, many of them foreign-owned) the centre of the rustlers' activity was Johnson County and its seat, Buffalo, in the northern part of Wyoming. In December 1891 the citizens of Buffalo were shocked by two murders within several days, just outside the town. One of the victims, a young cowboy, may well have done a little rustling, but the other victim, on his way home with Christmas gifts for his family, was a small but prosperous rancher who was outspoken in his condemnation of the association. The chief suspect in both cases was Frank Canton, an association detective and local informer.

The cattle shooting and rustling continued on an ever-increasing scale; the range country was in such a chaotic state that one newspaper declared that either the cattlemen or the "thieves" would have to go. Late in 1891 the Wyoming Stock Growers' Association decided to strike at the heart of the rustlers in Buffalo and drew up plans. (The president of the association, John Clay, was in Europe at this time, and it has never been made very clear what his role was in the events which followed.) Hiram Iams, the WSGA secretary, drew up a list of 70 men marked for execution—there were to be no prisoners in this invasion. The association also dispatched a man to buy horses in Colorado, and another to Texas to recruit gunmen. By April the cattlemen's invasion force was ready and assembled on a special train; the group included 19 cattlemen, 5 association employees, a doctor, 3 teamsters for the wagons, 2 newspaper correspondents, and 25 Texas gunmen.

The association's force travelled north by train as far as Caspar, then took to their horses and wagons. The telegraph line between Caspar and Buffalo was cut so that the rustlers could not send for help. The invaders were on the road for only a few days when they received word that a number of alleged rustlers, led by a cowboy named Nate Champion, were staying at a nearby ranch. The invasion force captured two men without a struggle and wounded a third. Champion, however, remained in the ranch's cabin and held off the attackers; they finally set fire to the building and riddled Champion with bullets as he tried to escape. (Champion kept notes of the fight in a small book which eventually got into the hands of one of the correspondents; the account, when published, transformed Champion into a hero and practically destroyed any sympathy which the public may have originally had for the association.) The sound of the shooting alerted people nearby who in turn roused the town. Buffalo was in an uproar when it received news of the invasion, and several hundred armed men, including businessmen and a preacher, marched out to defend their lives and property.

The invaders, realizing that the element of surprise was lost, hastily retreated to a nearby ranch. They threw logs up against the sturdy ranch house and barricaded themselves inside. The invaders suddenly found themselves the besieged.

The Johnson County defenders quickly captured most of the invaders' supplies, leaving the association's men in a desperate situation. Somehow, the invaders managed to get a message to the governor, demanding that he send troops to their rescue. News of the invasion reached Washington, and troops at Fort McKenney near Buffalo were ordered out to restore the peace. The besiegers agreed to allow the soldiers to arrest the invaders on condition that they could take the prisoners back to the civil authorities in Johnson County. The army commander agreed and took the invaders into custody.

Promises were made and broken in the events which followed. The prisoners were first taken to the state penitentiary where they were lodged in a comfortable wing at the expense of Johnson County, costs the young county could scarcely afford. Then the prisoners were released on their own recognizance. The case against them dragged on and on. It finally came to trial in January 1893. With the agreement of both parties, the case was dismissed, hardly an instance of justice being served.

But the glory days of the cattle kingdom were over. Everywhere the open range was fast disappearing and the basis of the cattle industry changing. The great train drives, the immense roundups, the extravagant speculation were already legend—the stories of old-timers remembering a lost world and a faded youth.

Chapter Two

CANADIAN BEGINNINGS

The cattle industry in western Canada began with the Selkirk settlers on the Red River. The Earl of Selkirk, a major shareholder in the Hudson's Bay Company, secured a grant of land from the company with the intention of establishing an agricultural colony which would serve a number of purposes. It would furnish provisions for the company's trading posts and boat brigades, provide both a place for retiring company servants and a supply of new men, and establish a stronger presence in the area in the face of increasing competition from the Montreal-based North West Company.

In 1811 the first group of settlers arrived at Hudson Bay and wintered on its inhospitable shores. The following spring they moved by canoes up the Hayes River towards Lake Winnipeg. En route the settlers paused at Oxford House, a Hudson's Bay Company post, where they were delighted to discover a pair of cattle, a bull and a yearling heifer, which they promptly purchased. The two young animals had apparently been brought from Europe as calves the year before; the settlers had great hopes for these animals and optimistically named them Adam and Eve. Training Adam and Eve to step into and out of the canoes was a major task, and the frequent stops for grazing the cattle slowed the group's progress, but eventually they all reached their destination safely in August 1812.

As the settlers established themselves near the confluence of the Red and Assiniboine rivers, they learned of a few other domestic cattle in the vicinity. The North West Company post on the Assiniboine had three animals, a bull, a cow, and a heifer calf. Peter Fidler of the Hudson's Bay Company purchased the three animals for the colonists. The settlers had plenty of problems with their few cattle, however. The bull from the North West Company turned mean and had to be destroyed, and Adam wandered away and drowned when he broke through the ice on the Red River, leaving the colony without a bull for breeding.

The Selkirk colonists wanted cattle more for their milk, cheese, and butter than for meat. With so many buffalo nearby, there seemed no real need for beef cattle. When Lord Selkirk visited the struggling colony in 1817, he proposed importing some good quality stock for the settlers from either Upper Canada or the United States. As Selkirk travelled south into the United States en route to Upper Canada, he became convinced that buying cattle from the American settlements was a more reasonable proposition than buying them in Canada.

In 1819 Robert Dickson, Selkirk's agent in the American northwest, contracted Michael Douseman, a merchant at Michilimackinac, to deliver to the Red River settlers some good milch cows, oxen, bulls, breeding mares, and a stallion. Douseman sold his part of the contract to Adam Stewart, collector of customs at Michilimackinac, for $1,000. Stewart travelled to St. Louis in the fall of 1819, bought some cattle in the area, and moved the herd north along the Mississippi valley. However, he managed to get no further than northern Illinois. Feed was scarce and the whole herd perished during the winter.

Undaunted by the disaster, Stewart purchased a second herd near St. Louis and started north again in 1821. This herd was lost to the Sioux, who found fresh beef quite as acceptable as buffalo. The persistent Stewart directed a third herd north in 1823 and managed to reach the Red River colony in late August. He brought in 170 head, even though his contract called for only 120; but considering the costs of the contract, wintering the cattle, and all the other hazards, Stewart had to sell more cattle than the contract stipulated if he were to make any profit on the deal.

While Stewart's cattle were a welcome addition to the colony, they had been preceded by a small herd delivered by Joseph Rolette, a French-Canadian trading at Michilimackinac and Prairie du Chien. Rolette drove his cattle north on speculation and sold them to a few of the colony's wealthier residents. The Canadian had, in fact, offered to deliver a herd when he had met Lord Serkirk some years earlier, but Selkirk had declined the offer as he felt Rolette's price was too high.

Altogether, about 650 head were introduced into the Red River colony from the United States. The size of the herd soon diminished owing to the severe climate and lack of appropriate care. However, subsequently their numbers grew sufficiently to meet the needs of the colony and the fur trade. By the late 1830s the cattle population was large enough for small herds to be driven south to American markets in Minnesota. The Red River cattle had a reputation for hardiness, and so were particularly valued by the American settlers on the northern plains.

The Red River settlers' interest in cattle was generally confined to milch cows, and later to work animals suitable for the transportation requirements of the Hudson's Bay Company for supplying its western posts. Much effort was also expended attempting to develop a wool industry, as it was considered that the country's conditions were ideal for sheep and the shipping and export of wool would present few problems. A number of sheep were brought into the colony as foundation stock, including a flock from Kentucky, but the results were disappointing and interest in sheep died.

During the same period in which the Red River settlers were struggling with their tiny herd, the foundations of a cattle industry in British Columbia were being laid. The first domestic cattle in that area were possibly introduced by the Spaniards. American settlers brought cattle to the American Fur Company's colony at the mouth of the Columbia River in 1814, and the Hudson's Bay Company systematically built up significant herds at some of its posts in Oregon. The numbers of cattle were further increased through the Puget Sound Agricultural Company, a subsidiary of the Hudson's Bay Company, and by the settlers who poured into the Oregon country during the 1840s. By 1850 there were approximately 42,000 head of cattle in the Oregon country, and by 1860 some 182,000 cattle were to be found in the state of Oregon and territory of Washington.

The country between the Rockies and the Cascade Mountains became a producer of excellent beef. The Durham strain predominated, and the animals were chunky and put on more weight than the Texas longhorns. The Oregon cattle were also good foragers and developed the stamina to withstand harsh northern winters; many were later driven across the Rockies to stock ranches in Montana, Idaho, and Wyoming.

As a result of the great gold rushes of the late 1850s and the early 1860s, the cattle industry expanded from the United States into British Columbia. The gold resources in British Columbia became known as early as 1855, when word leaked out that deposits of the precious mineral had been discovered near Fort Colvile at the mouth of the Pend Oreille River (actually in Washington). The news attracted miners into the area in 1856, but the rush really got underway in 1857 when news of more gold lured men to the Thompson River farther north.

On Sunday, 25 April 1858, the people of Victoria on Vancouver Island were astonished, as they returned home from church, by the appearance of a steamer from San Francisco jammed with gold seekers, only the vanguard of thousands who eventually flocked to the sandbars of the lower Fraser River in search of fortune. During the summer of 1858 most of the mining activity centred on the section of the Fraser between Fort Hope and Fort Yale. But the next year, many miners moved farther upstream to the district above Lytton.

The following year they spread eastward into the Quesnel country, attracted by increasingly rich discoveries. In 1861 gold was found in the canyon of Williams Creek, the great creek of the Cariboo gold country, and the strikes were richer than any yet found in British Columbia. Finally, in 1862, the richest find of all was made, and three ramshackle towns—Richfield, Barkerville, and Camerontown—sprang up along Williams Creek. In 1863 the gold boom reached its peak.

The miners needed food, and a few enterprising individuals saw as much opportunity in supplying beef as digging for gold. The first drive of cattle into the gold fields was organized by Gen. Joel Palmer of Oregon. Palmer, a native of Ontario (and whose account of his journey to Oregon became the standard guide for later immigrants to that country), started north from Fort Okanagan in Washington Territory in June 1858 with a number of cattle and several wagons pulled by oxen. He followed the Okanagan River northward, continued along the west shore of Lake Okanagan, and then to the vicinity of Kamloops, where he disposed of his cattle. Palmer made a second journey over much the same route in 1859.

The risks on these drives were, of course, considerable. Rushing rivers, especially during May and June, occasionally hostile Indians and fluctuating markets all presented problems. Sometimes a drover reached his destination only to find the miners on their way out of the country for the winter. He would then be forced to hold his cattle somewhere nearby for the winter. The grass around Kamloops supported cattle well, however, and a number of drovers began to look at that area for raising beef. About 1865, real ranching got underway in British Columbia when the first breeding stock were brought in.

The most famous of the early British Columbia cattlemen were the brothers Jerome and Thaddeus Harper. Both were born at Harper's Ferry in Virginia (though they were not related to the founder of the town), Jerome in 1826, Thaddeus in 1829. By 1850 Jerome was farming in California, and records show that in October 1859 he was operating a sawmill at Yale on the Fraser River. Thaddeus joined his brother in British Columbia and submitted a tender for constructing a portion of the Cariboo Road in March 1860.

The Harpers brought a herd of cattle across the border at Osoyoos in 1862, trailed it north past Okanagan Lake to Kamloops, crossed the Thompson River at Savona and continued north on the Cariboo Trail. The demand for beef in the gold camps was strong, and the brothers realized a good profit on their venture. They organized a second drive in 1863, and also acquired some grazing land east of Kamloops. For several years Jerome bought cattle in Oregon and Washington during the winter months, held them near Osoyoos until spring and then drove them north when the grass was fresh. When the drives reached Barkerville, the cattle were herded nearby, then driven to slaughter at a rate of about twenty a day, or fourteen hundred head a season. The Harpers also built up a large herd on their ranch near Kamloops.

Jerome Harper retired to California in 1870, and died there four years later after a lengthy illness. Thaddeus remained in British Columbia to look after his ranching interests, but found markets declining with the petering out of the gold fields. He drove a few small herds to coastal settlements such as New Westminster, but markets there were also limited. Prices were good at Chicago, however, and though that market was thousands of miles away, Thaddeus determined to sell his cattle there. In the spring of 1876 he started out from his ranch on the Thompson River with about twelve hundred cattle and headed for the nearest rail point—Kelton, Utah, just north of Salt Lake City. By the fall Harper and his outfit reached the confluence of the Snake and Columbia rivers, where a winter camp was set up. The railhead at Kelton was only six hundred miles away now, but Harper changed his mind and drove his herd first to Idaho, where it was summered during 1877, and then to California, where the market was particularly good after a prolonged drought had killed many thousands of head of local stock. Harper's cattle arrived in San Francisco, sleek and fat, and were sold at $70 per head. The drive had taken 18 months.

Although they were most famous for stock-raising, the Harper brothers' interests encompassed far more than just cattle. Their original property on the Thompson River, the Harper Ranch, was only the first of what were eventually to become vast holdings. In 1883 Thaddeus bought 19,000 acres of rangeland on the west side of the Fraser River and established the Gang Ranch, which today is still one of the largest ranches in North America. The brothers also invested in flour mills, lumber mills, and mining.

When Thaddeus Harper died in Victoria in 1888, the Harper interests were taken over by the Western Canadian Ranching Company, a London-based firm organized by Thomas Galpin. The British company sold the ranch to American investors in July 1948. In 1978 the Gang Ranch passed into Canadian hands for the first time, to a company organized by Dale Alsager of Alberta, after accusations and controversy in the British Columbia legislature that the absentee American owners were overgrazing and mismanaging the leases which comprised a large part of the operation.

As the American ranching frontier expanded north and the Canadian frontier west, the attention of stockmen focused on the plains and adjoining hill regions of southern Alberta and southwestern Saskatchewan. These glacial till plains vary from gently undulating to hummocky terrain. They generally suffer from poor drainage, and are marked by potholes, permanent sloughs, small shallow lakes, and numerous evaporation basins into which water drains and then evaporates, increasing the salinity of the depression each year. Stretching across southern Alberta is an unusual series of steep-sided, flat-floored valleys, or coulees, which thousands of years ago carried the glacial meltwater away to the south. The largest of these channels are Lonely Valley, Whiskey Gap, Verdigris, Etzikom, Chin, Middle, Kipp, Forty Mile, and Pendant d'Oreille coulees.

The plains of the range country slope gently from west to east, dropping from an elevation of 3,500 feet at the edge of the foothills to 2,800 feet at the eastern border of Alberta. This declination controls the alignment of the major rivers of the region—the Bow, Oldman, and South Saskatchewan rivers in the south, and the Red Deer River to the north. These rivers draw their flow principally from the melting glaciers and snowfields of the Rockies, and their volume varies according to the seasons. The smaller streams of the foothills and the front ranges of the Rockies are fed mostly by melting snow, with a heavy flow in the early spring and low water by midsummer. In the early days the foothills streams often flooded, and the Highwood River, Willow Creek, and the Oldman River created many problems for the early ranchers and travellers.

The climate of southern Alberta and Saskatchewan was one of the great attractions for cattlemen, even though the daily weather was subject to sudden and dramatic changes. There is an old saying in the country that "if you don't like the weather, just wait a minute!" Although the prevailing winds are from the west and southwest, the moderating influence of winds from the Pacific Ocean is largely cut off by the mountain barrier. The winds shift direction as Arctic and Pacific storm centres and high and low pressure areas follow each other. The most important climatic feature for the cattlemen, though, was the chinook, the westerly midwinter wind which made southern Alberta and Saskatchewan one of the few year-round grazing areas in Canada. While the rest of the western plains were blanketed in snow, the warm, dry chinook winds swept the range country bare, allowing the cattle to graze.

The early travellers and residents on the range often commented on the phenomenon of the chinook. Dr. Richard Nevitt, the first surgeon with the North-West Mounted Police in Fort Macleod, noted in his diary on February 6, 1875: "Still cold and the snow on the ground about six inches deep. At about 4:30 a strong wind from the west sprang up and in nine minutes the thermometer had risen 32 degrees! From + 8° to 40°." On 8 February 8, 1875, Nevitt wrote: "You never saw such a change in your life. A few days ago, so white and cold and hard, now so black and brown and wet ... "

Meteorologists still do not fully understand the chinook. Basically, what happens is westerly winds from the Pacific scoop up warm, moist air from British Columbia and Washington and carry it across the mountains. As the air rises to sweep over the mountain barrier, it cools and loses its moisture. Then, as it descends on the eastern side of the mountains, it warms again— about three degrees Fahrenheit for every thousand feet—and rushing across the plains, it melts the snow and sometimes causes it to disappear by the process of sublimation—moving directly from snow to water vapour.

For the ranchers and the cattle, the chinook was a welcome, and sometimes saving break in the winter. Moira O'Neill, the wife of a rancher west of Nanton, wrote:

> While the north wind blows, every breathing thing shrinks and cowers. The mere holding onto life is a struggle for poor unsheltered animals, and the longer it lasts the harder is the struggle, and the less their strength for it. But there comes a change in the air. Some nights on looking out we see that the clouds have rolled upwards, as if a curtain were lifted in the west, leaving a well-defined arch of clear sky with stars shining in it. That arch means that the west wind, the preserver, is on his way; and sometimes we hear his voice beforehand in a long distant roar among the mountains. When next morning breaks, the north wind has fled ...

The chinook, such an important element of life on the range, was naturally the subject of many tall tales. There was, for instance, the man who drove out in his sleigh to visit some friends in the country. While eating dinner, he glanced outside and noticed the chinook arch developing over the mountains. He quickly hitched up his team to the sleigh and started home at a gallop, with the warm wind so hot on his heels that he had to keep the horses going lickety-split all the way. Even so, while the front runners were sliding on snow, the rear runners were dragging in mud and water.

Winter, summer, spring, or fall, the wind was a constant companion in southern Alberta. Many settlers blamed it for nerves and bouts of crankiness as it roared and shrieked and whistled around their houses. A reporter for the Calgary *Herald* wrote in 1897:

> Nothing too good can be said of the Pincher Creek district and about all that can be said on the bad side is that for genuine able-bodied, wild west, three-ply, irresistible wind it can outblow any part of the world. In Macleod they tell the tenderfoot that the reason the stones on the main street are so round and smooth is that the wind sweeps them to one end of the street one day and back the next. At Pincher Creek the

jutting rocks on the hill tops have had their corners nearly rounded and polished by the same gales, and it is a curious study to watch the wind's artistic work in this line ...

And, of course, there was the story of the dog which was blown up against a house and held there for three days until the wind died down.

The dry winds and low precipitation made the southern plains unsuitable for tree growth and these elements, combined with frequent prairie fires, helped maintain the grassland environment. There were three basic zones of grassland in the range country. The southeast corner of Alberta and southwest corner of Saskatchewan comprised the shortgrass prairie, an area with only 10 to 14 inches of annual precipitation and dominated by such grasses as blue grama, June grass, and speargrass (often called needle and thread grass because of its sharp seed head and long, wiry tail). These grasses were high in nutritive value, and as they cured on the stem during the dry late summer and early fall, provided excellent forage in the winter. The grama grass achieved its main growth when the June rains came, and it was easily identified by its flaglike, dark-coloured head which was upwards of three-quarters of an inch in length. Blue grama was especially good forage during the spring and the late fall and early winter. The eroded hillsides and valleys of the Red Deer, Frenchman, Big Muddy, and Milk rivers supported semi-desert plants such as greasewood, Spanish bayonet, and sage.

Surrounding the shortgrass zone was an area characterized by greater precipitation and a mixed June grass and wheat grass prairie. The dry south-facing slopes, however, were still dominated by the shortgrass varieties, and as one zone merged into another, there were combinations of speargrass, blue grama, wheat grass, and June grass.

Along the base of the foothills and the mountains was a third distinct zone, the rough fescue prairie. An area of still greater precipitation than the mixed-grass zone, the rough fescue country was also interspersed with many groves of aspen poplar. This zone along the foothills and the Porcupine Hills was particularly attractive to the early cattlemen. Unfortunately for the ranchers, much of the zone also contained good black soil and so was eagerly sought by farmers as well.

The natural grasslands, of course, provided a vast pasture for the ranchers, and so it was with profound dismay that they watched settlers move into the range and turn it over with plows and seed it to crops. Although in many areas farmers failed and the land was allowed to return to grass, the range was never the same again.

Rising above the general level of the plains are several hill regions which played an important role in the development of ranching. The Porcupine Hills, approximately 55 miles long and 15 miles wide—from Willow Creek in the north to the town of Cowley in the south—run in a direction parallel to the front ranges of the Rockies. While the higher elevations support coniferous forests of Douglas fir, lodgepole pine, and white spruce, the lower areas carry extensive grasslands of fescue and wheat grass. The grasslands, combined with shelter provided by many coulees and water supplied by springs and creeks, made the hills some of the choicest lands for the early ranchers.

The Milk River Ridge, a prominent height of land running across southern Alberta from the Rockies to the town of Milk River, rises 900 feet above the nearby plains. The formation, about 25 miles wide, is an area of rolling prairie and also supports a nutritious mixed-grass plant community.

Farther east, straddling the Alberta-Saskatchewan border, are the Cypress Hills, a region of nearly level plateau and rolling hills rising to 2,300 feet above the plains at its western end. The hills support a mixed coniferous and deciduous forest and fescue grassland, a natural environment very different from that of the adjoining shortgrass prairie. The luxuriant grassland on the plateau of the hills and the shelter and springs of the coulees made the Cypress Hills very attractive to ranchers.

The Americans were the first group successful in exploiting the commercial possibilities of the southern Alberta and Saskatchewan range during the late 1860s and early 1870s. Their interest was trade in the hides of the buffalo which still grazed the plains in enormous numbers, and the northward and westward thrust of the American frontier pushed across the international boundary as traders and assorted adventurers from Montana began to tap the resources of the Canadian plains. While the area north of the 49th parallel was under the jurisdiction of the Hudson's Bay Company until 1870, at which time the country was transferred to the Dominion of Canada, neither the company nor the Canadian government was able to sustain a firm presence in the area, let alone enforce the law. The traders from Montana were a constant source of irritation to the Hudson's Bay Company, as they not only operated with impunity—and impudence—but also presented the company with stiff and unwelcome competition.

The Montana traders dealt in both dry and wet goods, but their most potent and profitable stock-in-trade was whisky, and a very brisk commerce in buffalo robes and liquor developed. This ruthless trade had a devastating two-fold effect—it rent the fabric of native society and contributed to the destruction of the buffalo herds. The whole unsavoury business burst into the awareness of the Canadian public with the 1873 massacre of a number of Assiniboine Indians by American traders and adventurers in the Cypress Hills. This incident hastened the formation of the North-West Mounted Police and their dispatch to southern Alberta in 1874. In that year, Fort Macleod was established as the headquarters for the force in what was then the North West Territories.

The arrival of the police on the plains signalled the real beginnings of white settlement in southern Alberta. There was already some settlement farther north around Edmonton and along the North Saskatchewan River. To the south the Methodist missionary John McDougall and his trader brother David established a mission at Morley on the Bow River, in the foothills, in 1873, and the next year John McDougall travelled south to Montana, brought back about one hundred head of cattle—the first range cattle in Alberta—and put them out to graze near the Morley mission. McDougall's purpose was not so much commercial as an attempt to place the mission on a self-sufficient basis. Nevertheless, John McDougall is often credited as one of the founders of the cattle industry in southern Alberta.

The following year, 1874, witnessed several developments in the livestock industry. Two enterprising men from Montana, Joe McFarland and Henry Olsen, brought small herds into the country and established operations near Fort Mcleod, where they found a good market among the police for their milk, cheese, and butter which they sold at 75 cents per pound. Even though the price of their butter was considered high, demand was such that the two men could not satisfy it. McFarland's and Olsen's success encouraged several others to locate dairy operations near the fort, among them a Mrs. Armstrong and her hired man, Mr. Morgan.

The presence of the Mounted Police was significant for the settlers in two ways. First, they were a market, albeit a small one, for suppliers of dairy and beef products. Second, they provided an element of protection and security for the settlers, though the buffalo in the country initially constituted a greater hazard to domestic stock than did the Indians. The danger lay in the buffalo herds sweeping away domestic stock, as happened to John McDougall when he drove some cattle south from Edmonton in 1873. One morning he awakened to find his animals gone, carried away in the night by a herd of buffalo. Fortunately, he was able to retrieve his animals, though a bull which had fancied the wild life had been savagely and bloodily rejected by the buffalo.

In 1876 George Emerson, who became know as the Grand Old Man of the southern Alberta range, began to drive cattle and horses into the country. Born in 1841 and raised in Danville, Quebec, Emerson left Canada as a young man, headed west and homesteaded at Council Bluffs in Iowa. He joined the rush to the gold fields of Montana in 1865, but finding little luck there and hearing of gold along the North Saskatchewan River, headed north in 1866. There he achieved some success, occasionally panning about eight dollars a day in gold. But the life of a gold seeker was an insecure one without much future, and Emerson took a job with the Hudson's Bay Company as a freighter.

For several years Emerson worked on the Red River cart brigades which moved across the northern prairies. He became thoroughly familiar with the plains and their changeable moods and conditions. Then, developing confidence in his abilities, he established various enterprises of his own and formed a partnership with Tom Lynch, a Montanan whom he met prospecting along the North Saskatchewan River. Lynch was an experienced cattleman, having worked with outfits in California, Washington, Oregon, and Idaho. The two partners rode south to Sun River, Montana, bought about two hundred head of cattle, drove them north, and sold them in and around Fort Mcleod, numbering some of the police officers among their customers. In subsequent years, Lynch and Emerson brought in more herds for other ranchers.

The Mounted Police wintered their horses on the prairie and naturally noticed their good condition in the spring. They also observed that the buffalo seemed to suffer few ill effects from the winter. In 1876 Sgt. D.J. Whitney bought a bull and 14 cows, some with calves, from a Montana trader. When he was unable to find sufficient feed for the winter, Whitney simply turned his cattle loose on the range, and in the spring was happily surprised with the fitness of his small herd. In fact, Whitney was so encouraged by the condition of his cattle that he managed to obtain an early discharge from the force in order to take up ranching full time.

Other policemen, including the brothers Edward and George Maunsell, took notice of the opportunities which the country presented and also went into ranching after their discharge from the force. Edward Maunsell served with the Mounted Police from 1874 to 1877. After his discharge he returned to Ireland briefly to visit relatives and then returned to southern Alberta by way of the Missouri River and Fort Benton.

Maunsell's trip up the Missouri was an eventful one. The muddy river clogged the steamboat's boilers, which had to be blown and cleaned frequently. On one occasion, while the boat was delayed and tied up to shore for repairs, Maunsell overheard a passenger remark that the boat would remain tied up until another vessel came along. Feeling restless and confined on board, Maunsell took his rifle and jumped ashore, hoping to find some game on the plains by the river. After a successful hunt he returned to the river, only to discover the boat steaming off into the distance.

Maunsell was aware of the dangers of staying alone on the prairie, far from any settlement and without provisions. Then remembering that the boat had to steam around a wide bend in the river, he ran to catch it as it looped back. As he cut across the loop and lost sight of both the river and the steamboat, Maunsell could hear nothing but his pounding heart. When he reached the river, everything was quiet, there was no boat in sight, and he had no idea whether it had passed. Scrambling down the bank to the water's edge, feeling cold and very alone, Maunsell built a fire and sat down to think out his predicament. He was sure that the boat would not pass him in the night if he slept, for it never ran at night. While these thoughts were running through his head, Maunsell heard a faint shriek downstream, the sound of the boiler blowing off. Immensely relieved, he decided to wait until the morning to try to reach his boat.

The next morning, in the early light, Maunsell pressed along the bank, saw the boat, and watched the crew haul out a cable to shore. Pushing through the bush until he was beside the vessel, Maunsell managed to sneak on board again. Safe at last, he said nothing to his fellow passengers of his misadventure after he realized that nobody had even missed him.

Colonel Macleod of the North-West Mounted Police was in Fort Benton in Montana on business when Edward Maunsell's boat tied up at that town's long levee, and he offered Maunsell a ride with the police party to Fort Walsh in the Cypress Hills. However, as he was anxious to get back to Fort Macleod, Maunsell declined the offer and caught a ride with a freighter driving north with supplies. When he arrived at Fort Macleod, Edward found that his brother had re-engaged with the police as a special constable for several weeks and, for the time being, was not able to help with their own plans for starting a ranch.

Edward Maunsell set about on his own to find out where and how to buy cattle. Howard Conrad of the I.G. Baker store in Fort Macleod offered to help the brothers obtain cattle, and Conrad and the Maunsells signed a contract for 100 head of cows and 3 bulls for delivery in the fall, with half the price as down payment. Henry Olsen, however, advised the Maunsells to wait until spring to bring in their cattle, as they would likely arrive in poor condition after a long drive and be poorly prepared for winter. Conrad was quite agreeable to the delay, as he was having unexpected trouble locating cattle for the Maunsells.

George Maunsell received his discharge from the NWMP and he and Edward cut fence rails, constructed a cabin and put up a stable and some corrals during the winter. In February 1879 the money which they had been expecting finally arrived. Unfortunately, it was in the form of a letter of credit drawn on a bank in Deadwood, Dakota Territory. Edward Maunsell took the letter to the I.G. Baker store in Fort Macleod, but the manager would not cash it. Maunsell decided to take the letter to Fort Benton, the nearest bank. Tony la Chappelle, an early resident of Fort Macleod, joined Maunsell for the trip. They both almost froze to death on the way and, in fact, never reached Fort Benton. Maunsell's feet were so badly frozen that he had to be carried back to Fort Macleod, where he recovered in the Mounted Police hospital. Eventually, the letter of credit was sent to Helena and cashed there.

Tom Lynch had contracted to drive the Maunsell's cattle into Fort Macleod, which he did in late June. Edward Maunsell later recalled:

> It was late when we got them branded and my brother and I started for home. Neither of us knew anything about driving wild cattle. They had been in the corral overnight and were thirsty and excited after branding, and when let out they started to run. I will never forget that drive. We thought the cattle were going to keep on running forever, and it was after dark when we got them near our cabin, where there was fortunately a slough. Here they drank and immediately began grazing, which was a great relief, as both we and our horses were completely worn out.
>
> Fearing that the cattle might take it into their heads to start running again after feeding, I undertook to nightherd them, but to my delight they lay down and started chewing the cud. I thus learned my first lesson in handling range cattle, for I saw that the reason they were so wild was that they were thirsty and hungry and that a full stomach made for contentment.

A few weeks after placing their herd on the range, the Maunsells counted their stock; they found that some animals were missing and decided that the cattle must have wandered away, for the herd was allowed to graze freely on the unfenced range. Henry Olsen, however, said that the cattle had probably been killed by Indians.

The native inhabitants of southern Alberta were on the verge of starvation. Treaty No. 7, signed in 1877, and by which the Blackfoot, Bloods, Peigans, Stoneys, and Sarcees relinquished their claims to the range country, seemed to portend evil times. The winter of 1877–78 was mild, the ground remained bare of snow, and prairie fires roared across the dry grassland, destroying the grazing grounds of those few buffalo left in the country. The Blackfoot waited for the buffalo to move towards the foothills, but the herds did not come.

Spring brought green grass and fresh pasture for the buffalo, but though they returned from their wintering grounds, their numbers were sadly depleted. Instead of great spreading herds, the buffalo appeared only in scattered bunches. There were enough animals for the Blackfoot, but other tribes pushed into the Blackfoot hunting grounds and the competition for game became intense. The Indians contemplated their future with fear and hopelessness. The treaty commissioners had assured them that the buffalo would last another ten years, but already, within a year, the end of the animals was in sight.

By early winter 1878 there was not enough meat in the country to feed the Blackfoot people. Only a few buffalo grazed within their hunting grounds. In desperation the Indians turned to pronghorn, deer, elk, porcupines, and even gophers and mice for food. That winter was a hungry time, and the following summer brought little relief. Summer hunting was poor as few buffalo moved north from the United States. The country just south of the boundary was ravaged by fires and this hindered the northward movement of the herds. Canadian authorities suspected that the fires were deliberately set by the Americans in order to starve Sitting Bull and his refugee Sioux who, after the Battle of the Little Big Horn, had moved north into the Cypress Hills and Wood Mountain districts. In late 1879 the Canadian Blackfoot crossed into Montana to hunt buffalo, but the American authorities pressed them to return. The Blackfoot straggled back into Canada, hungry, dispirited, and broken.

In his report for 1878, Colonel Macleod recommended that a large band of cattle be bought and herded in the Bow River country to provide food for the Indians; pasture was abundant and the cattle could graze all winter. Macleod added:

> There is no question in my mind as to the investment; many men in Montana have made fortunes in this business; why should not the Government utilize the magnificent domain lying idle in the West, and have at any moment such a supply of food as would meet any necessity that might arise.

The next year a herd of a thousand cattle was purchased for the Indians and pastured at the foot of the Porcupine Hills. This provided some relief for the next few years.

The cattle herds of the white settlers grazing freely on the range were an almost irresistible temptation and undoubtedly a number were killed by the Indians. During the late 1870s, ranchers' complaints about cattle-killing by Indians poured in to the Mounted Police. Superintendent Winder at Fort Macleod reported that from March to October 1879 complaints were made to him almost daily by cattlemen about Indians killing cattle. Winder and other officers investigated the complaints, but it was difficult to identify the guilty parties. In spite of careful enquiries and the vigilance of both the police and the ranchers, in only one case was a conviction obtained—a case which featured the most extenuating circumstances.

According to Winder, this was how the story went:

A Stoney Indian and his family had been without food for many days, and were in the most deplorable condition. The Indian when in search of game killed a cow, and went to a rancher in the neighborhood, to whom he supposed the animal belonged, and offered his horse in payment. The owner prosecuted, and the Indian ("Little Man") after laying in jail for a considerable period awaiting the trial, was ordered ... to pay twenty dollars, the value of the animal.

Winder also received complaints about houses being entered and provisions stolen, and gardens being robbed by Indians; he sent parties to the Indian camps in the vicinity but could find no trace of the stolen provisions. The Mounted Police advised the ranchers that if the stockmen could identify the Indians who killed their cattle, the culprits would be punished, but since most of the cattle were killed at night or in remote places, identification was impossible.

Henry Olsen informed the Maunsells that the country east of Fort Macleod and straddling the Oldman River had been selected by the Peigans for their reservation, and that he was planning to sell his land in the district to the government and move his cattle and interests to Montana. He advised the Maunsells that, under the circumstances, they might as well move, too. Before acting on this advice, the Maunsells decided to check with other cattlemen in the area and see what they were planning to do. A group of settlers came together and discussed their common concerns, then met with Colonel Macleod to see whether he could do anything to protect their herds.

The stockmen presented Macleod with a proposal to put all their cattle together, herd them during the day and corral them at night. Would the stockmen be able to defend their property if Indians came to kill the cattle? Macleod's answer was short and clear; if any rancher killed an Indian he would certainly be hanged. The ranchers then proposed that they receive compensation for any cattle killed by the Indians; that is they should be able to sell that animal at cost to the government. Again, Macleod's answer disappointed them: the stockmen were in the country at their own risk—the country could not yet be considered open for settlement.

A delegation of stockmen who went to appeal to Lt.-Gov. Edgar Dewdney met with no greater success. Colonel Macleod assessed the ranchers' situation and the role of the police in his report for 1879:

> I think it a matter of congratulation that the Indians throughout the
> territories generally have behaved so well. They have, however, been ac-
> cused of killing large numbers of cattle in the "Bow River District," and
> some in the neighbourhood of Fort Walsh. It is undoubtedly the case
> that they killed some, but nothing like the numbers claimed. It is the
> opinion of many respectable stockmen that whites had more to do with
> it than the Indians. A great many cattle have strayed back to Montana,
> and a great many more must have perished in the storms which have
> passed over the country in March last. The fact that seventy carcasses
> were found in one coulee shows the damage to be attributed to this
> cause. When I visited Fort Macleod for the Blackfoot payment, in Sep-
> tember, I was called upon by several stockmen who were then driving
> their cattle across the line. I pointed out to them, that if they herded
> their cattle in certain localities, it would be possible to do something
> for them, but as long as they turned their cattle adrift on the prairie,
> and only looked after them twice a year, they were themselves to blame
> if they lost a great many. To have done what they asked would have
> amounted to this; That the police would have had to act as herders over
> a country about one hundred miles wide, and over two hundred miles
> long, as the ranchmen who have squatted through that section are scat-
> tered over a country of that extent.

Some of the ranchers decided to move south into Montana, and, in
preparation, began to round up their cattle. This was the first roundup on
the Canadian range, the forerunner of many and much larger roundups, but
with an altogether different purpose—to pull out of the country. Sixteen men
took part in the roundup: W.F. Parker, William Winder, Jack Miller, Edward
H. Maunsell, Thomas Lee, H.A. ("Fred") Kanouse, Robert Patterson, J.B.
Smith, Joe McFarland, Henry Olsen, Sam Brouard, J.W. Bell, W.J. Hyde,
Morgan and Allison. Parker, Winder, Maunsell, Patterson, and Bell were all
former Mounted Policemen. Although Parker worked on the roundup, he decided to stay in the country, as he had lost all his cattle anyway. Joe McFarland
also decided to stay, but Miller, Patterson, Bell, Smith, and Morgan took their
cattle south to the Marias River range in Montana.

Edward and George Maunsell could find only 56 head to take out of the
country, though they had paid duty on 103 cattle brought into Canada. Most

of the ranchers suffered substantial losses. To make matters even more painful, the cattlemen discovered that they had to pay duty entering the United
States on the very cattle they had so very recently taken out of that country.
And to further rub salt into their wounds, reports in Fort Benton claimed
that the Canadians had to move to Montana in order to get protection which
the Dominion government and the Mounted Police would not provide. The
Maunsell brothers, after settling their cattle in Montana, made their way back
to Fort Macleod to maintain squatters' rights to their property, and to take up
farming until such time as they could resume ranching.

By early 1880 the Indians in southern Alberta began to move to their
roughly mapped-out reserves where the government provided food, some
tools, and assistance for farming. With the Indians more settled and the country secure, the outlook for stock-raising improved, prompting the Maunsells
and other cattlemen to try again. The brothers brought their cattle back into
the country in 1881 and were joined that year by a third brother, Harry.

Edward Maunsell travelled to Fort Benton to meet Harry, and while
there, talked briefly with James Walker, who was in the town en route to
take up management duties on the Cochrane Ranche near Calgary. The two
Maunsells started north; near Choteau, Montana, they came upon the ruins of the house which belonged to Mrs. Armstrong, who had left southern
Alberta with the other ranchers in 1879. She and her hired man, Morgan,
had been brutally murdered by a drifter; her little girl, however, had been
playing outside the house at the time of the killings and was able to identify
the murderer, who was apprehended and summarily strung up by a group of
neighbours. As a former policeman, Edward Maunsell wondered about the
processes of Montana justice.

The brothers continued north to the Marias River to take charge of
their cattle, which they had left with a rancher named Miller. It took Miller
several days to round up the Maunsell's cattle. When the count was complete,
the brothers learned that their little herd had dwindled even further, from 56
head to 50. Miller explained that blackleg was a serious problem on the range,
particularly among the calves. Edward Maunsell noticed that there were no
yearlings in their herd, whereas Miller's herd had more than the usual number. Maunsell remarked that he knew that blackleg was a fatal disease, but
hadn't been aware that it would attack one brand and not another.

Nonetheless, the brothers took what cattle remained to them and drove
them north. The winter which followed was a good one, and in July 1882
the three brothers could take pleasure that their herd had increased and their
venture was progressing.

In the early 1880s the cattle industry made a rapid and dramatic recovery from the collapse of the previous years. A number of developments favoured the expansion of ranching on the plains. The Conservative government of Sir John A. Macdonald pushed the construction of the Canadian Pacific transcontinental railway, a project which provided easier access into the country for settlers from the east, and out to eastern markets for the ranchers. The urgency of establishing a solid Canadian presence in the North West Territories grew each year as pressures mounted from the United States. The Canadian government was aware that free land for homesteading and open range was disappearing in the American west, while there was plenty of land lying empty and unused north of the border. It was therefore imperative that the North West be occupied and secured by Canadians. Settlement was likely to take a long time, but a western ranching industry seemed a sensible and economic means of enforcing Canada's claim to the North West.

A Canadian ranching industry would provide additional benefits. There were obvious advantages to supplying the demand for beef, both in the North West and the central provinces, from domestic sources. There was, of course, also a need to develop some traffic on the Canadian Pacific Railway to pay for the enormous costs of construction and government subsidies.

However, the North West was remote from central Canada, and investors were reluctant to risk their capital in that distant country when there were better-known and less risky opportunities in the United States. Furthermore, the Dominion Lands Act of 1872, framed to encourage agricultural settlement in Manitoba and the North West, made no provisions for large-scale grazing operations. Indeed, the act treated grazing lands as mere adjuncts to the operations of homesteaders on their 160-acre plots. All land was open for homesteading, and grazing leases granted under the Dominion Lands Act could be cancelled on six months' notice.

By 1876 the suitability of parts of the North West Territories for stockraising rather than farming was becoming apparent. The reports of the Mounted Police, surveyors, and various travellers were gradually changing the public's and the government's perception of the North West. In 1881 the Dominion Lands Act was amended to permit the granting of leases on large scale to nonresidents of the territories, though these leases could be cancelled on two years' notice if they were required for settlement purposes.

Few of the early stockmen in the North West had bothered to obtain grazing leases or homesteads. They simply squatted on the land and ran their cattle on the open range. In 1880, however, there were enquiries for grazing leases, the first one apparently coming from Senator Matthew Cochrane of Montreal. After discussions with Cochrane, Col. J.S. Dennis, deputy minister of the interior, submitted a number of recommendations to the government in a confidential memo. These recommendations formed the basis for the new lease policy which was promulgated by order-in-council in 1881.

The new policy contained seven provisions. First, the minister of the interior was to satisfy himself of the good faith and ability of the applicant for a grazing lease to carry out the enterprise involved in such application. Second, the leases were to be put up at auction and sold to the highest bidder. Third, such leases were to be for a period of 21 years. Fourth, the leaseholder was expected to stock his lease at the rate of one head of stock for every ten acres, and failure to stock the lease accordingly within three years would be grounds for the government to cancel the lease or reduce it proportionately. Fifth, leases were not to exceed 100,000 acres, and the lessee had the privilege of purchasing land covered by the lease on which to construct buildings, but this land was not to exceed 5 percent of the area of the lease. Sixth, the rent for a grazing lease was set at ten dollars per annum for each 1,000 acres, and the price of the land which might be purchased for the cattle station was set at $1.25 per acre. Finally, and curiously, "the Minister of the Interior shall have authority to grant leases on the above terms, without putting the lands severally applied for up to public auction, to the several persons to whom promises have been made to that effect ... "

Various provisions generated controversy almost immediately, but three in particular drew public attention—those dealing with the terms of 21 years, 100,000 acres, and rent of ten dollars per 1,000 acres (or one cent per acre). The new policy, however, combined with the strengthening interest in cattle as an investment opportunity, generated a rush among investors for grazing lands in the North West.

There was no lack of propagandists for the Canadian grazing regions, and the country received its biggest boost in 1881, when the Governor General, the Marquess of Lorne, toured the North West Territories. A number of correspondents from Canadian and British newspapers accompanied the tour, and sent back glowing reports to their readers of the manifold resources and opportunities to be found on the Canadian range.

In Scotland, Edinburgh was a major centre of interest and investment in North American ranches, and both the *Edinburgh Courant* and the *Scotsman* carried articles by journalists who accompanied the royal tour. The *Scotman's* correspondent, Dr. James McGregor, reported in September 1881 that "the fifty-seven miles from Blackfoot Crossing (Cluny) took us long to accomplish. The way lay along the high prairie and the rich level plain that skirts the left bank of the Bow River, a country unsurpassed for its qualities as a stock raising country." After passing through the country between Calgary and the international boundary, McGregor wrote that

A glance at the map will show that this is a well watered country, numerous creeks and streams—some of them, like the Little Bow and Old Man's River, being of very considerable size—flowing clear and ice cold eastwards from the Rocky Mountains ... the best land seems to be along what are known as the Foot Hills at the base of the mountains, and along the banks of the principal streams, there is no portion of it that is not more or less good for stock-raising.

So favourable are the conditions, climatic and otherwise, of the country we have now traversed that men hereabout speak of it as "God's country". With regard to the mildness of its winter climate there is a uniform and universal testimony. There are frequent cold snaps of great intensity but they do not last above a day or two. It is quite unusual to have a persistent low temperature. After one of these snaps, Lieutenant Clark, of the Mounted Police, has played cricket on the 3rd February.

When snow does fall it is in a fine powdery state, and is either blown away or melted away in a day or two by the warm Chinook winds. Horses and cattle live without shelter on the open prairie the whole winter, and are in excellent condition in the spring.

The Governor General's party visited Senator Cochrane's newly acquired lease west of Calgary. McGregor reported that "one is glad that so good a farm has fallen into such excellent hands." Farther south, the party found themselves

almost beneath the snow of the Rocky Mountains. The country selected is known by the ugly name of Pincher Creek, because some whisky-seller possibly under the influence of his own merchandise, dropped his pincers into the pretty stream and could not find them. "Why," the question has been often asked of the settlers, "should their beautiful little river, as is the case with almost every creek and river we crossed, be disfigured for all time by such a name?"

At the conclusion of the Governor General's tour, McGregor stopped briefly in Montreal before returning home and, after pronouncing Mount Royal Cemetery an ideal burying place, expressed his delight with the North West and repeated his conviction that as a grazing country, the territories could not be surpassed. The country he most admired was the Bow River district west of Calgary and he wished that he could place plenty of Scottish settlers out there.

John Macoun, a University of Toronto biologist who led a scientific expedition to the North West, published his encyclopaedic *Manitoba and the Great North West* in 1882. Alexander Begg, an indefatigable promoter of the North West, contributed two chapters, one of which compared stock-raising in the Bow River district with that in Montana.

> As a stock-raising country the Bow River district is the best in America. I say this advisedly, as I journeyed through a large portion of Montana and through the Bow River district, as far north as Edmonton ... in August, September, and October 1881, and closely observed the capabilities of each section along the route. Cattle owners from Montana and Texas, who have resided in the Bow River district for the past six or eight years, and raised stock west of Fort Macleod and north towards Calgary, testified freely to the superior grazing properties of the country; whilst the excellent condition of the cattle which had all wintered out in the severe winter of 1880–81, was ocular demonstration of the truth of their statement.

Begg also quoted from a lecture by Prof. W. Brown of the Ontario Agricultural College at Guelph. According to Brown, the arithmetic of stock-raising was both simple and financially appealing. For a ranch of 2,000 acres, Brown estimated capital needs at $10,050 for livestock (yearling bulls, heifers, cows, oxen and saddle horses); $2,500 for buildings, corrals, fencing, tools and equipment; $3,000 for incidental expenses, and $165 for a lease and homestead of 100 acres. Total cost—$15,765.

Professor Brown emphasized that the 2,000 acres could just as easily be 20,000, with obvious advantages of scale, so long as the range remained uncrowded. But more important than the costs, of course, were the anticipated gains. Barring any serious set-backs, such as epidemic diseases, bad weather, weak markets, or extensive theft, Brown calculated a net increase in capital of $9,550 over two and a half years—a healthy 60 percent. Could anyone seriously doubt the profitability of such a venture?

Perhaps the most frequently quoted booster (at least by historians) was the Governor General himself, the Marquess of Lorne, who exclaimed that if he weren't the Governor General, he would certainly be a rancher in Alberta. And indeed, a number of his party did invest in ranches in Alberta.

In 1881 there were some 9,000 head of cattle in the North West Territories, comprising a few herds around Fort Macleod, Pincher Creek, High River, and Calgary. The next year there were 154 applications for leases, 75 of which were authorized by the Dominion government and which covered

4 million acres. Over the next few years, however, the acreage under lease decreased, so that by 1884 authorized leases covered just over 2 million acres and 1885, about 1 million acres. Many leases were taken strictly for speculation by investors who expected to profit simply by holding the land until values rose. The Maunsells, like many early cattlemen, discovered after their return from Montana that the range they had been using had become part of a lease granted in Ottawa to someone else, and all that remained for them in the area was poor and rocky land. The large lease next to them, however, had been taken for speculation and was never stocked, and so they simply continued to let their cattle graze there until they acquired land for lease on their own. Many of the early leases were never stocked, or if they were, stocked with insufficient cattle, and were consequently either cancelled or reduced.

The leases formed a fairly compact block stretching from the international boundary to the Bow River, but were particularly concentrated along the trail between Fort Macleod and Calgary. The early stockmen did not venture very far east of the Calgary-Fort Macleod axis; the shortgrass country held little attraction for them while there was still room nearer the foothills and the Rockies. The main centres of the range country during the 1880s were Pincher Creek, Fort Macleod, High River, and Calgary.

One of the early ranching outfits was that of Lafayette French and his partner O.H. Smith at High River. Their brand was OH and their main business was trading, and as independents they were not very popular with the dominant firm of I.G. Baker Company. They were favoured, however, by Chief Crowfoot of the Blackfoot. French had saved the chief's life during an assassination attempt and was given permission by Crowfoot to establish a store at Blackfoot Crossing on the Bow River east of Calgary. At High River, French and Smith operated a busy trading post and stopping house on the Calgary-Fort Macleod trail, and ran a few cattle to furnish fresh beef for their customers. In 1883 they sold their brand and cattle to Fred Ings, who moved the outfit west into the foothills and started the Rio Alto Ranch on the Highwood River.

Ings was a native of Prince Edward Island and member of a prominent merchant family. After spending two years in Spain and other parts of Europe, he and his brother Walter attended Ontario Agricultural College where their fellow students included Lord Richard Boyle, his brother the Honourable Henry Boyle, and young De Winton, son of the Governor General's aide-de-camp, Francis De Winton. At the completion of their course, Fred Ings, the two Boyles, and De Winton set out together for the North West. Walter Ings later joined his brother on the OH.

Lord Boyle, the son of Lord Shannon of county Cork, Ireland, was born in London. After attending Eton he studied at the Royal Military College, Sandhurst, and spent two years in a rifle brigade. He retired from service in 1882 with the rank of lieutenant, came to Canada, and took up ranching near Pincher Creek. In 1885 he was elected to the North West Council for the Macleod District, beating out his competitor, fellow rancher George C. Ives, by a large majority. According to *Robertson's Political Manual of Manitoba and North West Territories, 1887,* Boyle was "now one of the largest stock raisers in Alta … and is a very popular member of the Legislature."

Lord Boyle later joined the stampede to the gold fields of the Klondike, where he disappeared for a time. He reappeared, however, and, succeeding to the earldom of Shannon, returned to Ireland. The Honourable Henry Boyle did not take to the life of the range very well, according to one of his contemporaries, he was always bored and spent much of his time driving around and cracking his horsewhip.

Dan Riley, another native of Prince Edward Island, arrived in the cattle country during the early 1880s. After teaching school on the island for several years he made his way to Winnipeg in 1882 via Chicago and Minneapolis. He worked for the Canadian Pacific Railway in Winnipeg for a winter and then, with four companions, struck out for the west in the spring of 1883. The party went as far as it could by rail, then bought a wagon and team for the rest of the journey. Riley lost his watch and wallet when he and his friends had to ford their outfit across the South Saskatchewan River at Medicine Hat. When he arrived at the crossing of the Highwood River in May, he immediately went to work for French and Smith in order to replenish his funds.

During the next few years Riley worked for several outfits in the High River district, including the Bar U and the "25." When the rebellion of 1885 erupted, he signed on as a dispatch rider between Edmonton and the Peace Hills near Wetaskiwin. In 1889, accompanying a shipment of cattle to Montreal, he took the opportunity to visit his family in Prince Edward Island. When he returned to High River, he brought back both a bride, Edith Thomson, and a brother-in-law, Fulton Thomson.

Riley and Thomson then began a long and profitable business partnership in the High River district. Thomson developed a ranch based on Langford Creek west of Nanton, while Riley ran a land business centred in High River. As Riley became more experienced in land sales and an expert on land matters generally, he made many trips to Ottawa on land questions and issues. Over the years he became well acquainted with many people in the capital, and so it was no great surprise to his friends in the North West when he was appointed to the Senate. As well, Riley was a director and a long-time president of the Western Stock Growers' Association.

John Quirk was another early rancher. He drove a herd of cattle from Montana to the Highwood River in the early 1880s and settled near High River. A native of Ireland, he had married in that country in the 1870s, then sailed to America to seek his fortune, intending that his wife should join him once he was established. Apparently he forgot all about his bride, or at least he didn't write to her. After several years of not hearing a word from him, the redoubtable lady set out by herself to find him in the sprawling west. Catching up with him in a Montana gold camp, she decided that there must be something better than the life of a gold miner. Mrs. Quirk helped her husband wind up his interests in Montana, and then together they trekked north to Canada. After a few years in the High River district the Quirks moved their operations farther west to the north fork of the Sheep River.

William Roper Hull was another early arrival in southern Alberta. When he was 17, he and his brother John left their native England to join their uncle, Robert Roper, on his ranch in the Kamloops district of British Columbia. The two brothers took passage to Panama, walked across the isthmus, and then sailed up the coast to the mouth of the Fraser River, from which point they walked the final leg of their journey to Kamloops. William and John Hull started a small ranch on the North Thompson River and raised horses and cattle, selling some of their beef to the CPR crews working east from the Pacific coast. The Hulls, like many British Columbia ranchers, had a serious problem with surplus horses which were rapidly increasing in numbers, but for which there was no accessible market.

Hearing that there was strong demand for horses in southern Alberta, the Hull brothers rounded up a herd of 1,200 wild and spirited animals from the Kamloops district, and in late 1883 started out for Alberta. There was no direct route to their destination, so they headed south along the old cattle trail of the 1860s, past Okanagan Lake and Osoyoos to the Columbia River where they turned east. The brothers trailed their herd of horses right through Spokane and Bonners Ferry, then turned north, crossed back into Canada, and pushed through the Crowsnest Pass on a newly cut trail into southern Alberta. They found a small market for horses around Fort Macleod and sold a number there. They drove the rest of the herd to the Calgary district where they managed to sell them, then returned to British Columbia.

The Hull brothers returned to Alberta in 1884 and started a butcher business. In the fall of 1886 they and their partner W.P. Trounce brought in for sale a large herd of cattle from Kamloops. Those cattle they didn't sell they put in the charge of Dan Riley. Riley, together with Henry Minesinger, looked over the country for a suitable wintering ground, and moved the Hulls' surplus cattle into the north end of Pine Coulee in the hills west of Nanton. The location proved to be almost ideal. The winter was unusually severe, but the deep coulee provided shelter while the hills were blown clear of snow, thereby allowing the cattle to get at the grass. Losses were so light compared with other outfits in the district that Hull and Trounce established their own ranch, the "25," in the Pine Coulee hills. This operation was later sold to Alberta Estates, a Scottish syndicate which also had large holdings in South America.

The Hulls expanded their business interests in Alberta, though the two brothers eventually dissolved their partnership, first with Trounce and then with each other. John took over the Kamloops and British Columbia operations, and William, those in Alberta. One of William Roper Hull's important acquisitions in Alberta was the 4,000-acre Government Supply Farm south of Calgary. This farm, where Fish Creek flowed into the Bow River, included the original homestead of John Glenn, who established the first permanent farm in the district about 1875. Glenn sold his property to the federal government as an instructional farm for Indians for $350, a cow and a calf. Hull developed the government farm into the Bow Valley Ranch, one of the premier ranches of the Calgary district. His prosperity and well-publicized success—Hull was a very effective showman as well as rancher and businessman—gave Bob Edwards of the Calgary *Eye Opener* an opportunity to exercise his wit:

> The statement attributed to Mr. W.R. Hull in a recent interview that he intended purchasing the late pontiff's herd of papal bulls to put on the range adjacent to the New Oxley Ranche for the purpose of improving the breed, is entirely without foundation. Mr. Hull has no such intention.

During the 1880s many farmers and stockmen sought opportunities on the range. The McNab family from the Ottawa valley settled near Fort Macleod, and in 1883 Joe McNab, aged 15, helped drive his family's stock from the end of the CPR rails at Calgary to their homestead. McNab later recalled that the drive was a long walk, and that the cows thought the Rocky Mountains were the big barns of the east. Consequently, they travelled too fast, and McNab had to bawl like a calf to hold them back.

In the south, O.S. ("Hod") Main, who ran cattle on the Marias and Teton ranges in northern Montana, also drifted many cattle across the border and supplied foundation stock to many of the ranches in southern Alberta. Main located his Canadian headquarters near Kipp, but in 1883 sold both the headquarters and his cattle to Walter Huckvale, a young Englishman who chose as his brand the Fiddleback. Huckvale operated on the Kipp range for about ten years. Then, with his partner Syd Hooper, he moved southeast to the shortgrass range on Manyberries Creek and built up his outfit into one of the district's largest ranches.

The Maunsells also continued to expand their cattle business. Edward Maunsell acquired a lease of about forty-five hundred acres in October 1883; he had about three hundred cattle on this range in 1885 and about four hundred and ninety in 1886. In 1902, with government permission, the Maunsells fenced some 130,000 acres of the Peigan Reserve with four strands of wire, and in 1905 they bought the Cochrane Ranche cattle, one of the biggest and finest herds in the country.

Both Tom Lynch and George Emerson settled in the range country, Lynch developing a ranch a few miles upstream from High River. When drought hit the country and it was impossible to put up any hay on the prairie with which to winter his cattle, Lynch started a ranch, the TL, on Sullivan Creek in the foothills, where there was plenty of grass and water. To move his cattle to Sullivan Creek, Lynch hired George Baker to pilot his four-horse outfit. Baker, though a top rider, was rumoured to be an ex-outlaw from Wyoming. When the outfit pulled into the OH Ranch for dinner, the OH owners feared that Baker may have been planning to locate near the range where their own cattle were grazing. They decided to keep an eye on him and if their suspicions were true, they would run Baker and the cattle he was herding out of the area. As soon as Baker and his outfit left the ranch, the OH hands saddled their horses and followed in their tracks. Seeing Baker was headed for Sullivan Creek, they decided to beat him to it.

Riding up Flat Creek, which parallelled Sullivan Creek, the OH hands quickly gathered up some of their cattle and herded them down onto the Sullivan Creek meadows. Baker arrived at the same time and, sizing up the situation, unstrapped a Winchester rifle from the back of the wagon seat. He rode up to the OH men with his rifle resting across the front of his saddle. The OH men claimed that the meadow was their range. Baker said it wasn't and that he knew their cattle had just been driven in. He suggested that they'd be going out a damn sight faster than they came in, and that he was starting a ranch right there in half an hour. He then set his dog on the OH cattle. Convinced that, in this instance, discretion was the better part of valour, the OH men gathered up their cattle and headed home. The TL Ranch was underway.

Emerson built up a ranch on the middle fork of the Highwood River, a few miles above the Bar U. He stocked his range with a large number of choice cows, starting with about three hundred head. After carrying on operations there for many years, he sold out in 1905 to the reorganized North West Cattle Company, and moved his principal interests east to the Red Deer River country.

Emerson kept all his business in his head, a practice which led to an oft-repeated story about the pioneer cattleman. William Fares of the big cattle-buying firm, Gordon, Ironsides, and Fares, drove out to Emerson's ranch one day to find out what had become of a cheque for $60,000 which the firm had paid Emerson the previous fall after a large deal, and which after several months, had still not cleared the bank. When Fares entered the ranch house, he found Emerson intently watching a couple of his cowboys playing a game of Seven Up while the Chinese cook, with dinner all ready, was trying to get them to eat it before it went cold. After chatting with Emerson for a few minutes, Fares broached the subject of his visit and asked what had become of the cheque. Emerson said that he supposed it had been credited to his account in his Calgary bank; but on being told that it had not gone through a bank at all, he allowed that the situation was rather strange. He hunted around the house for the cheque, and finally found it in the pocket of an old vest hanging on a nail behind a door, just where he had stuffed it six months earlier.

One of the country's most successful ranchers, Alfred Ernest Cross, arrived in Calgary in 1884 to work as bookkeeper, veterinarian, and ranch hand on the Cochrane Ranche west of the town. Born in Montreal in 1861, Cross was the fourth son of a Queen's Bench judge and took several years of formal schooling in England before returning to Canada to attend the Montreal Business College. Spending his holidays on an uncle's farm in the Eastern Townships, Cross developed an interest in agriculture which led to studies in animal husbandry at the Ontario Agricultural College at Guelph, and then in veterinary medicine at McGill University.

Cross did not stay long at the Cochrane Ranche, and in 1885 he took up a homestead on the prairie along Mosquito Creek. The following year he purchased a quarter section in the hills to the west of land belonging to his brother, William H. Cross. The new location provided better pasture and later developed into the home place of the a7, which was to eventually grow into one of the largest ranches in Alberta.

West of Calgary, A.P. Patrick obtained a lease north of the Bow River near the Ghost River. Patrick, a native of Montreal and the son of Alfred Patrick, clerk of the House of Commons, was educated at Upper Canada College in Toronto, and also attended Royal Military College at Kingston. In 1877 he was one of six commissioned Dominion topographical surveyors, and travelled to the far North West by Red River cart in 1878. He surveyed a great deal of southern Alberta, including the Stoney and Sarcee Indian reserves, many of the townsites between Edmonton and Fort Macleod, and much of the city of Calgary.

After obtaining his lease, Patrick returned east, and from there he shipped 208 good head of Ontario stock to the west. In 1883 he assigned his 12,000-acre lease to Edward A. Baynes, the son-in-law of Sen. Matthew Cochrane. Baynes in turn sold the lease in May 1884 to a group of investors forming the Mount Royal Ranche Company Ltd. Patrick, his father, and Baynes, as well as Alexander Gunn and William Benson, both members of Parliament, were shareholders in the company. With Baynes as manager of the ranch, the Mount Royal intended to raise horses, but the venture was plagued with problems and went into receivership. The creditors sold the horses at public auction in May 1886, the company was liquidated, and the ranch sold to W.C. Wells and Nelson Brown.

While the decade of the 1880s witnessed the development of many small and medium-sized holdings, the ranches which attracted the most attention were the large companies—the Cochrane, the Oxley, the Bar U, and the Walrond. The 1881 grazing regulations, the cattle boom in the United States, plentiful capital and the need for investment outlets, as well as the prospect of spectacular profits in western cattle and a growing awareness of the North West and its resources, all helped focus attention on the Canadian ranges.

Charles Edward Harris, manager and one of the founders of the Chipman Ranche (part of which lay within the present boundaries of Calgary under the waters of Glenmore Reservoir), described the spirit of the time:

In the year 1881 ... when the great possibilities of the Prairie Country, between Winnipeg and the Rockies, were being written up by paid agents, a few Halifax business men conceived the idea of being the first, or amongst the first to grasp, some one of the many chances then offering, at the very beginning, to reap a fortune, to say nothing of fame.

Well do I remember the sly, quiet gatherings that were held by this chosen few, in the back office of the firm whose leading members were the promoting spirits in this scheme. The undertaking decided upon, after the most profound research and calculation, being a Cattle and Horse Ranche beneath the Rocky Mountains, where, according to written reports, the seasons were about like an Eastern summer and autumn all the year round. There was no question, at those meetings, about the climate—that was a settled matter, and useless to discuss. It was merely a matter or taking hold promptly and with determination—the result was certain.

I was one of the select party ... My business was a good appearing one, but the net profits very small. I was eager for gain and glory. This Cattle and Horse Ranche business was very enticing. I was offered the management of the business, the salary being $1,200 per year, besides

my living. The result was I closed my business and accepted the position. I was a partner in the undertaking also, having subscribed, and was
then prepared to put in Three Thousand Dollars ($3,000). I did put in
this sum. My duties as then discussed were very attractive. I was to do
the business, including correspondence; superintend the men; I was to
have horses and men at my command, and it naturally got fixed in my
mind, that I was going to have a most enviable, free sort of life; but oh!
The horrible reality!

The Chipman brothers of Halifax were major shareholders in both the
group's ranch near Calgary and its 100,000-acre Halifax Ranch near Fort
Macleod; they also operated a hardware store in Calgary. However, by 1885
the hardware business was up for sale, as was the property and herds of the
southern ranch. The ranch near Calgary concentrated on horses, but in 1887
it too was offered for sale. The auction notices advertised "Sale positive." No
postponement on account of weather," with 650 horses, including 13 Perche-
ron stallions, and 1289 acres of the best land.

The Mount Royal and Chipman ranches were two of the more spectacular early failures, but many of the large ranches not only managed to
survive, but prospered.

Chapter Three

THE COCHRANE RANCHE

There were few white people in the 1880s who were more familiar with the plains and foothills of southwestern Alberta than John George ("Kootenai") Brown. The experienced frontiersman was leading a solitary life in the country around the Waterton Lakes, a great departure from the activity and excitement which had characterized his earlier career.

Kootenai Brown was born in England in 1839, and after a brief career in the British army he left that country for the New World, landing in Panama in 1862. He and a friend, Arthur Vowell, quickly headed north for the gold fields of British Columbia, where their experiences in the diggings and mines of the Cariboo were typical of hundreds of others—great hopes, but little reward for their efforts. From the Cariboo, Brown moved on to Wild Horse Creek in the east Kootenay region of southern British Columbia where he got work as a special police constable. News of a gold strike at Wild Horse Creek attracted hundreds of gold seekers from British Columbia and the northern United States, but the shallow diggings were quickly exhausted and the rowdy mining camp suffered a quick demise.

Like the other miners and hangers-on, Brown moved on again, still in search of the elusive big strike, this time heading for Edmonton after hearing rumours of placer gold in the North Saskatchewan River. With several companions he crossed the mountain ranges and emerged from the South Kootenay Pass into the foothills near the Waterton Lakes. Climbing to the top of one of the lower mountains, Brown discovered that "the prairies as far as we could see east, north and west was one living mass of buffalo. Thousands of head there were, far more than ever range cattle grazed the bunch grass of the foothills."

During the following years, Kootenai Brown travelled and lived on the plains in both Canada and the United States. For a short time he traded whisky to the Indians near Portage la Prairie, and then carried mail between army posts in the northern United States. Once, while acting as a courier, he was taken prisoner by Sitting Bull and his Hunkpapa Sioux, and managed to escape with little more than his skin and his life.

In Dakota Territory Brown met a young, pretty Métis girl, Olive Lyonnais, and they were married at Pembina in 1869. A few years later Brown left the employ of the United States Army and joined his wife's people in the last of their great buffalo hunts in the country between the Milk and South Saskatchewan rivers. After three years, however, he gave up that life as well, and joined a group of wolf hunters operating in the Sweetgrass Hills of northern Montana and southern Alberta. There was money to be made in the wolf-hunting business, but his experiences with the wolfers ended in tragedy when, in a moment of uncontrollable rage, he killed a fellow hunter at Fort Benton and was arrested and charged with murder. A grand jury at Helena, Montana, considered the nature and extent of the evidence against Brown, but found it insufficient to warrant a trial and decided that an indictment should not be returned against him. Free again, Kootenai Brown took himself and his family to a quiet corner of Canada near the Waterton Lakes, just north of the international boundary.

Like most people on the plains, Kootenai Brown appreciated the appearance of company, which was rare, so one day, when he met a man driving a buckboard across the prairie, he happily entered into conversation with the stranger. The driver began to question Brown about grazing possibilities of the surrounding plains. Surely, the stranger remarked, cattle should be able to live where the great herds of buffalo had once roamed, and that it should not be necessary to feed them in such a mild climate where there was so little snow during the winter.

Brown, reflecting on his own long experience on the plains, disagreed with the stranger. It was a delusion, he said, that cattle could just as easily survive on the plains as the buffalo once did. Unlike cattle, buffalo ate the grass right down to the roots, and then moved onto new range. They might cover hundreds of miles in a season, always moving in search of new range. Besides, Brown pointed out, buffalo faced and travelled into the cold north wind, while cows and steers simply turned their backs and drifted with it, regardless of where it might lead them. And cattlemen, Brown added, should definitely cut hay for winter feed, for they could not always depend upon the chinooks and mildness of the country. The stranger laughed, thanked Brown for his advice and pushed on. In the following years, however, he had many occasions to consider Brown's sound advice and to calculate the cost of disregarding it. The stranger was Matthew Cochrane, who was one of the greatest stockmen in Canada.

Cochrane established the first one of the "big ranches" on the western plains, and in many ways exemplified the origins and workings of the ranching community which developed in the late 19th century. Matthew Henry Cochrane was born in 1823 in Compton County, Quebec, an area noted for its fine cattle and careful breeding. He was the son of an immigrant from Northern Ireland and lived on the family farm until he was 18, when he set off for the bright opportunities of Boston to seek his fortune. As frequently happened in his life, Cochrane achieved his goal, building a very successful leather and shoe business in that city. In 1864 he returned to Canada and settled in Montreal, but continued in the same line of work, this time in partnership with Samuel G. Smith.

When Smith died in 1868, Cochrane entered into the business with Charles Cassils, and together they established the firm of Cochrane, Cassils, and Company. By the mid-1870s the company employed about three hundred workers and was generating annual profits of about $500,000. Cochrane was not content to confine his interests to one field; his other ventures included agriculture, railways, and banking. As well, he was a trustee of Montreal High School and of Bishop's College School in Lennoxville. Although never politically active, Cochrane was acquainted with many of the leading Conservatives in Canada, and in 1872 the government of Sir John A. Macdonald appointed him to the Senate.

In 1849, Matthew Cochrane married Cynthia Maria Whitney, a direct descendent of Eli Whitney, inventor of the cotton gin. They raised nine children, three boys and six girls. All the boys were to be active in the affairs of the Cochrane ranching ventures; James was a director for many years, even though his principal activities related to the family interests in Quebec; the other sons, William and Ernest, managed family-owned ranches in the North West. One of the girls, Eleanor, married Edward A. Baynes, who at various times ranched and homesteaded on his own and with the Cochranes, and later managed the Mount Royal Ranche near Calgary. Senator Cochrane apparently had little regard for Baynes, however, and it was ensured that his son-in-law would not get any of the Cochrane money when the senator died; the senator settled only an income, and no cash, on Bayne's wife.

In spite of his many successful business ventures, Cochrane's first love was stock-raising, and in 1864 he bought Hillhurst, a large farm of about eleven hundred acres near the original Cochrane home in Compton County. Then, in 1866, he attended the provincial agricultural exhibition in Hamilton, Ontario, where he met and visited with John Miller, a leading cattle breeder. Cochrane purchased two of his purebred heifers and insisted that Miller accompany him back to Hillhurst and advise him on the proper care of his cattle.

Miller and Cochrane travelled back to Compton County together, but when Cochrane took his guest out to the stables to inspect the stock, Miller was appalled by what he saw. The mangers were half-full of straw and meal, some of which was packed down and had turned sour. The feed troughs of cattle must be kept clean and sweet, Miller informed Cochrane, and if an animal failed to clean up its feed, the residue should be removed and less feed given at the next meal.

Cochrane was not one to shirk physical labour and immediately got a fork and shovel and handed one of the tools to Miller. The two of them cleaned out all the mangers before they quit and went into the house. On one occasion, when Cochrane was visiting at the Miller farm, Miller was awakened early in the morning by the sound of chopping wood. Getting up to investigate, he found Cochrane out in the woodyard. His guest explained that he liked to rise early in the morning and get in some hard exercise.

It was through John Miller that Cochrane met Simon Beattie, a native of Scotland and nephew of one of that country's leading breeders. Beatty had acquired considerable knowledge of cattle in Scotland and was renowned both there and in North America for his fine judgement and superb sense of showmanship. For many years he worked in Ontario, before beginning a long and spectacular association with Matthew Cochrane.

In 1867 Cochrane and Beattie made a major purchase of Shorthorn cattle, a breed raised for both beef and dairy purposes and which was highly favoured by stockmen at the time in both England and North America. There were two competing strains of Shorthorns; one prize bloodline belonged to the Thomas Booth family of Yorkshire, and the other important line, developed by Thomas Bates, was controlled by Sir Robert Gunter of York. There was tremendous rivalry between champions of the two lines.

In 1868 Cochrane imported 11 more head of Shorthorns to Hillhurst, including some of the first pure Bates cattle to come to Canada. For one of these animals, Duchess 97, Cochrane paid $5,250, at that time the highest price ever paid for a Shorthorn and the highest for a female of any breed. With Beattie's considered advice, Cochrane was prepared to buy the best cattle he could, and within a short time he was dealing in the most fashionable Bates pedigrees and exporting cattle from Canada as well as importing them.

The story of Duchess 97 makes an interesting study of the cattle-breeding business. Sir Robert Gunter, who had the select herd of Bates Shorthorns, refused to sell any of them to his fellow breeders in Britain. He would, in fact, sell only for export, since the animals would then cross the ocean and therefore not get into the hands of Gunter's rival British breeders. Gunter's greatest rival, the Earl of Dunmore, offered him $15,750 for a pair of Shorthorn cows,

Duchess 101 and Duchess 103, but Gunter refused the offer. Instead, he sold them to Cochrane for considerably less, on condition that they would not be returned to Britain. There was, however, nothing in the agreement concerning the cows' calves, and the Earl of Dunmore contracted with Cochrane to pay 2,500 guineas (the price of the two cows) for their calves. The two cows were bred in Britain and placed on board a ship for Canada; both were due to calve shortly after landing there. The earl sent his herdsman with the cows to await the birth of the calves. Both happened to be females, and when they were five months old, they were shipped back to Britain.

In the end, Gunter was more amused than angered by the incident, and finally withdrew the stipulation regarding the cows and allowed them to return to Britain as well. The Earl of Dunmore subsequently purchased Duchesses 97 and 101 from Cochrane and took them back to his farm. He also purchased Duchess 103, but she died before the crossing.

Cochrane did not limit himself to Gunter's line of Shorthorns; whenever a good opportunity arose, he also purchased cattle of the Booth strain. According to Duncan Marshall, a historian of the Shorthorn breed in Canada, Cochrane was "never afraid to enter into a large deal, but ... revelled in buying and selling livestock, and perhaps got more pleasure out of seeing the cattle he imported win prizes for the people he sold them to than he did out of any other business he carried on." All this time he was also dealing in American cattle and buying and selling across the border.

In 1876 Cochrane sold some of his Shorthorn stock at Toronto. This sale fetched record high prices, prices which were purely speculative; the cattle were never worth a fraction of the amounts paid for them, except to sell again to some person who valued them so much that he was willing to pay many times their worth.

Cochrane seemed to sense that the rage for Shorthorns was easing and that prices might shortly begin to decline. By the mid-1870s the popularity of the Booth cattle was already declining in North America, though there were still many interested breeders in Britain who set the Booth line in competition with the Bates line. Cochrane decided to take advantage of the situation there and shipped his Booth cattle to Britain for sale by auction at Bowness, on the shore of Lake Windermere. He also shipped some of his Bates cattle, thus attracting buyers from both camps of the Shorthorn fraternity. This strategy worked up tremendous interest, and again the sale set record prices for Shorthorns.

However, the Shorthorns were indeed reaching their peak, and the effects of inbreeding were beginning to show; the cattle began to lack the constitution and vigour necessary for good beef and dairy animals. In 1882 Cochrane sold the remainder of his Bates cattle and withdrew from the Shorthorn field, at least for the time being. By this time, however, his interest was increasingly taken up by a new venture—a ranch in the Canadian North West.

Cochrane was certainly aware of the affairs of the Canadian Pacific Railway syndicate in Montreal. As a staunch Conservative he could hardly remain ignorant of the close ties between the party and the railway, nor of the opportunities which the completion of the railway would present. He was also familiar with the reports of the North West which came east on a regular basis from travellers, surveyors, and the Mounted Police.

In November 1880 Senator Cochrane first outlined his plans for a western ranch in writing to Col. James S. Dennis of the Department of the Interior. A subsequent letter to Sir John A. Macdonald, who was minister of the interior as well as prime minister, explained his object of establishing a stock farm in the North West "with the view of affording emigrants settling in that part of the Dominion an opportunity of stocking their farms with improved breeds of Cattle and Horses, and also in the belief that a large foreign trade can be developed in the Export of stock from the Canadian North West."

The senator also had his eye on the local market for beef in the North West:

> … owing to the limited number of domestic cattle in the country the government have in the past been obliged to purchase the cattle and beef supply for the police force and for the Indians from Montana Territory. The amount thus paid to foreigners for food supplies has been very considerable … it is obviously in the interest of the Dominion to favour in every legitimate manner an industry that will enable the Government to purchase food supplies within its own border …

Another person who became deeply involved in the establishment of the Cochrane Ranche was Dr. Duncan McEachran of Montreal, who handled much of the actual organizational work and negotiations with the Department of the Interior. McEachran was later even more active in the western ranching industry as Dominion veterinarian and manager of the Walrond Ranche.

A third party in the venture was James Walker, the resident manager of the ranch. Walker was born in 1846 in Carluke, Ontario, where he served in the militia and fought the Fenians when they pushed across the border into Canada in 1866 and 1870. He later joined the North-West Mounted Police, serving with them from the force's inception in 1873 until 1881 when he retired with the rank of superintendent.

While he was with the Mounted Police, Walker came to the attention of Edgar Dewdney, lieutenant-governor of the North West Territories, for his firmness with the Indians and his efficiency in distributing thousands of dollars and supplies in treaty payments. In 1880 Walker was at Fort Walsh in the Cypress Hills when he received orders to escort the widow of an officer who had recently died at the fort back to Ottawa. The widow turned out to be the niece of Lady Macdonald. In Ottawa, Dewdney had apparently suggested to Cochrane that Walker would make a good manager for his ranch, and this proposal was put to Walker by the prime minister himself. The salary for managing the ranch was $2,400 compared with Walker's $1,400 stipend from the police. Walker accepted the prime minister's offer.

The business manager of the Cochrane Ranche was John Milne Browning of Longueil, Quebec. Browning was one of Quebec's leading real estate agents who also had broad interests in agriculture. He remained with the ranching company until 1888, at which time he left for British Columbia to manage the affairs of a real estate syndicate in which the CPR had an interest.

The Cochrane Ranche Company was incorporated in May 1881 with an authorized capital of $500,000 divided into 5,000 shares of $100. At incorporation, $270,000 was subscribed: Matthew Cochrane bought 1,000 shares; James Cochrane, 500; McEachran, 1,000, and James Walker and Browning 100 shares each.

Cochrane had already travelled to England to obtain good breeding stock which he planned to place on the range where they would mix with the native cows and thereby improve the quality of the range cattle. The *Montreal Gazette* in April 1881 noted that the Dominion Line steamship S.S. *Texas* had arrived in Halifax with the largest consignment of purebred cattle ever brought into Canada. Included in the shipment were 60 purebred polled Angus, Hereford, and Shorthorn bulls, and two Clydesdale stallions—all destined for the Cochrane Ranche. In October James Cochrane, who had also travelled to Britain to search for stock, shipped back cattle he had purchased from several leading breeders, including the Earl of Lathom, a shareholder in the Oxley Ranche. This consignment included 86 Hereford bulls. One of the Liverpool newspapers noted that these shipments might be of interest to English beef consumers—and of considerable importance to producers who were already concerned about the flood of beef from North America.

Originally the Dominion government planned to auction off grazing leases in the North West, but this plan was soon discarded since so many of the leases were already promised to various supporters of the government and other interested parties. Cochrane was confident of getting what he wanted anyway, and in June 1881 he and Dr. McEachran went west to choose their land. It was at this time that Cochrane met Kootenai Brown. Ranch manager James Walker had already staked out a choice area along the Bow River with ranch headquarters at Big Hill, about twenty-five miles west of Calgary; his selection was confirmed by Cochrane and McEachran when they visited the area. The original Cochrane lease consisted of those parts of townships 24 and 25, range 3, north of the Elbow River; townships 25 and 26, range 4, and the east half of townships 25 and 26, range 5, all west of the fifth meridian. McEachran described the company's lands for a Montreal newspaper:

> The land is rolling, consisting of numerous grassy hills, plateaux and bottom lands, intersected here and there by streams of considerable size issuing from never-failing springs. The water is cool and clear. Every one of them, as well as Jumping Pond [sic] Creek and Bow River, is full of trout, brook and salmon, which are most delicious to eat. There is an abundance of pine and cottonwood on Jumping Pond Creek and the hillsides, besides numerous thickets of alder and willow scattered here and there over the range, which afford excellent shelter for stock in winter ...
>
> The site selected for the ranch buildings is a beautiful one, a level plateau covered with rich pasture, on the north bank of Bow River, about forty feet above the level of the water. It commands an extensive view of the range, and from here the snowcapped peaks of the Rockies are seen standing out in bold relief against the western horizon ... in a few years, probably, it will be fenced in and divided into beautiful fields with sheds and corrals necessary for the segregation of the different breeds of the male animals and otherwise assume the features of civilization.

The south-facing slopes of the river valley were considered an advantage in that they would warm up, be clear of snow and provide grass earlier in the spring than level areas.

Cochrane also ensured that he had sympathetic neighbours in the North West, whose lands would be available for his use. In addition to the 100,000 acres given to the Cochrane Ranche itself, Sen. A.W. Ogilvie, of flour-milling fame and fortune and a business acquaintance of Cochrane's, received a lease of 34,000 acres on the northeast boundary of the Cochrane lease, and the senator's son-in-law, Edward A. Baynes, 55,000 acres, also adjoining the company's lease. Altogether, Senator Cochrane had approximately 190,000 acres of what was considered the finest grazing lands in the Canadian North West. The actual leases were not signed until 1882, by which time the Cochrane Ranche had already occupied its land for over a year.

By early summer 1881 there was some stock on the lease along the Elbow River west of Calgary under the supervision of Baynes. In the autumn some purebred bulls arrived from Quebec via the usual route into the area—rail and river to Fort Benton in Montana and then north by trail. These cattle were principally Herefords, Angus, and Shorthorns; the Angus seemed to hold up best and the Shorthorns worst.

James Walker was given charge of purchasing range cattle to stock the lease, and he rode into Montana and Idaho to look for suitable livestock. He was disappointed to find that prices for both beef cattle and breeding stock were much higher than he had expected, for the cattle boom in the United States was gathering momentum and many ranchers made little distinction between the two groups of animals.

Walker purchased his first herd, 500 head, from a rancher in Walla Walla, Washington. The drive across the mountains was not only hard but tragic. Mose McDougall, who was supervising the drive, drowned in the Hell Gate River near Missoula.

Walker purchased another herd in Dillon, Montana, where he met a group of ranchers while waiting for the stagecoach. More cattle were acquired from six different operations; the terms were $16 a head, delivered to the international boundary. One of the vendors, Howell Harris, was quite familiar with the route from his days as a trader in Alberta, and he supervised the drive of the cattle to the boundary.

At the border the I.G. Baker Company took charge of the herd and was contracted to deliver it to Big Hill at $2.50 a head. About thirty cowboys and three hundred horses were brought together for the drive, all under the supervision of Frank Strong, the 23-year-old foreman of the I.G. Baker ranch.

The drive north got underway late in the season, so Strong divided the herd into two parts in order to speed up its progress. First, he formed a dry herd of steers and placed them in the charge of George Houk, an experienced teamster from Fort Benton. The second herd, consisting of cows and calves, followed, supervised by Strong himself and Frank Allen. The steers were pushed along at 15 to 18 miles a day, a very fast pace for cattle. The cows and calves made only slightly less time, averaging about 14 miles a day. All the cattle were kept on the move constantly during the day, the cowboys "tin-canning" and "slickering" them to push them on. At night the animals were so tired that they preferred to rest rather than eat, although they were so closely herded that they could have found little to eat in any case.

A number of wagons followed the second herd, picking up the calves which were unable to keep up. Many were simply too weak to follow, and soon the wagons were filled. As a result many calves were left to die along the way, or were simply traded off for food, tea and whisky. The number of calves lost represented a major cost to the ranch.

Strong met Walker and his outfit at the Bow River near Calgary, where the cattle were counted before the Cochrane crew pushed them across the river at Mewata and drove them to their new range at Big Hill. Walker was anxious to get the cattle on the range before winter set in so that they could become accustomed to the ground before the snow arrived, but he had a problem. The cattle had not been marked with the Cochrane brand and to do so would involve holding them for several days. On the other hand, to turn them loose without branding them would simply invite theft. In the end, Walker decided to turn the cattle out on the range and mark them with a hair brand scraped on with a knife or acid, as time allowed.

An early winter justified Walker's concern. The cattle were not familiar with their new surroundings before snow covered the ground and were unable to find good grazing area, shelter or water. They often simply drifted with the bitter north wind and huddled in the coulees.

In the spring of 1882 not only were Cochrane cattle scattered all over the country, but the hair brands had disappeared under the animals' new coats of hair. From Montreal McEachran sent Walker explicit orders to round up every unbranded animal he could find on the range and mark it with the Cochrane brand.

As the spring roundup began, the Cochrane cowboys were joined by many of the area's settlers, who were happy to hire on in order to earn some extra money and perhaps to enjoy a little visiting after the long, cold winter. But their willingness to help quickly dissipated as they watched the Cochrane people sweep up everything on the range, including their own cattle! The settlers protested, and even Walker's cowboys protested, but Walker was determined to execute McEachran's instructions to the letter.

The settlers soon quit the roundup and returned to their homesteads to protect their own property. Not surprisingly, many also took with them unbranded stock which obviously wasn't theirs. Unlike many of the Cochrane people, the settlers were familiar with the country and generally knew where to look for cattle still hidden in the coulees and brush. Many justified their actions by claiming that what Walker was doing would wipe them out. Whatever the respective merits of the quarrel, the result of the spring roundup of 1882 was a legacy of bitterness towards the Cochrane Ranche which never quite disappeared.

While there were losses from the winter and the roundup, they were not so heavy as to cause the Cochrane Ranche serious concern, and little hay was put up for the next winter. Not only that, but the company decided to expand its herd, and in the spring of 1882 Walker again rode down to Montana and arranged to buy 4500 head from Poindexter and Orr's outfit. He was about the close the deal when a messenger called him to Fort Benton, 300 miles away, for an urgent telegram from McEachran.

The Cochrane directors had been negotiating with the I.G. Baker Company, which was thinking of establishing a ranch in Canada. The two firms felt that they would be able to arrange a more advantageous purchase jointly than they could separately, and so they instructed Walker to break off negotiations with Poindexter and Orr. Walker rode back to Poindexter and Orr's ranch, called off the deal, and returned to Fort Benton.

No sooner had he arrived back in town than he received another urgent telegram from McEachran, informing him that the deal with the Baker Company had collapsed and that he should go ahead with the purchase of the Poindexter and Orr cattle after all. Once again Walker set out for their ranch; when he arrived, he discovered that in the meantime the price had risen by $25,000. Nevertheless, he signed an agreement to purchase the herd at $25 per head. (Prices were rising generally; Walker bought about five hundred three-year-old steers from the Baker Company in September at $40 per head.) By this time, however, he had become so exasperated with the contradictory orders from Montreal that he sent in his resignation, effective as soon as a replacement could be found.

The contract with Poindexter and Orr was signed on 16 May 1882. All the unbranded yearlings and calves over eight months old at the date of de livery were counted in the herd; the balance of the calves were given free and were not counted. Delivery was to begin on 1 July and continue until all the cattle were delivered to Big Hill. Poindexter and Orr also agreed to provide suitable corrals with branding chutes, and to assist Walker with the branding at the Cochrane Ranche.

The company, on receiving Walker's resignation, hired Frank White as treasurer for the ranch, and also sent James Cochrane and John Browning west to look into the ranch's affairs. In Fort Benton they hired William Kerfoot, a Virginian with experience on the northern ranges, as manager of the range operations. White joined Cochrane and Browning in Fort Benton, and the trio rode north to Big Hill, arriving on 17 September. Kerfoot showed up on 7 October. Walker was still at the ranch; he had agreed to remain until the new cattle from Montana were brought in and his replacements had time to settle in.

Frank White had little experience to prepare him for the operation of a large cattle ranch. He had emigrated to Canada from England in 1860 at the age of 16 and worked for the Grand Trunk Railway in Quebec before being hired by the Cochrane directors. Kerfoot, on the other hand, was very familiar with the cattle industry. He was the son of a cavalry captain in General Lee's Confederate army, and was born in the Shenandoah Valley in Virginia. He moved to Montana as a young man—southerners made up a considerable proportion of Montana's population after the Civil War—and established a cattle ranch. Unfortunately, he became caught up in a conflict between cattlemen and sheepmen, and suffered substantial losses. One of Kerfoot's family later pointed out the irony of Kerfoot's working for a ranch which was one of the first to introduce sheep into Alberta on a large scale.

For various reasons the Poindexter and Orr drive did not get underway until late in the summer, and this second drive was almost as hard on the cattle as the first one. The animals were exhausted when they reached Fish Creek south of Calgary in late September. To make matters worse, on 28 September a terrific storm with snow, rain, and cold blew in from the north, directly into the faces of the cattle. Phil Weinard at High River estimated that three feet of snow fell in the area over an eight-day period and the Macleod *Gazette* reported that the same storm left about one and a half feet of snow on the southern ranges. At Fish Creek the piercing wind piled the snow in big drifts, buried the trails and completely blocked the Cochrane cattle moving north.

At Big Hill the cowboys were busy trying to repair the roof of their bunkhouse and stretching hides over their beds to keep their blankets dry. Cochrane and Browning tried to reach Calgary to start their journey back east, but found the trails so deep in snow that they were forced to give up. Eventually, Walker set out ahead of them with a light wagon and four-in-hand to break a trail, while Cochrane and Browning followed in a buckboard.

Poindexter sent word to Walker at Big Hill that it would be best to leave the cattle at Fish Creek for a month or so to rest up and to wait for the trails to clear. For his part, Poindexter would leave his cowboys with the cattle to herd them to the Cochrane ranch when the trails were clear. Walker insisted that his orders from the directors were to get the cattle on the Cochrane lease as soon as possible, and pointed out that the agreement called for their delivery to Big Hill.

In spite of his misgivings, Poindexter prepared to oblige Walker. First, he rode ahead to Calgary, rounded up some strong native cattle, then jammed them south through the snowbanks to Fish Creek. There he turned them around and pushed them back to Calgary, breaking a trail through the snow. It was this trail that Poindexter used to drive the Cochrane cattle onto Big Hill.

The weather was cold but clear on the morning of 20 October as White and some cowboys gathered at the corrals at 6:00 A.M. to await the cattle.

Walker, however, seemed fated for endless difficulties. He didn't arrive for another two hours, and the counting couldn't begin without him. And when he
finally arrived, he had to spend another hour looking for a good horse. From
nine in the morning to five at night the cowboys counted cattle as the herd
passed them. By the end of the day the Cochrane crew had counted 4,290
head. "Here they are," shouted Poindexter to Walker as he rode up with the
cattle. "Count 'em now, because half of 'em will be dead tomorrow ... " White
noticed that the cattle looked thin and tired, and indeed the close herding and
counting of the past two days had kept them from feeding properly.

The Cochrane outfit needed more help and White succeeded in per-
suading 12 of the Poindexter and Orr cowboys, including a short Mexican
mestizo named Ca Sous, to remain at Big Hill for the winter. On 24 October
the Cochrane Ranche settled its account with Poindexter and Orr, and the
two Montanans left for home in the late afternoon. Meanwhile, the cowboys
started the long, hard process of branding the cattle before putting them on
the range.

With the arrival of the Poindexter and Orr cattle, Walker left Big Hill.
He had travelled into Calgary on 26 September to discuss his departure from
the Cochrane Ranche Company, not only as a manager, but as shareholder.
Under the terms of his resignation he was given a sawmill, considered to be
worth about $15,000, which the company had built on the Kananaskis River
to the west. Walker later expanded the sawmill operations to Calgary, and
with the building of the CPR and the growth of Calgary he found a large market for ties, lumber, and building materials. Walker branched into other fields
as well, and became one of Calgary's most respected citizens before his death
in 1936. (In 1975 he was declared Calgary's Citizen of the Century.)

While at the Cochrane Ranche, Walker had devised a "squeezing gate"
for holding and branding grown animals; though the idea was sound, the
cowboys found that the thing actually didn't work very well. The weather
remained cold and the Cochrane people struggled constantly with Walker's
gate as they tried to brand the cattle. White complained that they spent half
their time fixing Walker's wretched gate. By the end of October a bad snowstorm had buried the range, and White and Kerfoot gave up the branding
and turned the cattle loose. Already, thanks to the storm, some animals were
falling dead around the buildings, and the cowboys were killing some of the
weaker ones and skinning them.

The October storm was followed first by a warm spell and thaw, then by
bitter cold. The cattle could find little feed, as the grass was trapped under an
icy crust, and their hoofs were still so worn after the drive from Montana that
they could hardly negotiate the treacherous hills and slopes.

By early December the cattle were suffering terribly. Kerfoot and White looked everywhere for feed; they tried to purchase oats from the government farm at Fish Creek and hay from neighbouring settlers. White was tireless in his efforts to find feed and called on practically everyone in the area in his search. However, there was little feed available and little sympathy for the ranch's plight.

There was good grazing and open range to the southeast, towards Blackfoot Crossing; the cattle drifted persistently in that direction, seeming to know instinctively that their salvation lay there. Browning and Cochrane, however, were firm in their orders that the cattle be kept on the lease west of Calgary. White therefore established cow camps at Calgary, the mouth of Fish Creek, and the mouth of the Highwood River to check the drifting cattle. Every day the people of Calgary watched strings of cows walking downstream along the Bow River towards the open range, while the cowboys on the ranch and at the camps worked day and night pushing the cattle back towards Big Hill.

Just before the new year, Kerfoot rode out to check on some cattle north of the ranch buildings. A blizzard struck while he was on the range and he became lost while searching for the head of the Big Hill valley which would have led him back down to the ranch. For two days and a night he wandered over the plains, sometimes riding, sometimes walking, but never stopping. Several years earlier he had frozen a leg in a snowstorm in Montana, and so he knew the potential danger of resting. The storm finally blew itself out on the second day and he was fortunate enough to meet a rider who had left Calgary at the end of the blizzard. This man put Kerfoot on his own horse and walked beside him back to Calgary. Kerfoot's horse was turned loose in the hope that it would follow, but it collapsed and died from exhaustion and exposure.

In the spring of 1883 the thaw slowly uncovered the Cochrane range; snow remained on the ground until June. Finally, the extent of the disaster revealed itself—there were dead cattle everywhere, piled up in the coulees and draws. In some cases a person could cross a gully on the bodies of dead cattle without ever touching the ground. Alexander Staveley Hill, a shareholder in the Oxley Ranche, grieved to see the "vast numbers" of dead cattle along the Bow River near Calgary. The ranch estimated its losses at three thousand head, leaving only some four thousand cattle on the lease, and most of them in poor condition.

White and Kerfoot found that they had insufficient cattle to meet the ranch's contracts with the government, and so, like Walker before him, White set off for Montana in April to purchase additional animals. Just outside Fort Benton he met the northbound mail for Calgary, and after a search through the letter pouch found a message from Browning, informing him that the directors had decided to change the location of the cattle operations to the southern Alberta range, along the Belly River.

Despite the enormous losses of the past two years, Senator Cochrane was not ready to give up on his ranching venture. The disastrous winters seemed to have hit only the Bow River range; those ranges around Fort Macleod and Pincher Creek had come through them with little loss. Thus the decision was made to shift operations south.

Among Cochrane's acquaintances was Edward Brooks, the Conservative member of Parliament for Sherbrooke (1872–82) and a judge of the Superior Court of the District of St. Francis in Quebec. Brooks was solicitor for the Eastern Townships Bank and vice-president of the Waterloo and Magog Railway (Cochrane served as a director for both organizations.) Brooks was also a trustee of Bishop's College School in Lennoxville. In 1882 he had applied for and received a lease of 33,000 acres in southern Alberta under the name of the Eastern Townships Ranche Company. Adjoining his lease was that of Charles Colby and his Rocky Mountain Cattle Company; interestingly, the rent for the Eastern Townships Ranche in 1883 was paid by Colby, not Brooks.

In March 1883 both Colby and Brooks assigned their leases to Cochrane, while a third lease, held by Gagné, Pratt, and Company, was assigned to James Cochrane. The Cochrane Ranche now had about one hundred and seventy thousand acres of prime grazing land in the south, lying in a tract between Fort Macleod, the Peigan Reserve, and Waterton and Belly rivers. These lands were held by the Cochrane Ranche in addition to those along the Bow River, even though the lease regulations technically limited holdings by one individual or company to 100,000 acres.

Senator Cochrane now began to split his operations. While Kerfoot remained at Big Hill to manage affairs there, White moved to the southern range where he was assisted by Ca Sous as foreman. Ca Sous, unfortunately, and despite his ability and experience, never got on very well with the rest of the cowboys. One rancher also told White that he thought Ca Sous drove the cattle too much, and refused to herd his cattle where the Mexican might possibly handle them. In the end, it became necessary to replace Ca Sous as foreman with Jim Dunlap.

The cattle at Big Hill were divided into two herds and driven south in the summer of 1883. The first two winters on the southern range were mild, giving the cattle a rest after the two previous hard years. Ironically, the winters of 1883 and 1884 were very mild on the Bow River lease as well.

During the winter of 1885–86, however, the Cochrane cattle were grazing near the Waterton Lakes when a very heavy snowfall struck. The snow piled up in drifts, covering all the grass and leaving the cattle unable to rustle feed. The situation was grim and the Cochrane Ranche seemed assured of another heavy loss. Word of the company's predicament reached Frank Strong at Fort Macleod and he offered to save the herd if the company was prepared to pay him $1,000. Strong's offer was quickly accepted and he set to work.

Following Poindexter's example of 1882, Strong rounded up about five hundred Indian horses from the nearby reserves, and for two days whipped and spurred them towards the trapped cattle. The horses broke a path through the snow; once they reached the cattle, Strong turned them around and hustled them back. The hungry cattle, with an open trail before them, then followed closely behind, finally reaching the Peigan Reserve and spilling out onto the still bare and grass-covered range. Strong had good reason to feel that he had redeemed himself for the disastrous drive in 1881.

The first years on the southern range were hard ones, but gradually the Cochrane Ranche there developed into a well-run and profitable operation. By 1891 there were almost thirteen thousand head of cattle on the Cochrane lease along the Belly River.

The northern lease, meanwhile, was undergoing some notable changes. The senator had too much money invested in buildings and corrals to abandon the lease, and was determined to develop his Bow River holdings into a profitable operation. While he had originally been strongly opposed to grazing sheep in the country—taking into account the destruction of the grasslands by sheep in Wyoming and Montana—he underwent a thorough conversion and decided that the Bow River country would be ideal for sheep after all. Using all his own considerable influence and that of his friends, Cochrane put enormous pressure upon the government to allow sheep into range country, even though at that time they were banned, largely through his own previous efforts.

There was strong opposition to the senator's plans from other ranchers in the country, particularly from members of the South West Stock Growers' Association who petitioned the government to continue the ban on sheep. In 1884 the Dominion government did consent to allow sheep north of a line formed by the Bow and Highwood rivers; the country south of the line remained reserved for cattle.

The strains put upon the Cochrane Ranche Company by the losses of 1881 and 1882 also led to bitterness and conflict among the directors. In January 1884 Cochrane sent Frank White a telegram directing him to take an inventory of the company's cattle and other assets, and then proceed to Montreal for the firm's annual meeting in order to report on the company's affairs in the North West. White spent much of January travelling between the northern and southern ranges, checking the records of the ranch, its sales, herds and overall position. He left Calgary by train on January 24, 1884 and arrived in Montreal on February 1 where he was met by Senator Cochrane and John Browning.

The following day the company directors met at 97 St. James Street to consider White's report. The meeting was a stormy one. Dr. McEachran protested at being excluded from a meeting which he felt White, Cochrane, and Browning had held behind his back. For their part, Cochrane and Browning told the doctor that he had done all in his power to injure the credit of the company, and that his conceit and pomposity were standing in the way of his own advancement. There was a move among some of the directors to dismiss White, but McEachran opposed such action. White remained in the company's employ, but with the threat of dismissal hanging over him.

White realized that his position with the Cochrane Ranche was likely a tenuous one, and that he was probably being made the scapegoat for all the troubles that the company had experienced over the past several years. Consequently, he began to make plans for setting up his own ranch west of Big Hill. It therefore came as no surprise to him when Senator Cochrane visited the Belly River ranch in July and spoke of the smallness of the band of cattle and the necessity for economizing. The company would be glad, Cochrane said, if White would relieve them of the expense of his management as soon as he could do so without loss to himself.

In December 1884 White once again prepared to travel east to meet the directors of the ranch. Before he left, however, he had dinner with Colonel Walker in his new house in Calgary and it is likely they discussed their common experiences with the Cochrane Ranche. White arrived in Montreal on December 19 and met the senator's son, William F. Cochrane, at the company's offices. Together they agreed that White should finally cut his connection with the ranch and that he receive one month's salary as compensation. William Cochrane succeeded Frank White as manager of the southern operation.

The earlier meeting of the company's directors in February 1884 had also considered plans to dispose of the Bow River lease to a new company, a move necessary to keep within the regulations concerning maximum leases of 100,000 acres. The Cochrane Ranche Company sold its Bow River lease and all improvements to the British American Ranche Company for $55,000. This new company had been incorporated in January with Senator Cochrane, Hugh McKay, William Lawrence, William Ewing, and Charles and William Cassils as shareholders; William Cassils was the largest shareholder, and Cochrane held 300 of the 2,000 authorized shares. In 1885 Edward A. Baynes assigned his lease of 55,000 acres to the British American Ranche, as did A.W. Ogilvie his lease of 33,000 acres.

The first sheep were brought to the Bow River lease in 1884, mostly from Montana and Wyoming. The British American Ranche imported between seven thousand and eight thousand head, principally Merino and Rambouillet crossed with Shropshires or Oxfordshires; it also brought in about two hundred purebred Shropshire rams to improve the quality of the herd.

The sheep were driven to the British American lease slowly, and though they arrived on the range during a blinding September snowstorm, they were in fine condition. The first winter was a mild one and the sheep pulled through the cold weather well. Spring brought its share of problems, however. An early spring storm in April dumped a heavy snowfall on the range; a steady wind swirled the snow inside the corrals and drifted it up against the fences, eventually covering them. A large number of sheep walked out of their corrals on the snowbanks and wandered before the storm until they came to a slough which, by spring, had melted. Scores of sheep walked into the water, or were pushed in by those behind, and drowned. Later, with warmer weather and a tinder-dry range, a prairie fire trapped and killed another four hundred head. The company suffered further losses when several hundred ewes died during lambing.

The sheep operation ran into still more bad luck; the wool market was disappointing, the British American wool cut hitting the markets about the same time as the great production from Australia knocked down prices. As well, there was more trouble between management and the directors. William Kerfoot was ordered to fire a sheepherder after a large number of animals under the man's supervision were lost. He refused to do so, insisting that the man had done his best under the circumstances. There was an exchange of letters between Montreal and Big Hill, and in the end the company fired Kerfoot as manager and replaced him with Ernest Cochrane.

The Virginian did not leave quietly. He launched an action against the British American Ranche Company for the remainder of his salary on the original five-year contract he had signed. The case was heard in Calgary in April 1885; James Lougheed represented Kerfoot and Henry Bleecker the British American Ranche. Among those called to testify was Frank White. The court found in Kerfoot's favour and awarded him $1,650, all costs and interest. (Kerfoot's son later wrote that his father did not look back with any great pleasure on his experience with the company as it was run from the east, and that the company seemed to have the "happy knack of getting together a lot of good men and then ignoring their recommendations, usually with heavy loss to themselves.")

In November 1887 the shareholders of the British American Ranche gathered for their annual meeting and authorized the directors to sell, transfer, or otherwise dispose of the assets of the company and wind up its affairs. The next year the company advertised the sale of seven thousand sheep and 41,000 acres of leasehold, but it took a long time to dispose of the assets: the limited local market was simply unable to handle the dumping of so many sheep at one time.

The British American Ranche had briefly tried to raise horses as well. Kerfoot had initiated horse ranching on the part of the lease which lay south of the Bow River, with headquarters at the junction of Jumping Pound Creek and the river. In 1886 he brought in a herd of horses from the Harper Brothers' ranch in British Columbia, expecting to service the local market of cowboys, the North-West Mounted Police, and settlers. The horse market turned out to be limited, however, as the police preferred to obtain their mounts from the east and there were not enough settlers in the country to sustain a continued demand for draft animals.

The British American Ranche sold its horse-ranching operations in 1887 to the Bow River Horse Ranche, a company owned by a group of wealthy Englishmen and managed by G.E. Goddard.

Senator Cochrane retained an interest in the Bow River Horse Ranche, but later withdrew when its management concluded that he had not been completely candid in his description of the lease and stock. The lease on which the Bow River Horse Ranche operated was cancelled in 1894 after a long, bitter struggle between Goddard and homesteaders. Goddard purchased much of the land himself and went into business with E.H. Warner and W.P. Warner.

On the north side of the Bow River, the British American Ranche Company came under intense pressure from homesteaders and the government to open up its lands for settlement. Senator Cochrane finally decided to withdraw from the area and agreed to give up the remainder of the lease on condition that the government sell three quarter sections to the company at the going price of two dollars per acre, and give his son Ernest homestead entry for one quarter section. An agreement was finally reached, and on September 27, 1890 the sale was completed. Ernest Cochrane received his patent in 1892 and returned to Quebec.

With the death of Senator Cochrane in 1903, the driving force behind the Cochrane Ranche seemed to fade. William F. Cochrane returned to Quebec, leaving the management of the Belly River ranch in the hands of Col. Harry Mullins. The day of the big ranches seemed just about over—settlers were crowding in, taking the best land and waterholes—and the Cochrane family was ready to sell its holdings. Already a number of Mormon settlements adjoined the Cochrane Ranche, and there were more homesteaders coming up from the south, looking for land.

From their centre in Salt Lake City, Utah, the Mormons had spread out into Utah, Idaho, Nevada, and Montana. A very successful agricultural people, they also sent scouting parties into southern Alberta and British Columbia to search for areas to settle. The first group of 40 Mormon settlers arrived at Lee's Creek in southern Alberta in July 1887, under the leadership of Charles Ora Card, a son-in-law of Brigham Young. Card was dismayed to find that all of the lands in southern Alberta were leased, but then happily discovered that the lease along Lee's Creek had expired. The Mormons quickly acquired the land and settled in. By 1888 there were 126 Mormon settlers in the area, and by 1893 their numbers had grown to 593. They were joined by additional Mormon families moving up from the south in their covered wagons, and their settlements spread east and west of their Alberta centre of Cardston.

The Mormons first became involved with the Cochrane Ranche in 1890s, when William Cochrane contracted with them to put up his hay. When a Mormon businessman and settler told Colonel Mullins that he would like to purchase part of the Cochrane lands for a dairy operation, Mullins asked him whether the Mormon church would consider buying the entire holding. Encouraged by the response to his proposal, Mullins obtained a letter of introduction to Joseph F. Smith, the head of the Mormon church, and his counsellors. He travelled to Salt Lake City to formally offer them the opportunity to purchase the entire Cochrane operation—67,000 acres of good land in one tract which was close to already established Mormon settlements.

Later, Ernest Cochrane and the company secretary, Charles Holt, met with Smith and Mullins in Salt Lake City. After careful and prolonged consideration, the Mormons accepted the Cochrane's terms and purchased the land for six dollars per acre. The sale represented one of the largest real estate transactions in the North West to that time. All livestock was to be removed and legal possession and occupancy turned over to the representatives of the Corporation of the Alberta Stake of Zion with headquarters in Cardston.

When news of the sale became public, Edward H. Maunsell persuaded his banker in Fort Macleod, Cowdry Brothers, to join with him in purchasing most of the Cochrane cattle, about twelve thousand head. Maunsell and Cowdry later disposed of most of them to Pat Burns, the Calgary-based rancher and meat packer.

The Mormons were determined to make their newly acquired property self-supporting until they could decide on a policy to colonize and dispose of the lands. At that time, there were not yet enough Mormon settlers to farm that much land, and the property was too valuable to leave idle. Consequently, they purchased a number of good cows with calves from Pat Burns and placed them on the ranch, later adding more stock acquired from local ranchers.

In 1909 the Cochrane Ranche lands in southern Alberta were surveyed for the best sites for possible villages. Four potential townsites were selected on the basis of adequate water supply and favourable topography. Eventually, the choice was narrowed to two sites which became the towns of Glenwood and Hillspring. Mormon settlers gradually took up lots in the two towns and farms in the adjoining district. By 1923 most of the lands from Glenwood on the east to a few miles south of Hillspring were occupied by farmers who had purchased them from the Mormon church under a ten-year purchase plan. About one-third of the land on the south end of the ranch continued to be used by the church for raising livestock, this operation being under the overall supervision of the presiding bishop's office in Salt Lake City. In 1968 this land was sold for 3 million dollars to Morris Palmer, an American oilman and rancher living in Calgary.

When the Cochrane family sold its lands in 1906, the mineral rights were not included. With the discovery of oil and gas in Alberta in 1949, these rights suddenly became very valuable, and the Cochrane Ranche Company, the charter of which had never lapsed, was revived and reorganized to handle the new wealth.

In 1885, after leaving the Cochrane Ranche, Frank White purchased a herd of sheep along the Teton River in Montana and drove them to a range he had prepared west of Big Hill, between Beaupré Creek and the Ghost River. He soon came into conflict with the Reverend John McDougall of the Methodist mission at Morleyville, who protested that White was encroaching on land which belonged to him and on which he intended to build an Indian orphanage. McDougall warned White to be off the land within six weeks, and that he had filed a protest with the Dominion government. White replied that he could not move just then even if he wished to do so, as he had no other place to go. Besides, the matter was in the hands of the government and he, White, would abide by their decision.

The missionary replied that he would not abide by the government's decision unless it gave him and the settlers in the district what they wanted. Furthermore, he claimed, Sir John. A. Macdonald had promised him six years earlier whatever land he wanted up to 2,000 acres, and the promise had been repeated two years later. (McDougall's brother David told White that while John McDougall and the Methodist Conference had indeed obtained a promise of land, neither had taken steps to obtain title, and so there was no stipulation as to where the land should be.)

In June William Pearce, representing the federal government, visited White to see whether he would take cash and move to the other side of the Bow River, and to estimate the cost of building on that side. White finally agreed to move and drove his sheep across the river in July 1886. This marked the beginning of his Merino Ranch, and by 1890 he was running about five thousand head of sheep on 34,000 acres of good pasture. In 1901 he sold the Merino Ranch and moved to Fernie, British Columbia, where he took the position of coal commissioner for the Crowsnest Coal Company. He died in January 1924.

After he left the British American Ranche, William Kerfoot homestead-ed in the Grand Valley, just outside the western boundary of the company's lease. Kerfoot was considered to be one of the best horsemen of his day. He was riding in a parade at a summer show in Calgary in 1908 and a band began to play just as he passed. The noise scared his horse, causing it to rear up and fall over a cow. Kerfoot suffered a broken back and died from the injury.

Chapter Four

THE OXLEY RANCHE

The Oxley Ranche was another of the "big ranches" of the early days, and like the Cochrane Ranche its beginning years were difficult ones. The relationship between its first manager, John R. Craig, and the major shareholders, a group of English notables, was a troubled one. The ongoing quarrel eventually became public and the ranching community was sharply divided in its sympathies, a division which lasted almost a century.

After his dismissal as manager of the Oxley Ranche, Craig wrote about his experiences with the operation's gentlemen shareholders in a book called *Ranching with Lords and Commons*. The work was published in 1903 and created quite a stir in southern Alberta where a large number of the ranches were owned and operated by English principals. These owners considered any criticism of one of their number by a colonial manager to be the height of presumption and quite unacceptable.

It is difficult to determine just how accurately Craig told the early history of the Oxley Ranche. Alexander Stavely Hill, the managing director of the company and principal villain of Craig's book, also published an account of his adventures, travels, and sundry activities in southern Alberta under the title of *From Home to Home*. However, Hill, in his book, makes little mention of the actual operations of the Oxley. *From Home to Home* is, in fact, more properly a Victorian travel book, the colonial North West as seen through the eyes of an English gentleman.

John R. Craig himself was the original guiding spirit behind the Oxley Ranche. He was born in York County, Ontario, in 1837, the year of the rebellions in Upper and Lower Canada against the stifling grip of the Family Compact and the Chateau Clique. He was the son of Robert Craig, a prominent breeder and importer of pedigreed sheep and swine. For many years young Craig farmed in Peel County where he specialized in raising Shorthorn cattle and Berkshire hogs. Unlike Matthew Cochrane, he imported few Shorthorns from Britain, but he did buy and sell frequently in the United States.

John Craig was one of the first Canadians to exhibit at leading livestock shows in the United States, beginning in St. Louis in 1871. He was also secretary of the Arts and Agricultural Association of Ontario, and one of the group which founded the Toronto Exhibition, forerunner of the Canadian National Exhibition. Later, in the North West, he was acknowledged to be one of the best judges of cattle who ever went into the ranching business.

In 1875 Craig decided to sell his stock of Shorthorns, and the sale held in Toronto on December 3 fetched some of the highest prices ever recorded at a Canadian auction sale to that time. He sold 39 females in all, 11 of them at prices over $2,000, with the top price being $4,000.

During the next few years Craig gradually formed plans for a large cattle operation in the North West Territories. Both ranching and the North West were gaining attention among eastern farmers. Accordingly, he organized a company, the Dominion Livestock Company of Canada, with an authorized capital of $500,000, and in 1881 applied for and received a lease of 100,000 acres in the North West. From the map the tract looked very attractive. The terms of the lease were standard and called for one animal on the range for every ten acres within three years. The shareholders envisioned an eventual herd of ten thousand cattle.

Craig and his colleagues in the venture managed to raise about $200,000 among themselves, but felt that the company needed more capital. With the approval of his fellow subscribers, Craig travelled to Britain where interest in North American cattle companies was very strong. British investors considered cattle ranching in North America to be both a safe and profitable venture.

Among the potential investors in Liverpool, Glasgow, and Edinburgh Craig planned to call on was Alexander Staveley Hill, a lawyer and member of the British House of Commons. Hill had just returned from a tour of Canada that took him as far west as Manitoba. He had a country estate named Oxley Manor and had a strong interest in agriculture and ranching. Looking over Craig's plans and promotional prospectus, Hill expressed interest in the venture, but told Craig quite bluntly that he objected to the other subscribers to the company; he would undertake the project only with men of his own acquaintance, English gentlemen. Furthermore, Hill mentioned, he could obtain from his friends all the capital needed, and so there was no need for the other investors Craig had gathered.

The vision of unlimited capital for his ranch was understandably appealing to Craig, especially as conventional wisdom held that the larger ranch and the herd, the less proportionate the expense, and therefore the greater the profits. The $200,000 of the original subscribers would establish a fair-sized operation, but the resources Hill and his friends could muster promised far greater rewards. However, before dealing further with Hill, Craig decided to consult the other members of his company. They agreed to withdraw from the venture, thus clearing the way for Craig to work solely with Hill and his English friends.

Having cut his ties with the original investors, Craig suddenly found it difficult to obtain a firm commitment from Hill. The MP also hinted that Craig should, after all, find additional investors—subject, of course, to Hill's approval of their social standing.

Craig had previously met the Earl of Lathom, a prominent cattle breeder who fortunately happened to be an acquaintance of Hill's. Lathom agreed to join the venture and on March 25, 1882 the Oxley Ranche syndicate was formed. The members and directors of the company were Hill, QC, PC, DCL, JP, recorder of Banbury, deputy high steward of Oxford University, counsel of the Admiralty and judge-advocate of the Fleet in the administration of Benjamin Disraeli, and member of Parliament for Coventry and later West Staffordshire; the Earl of Lathom, owner of 11,000 acres of land in Lancashire as well as numerous mineral properties, and later Lord Chamberlain of England; and Mr. George Baird. Hill was elected managing director, and John Craig was appointed resident manager of the Oxley Ranche at a salary of $3,000 per year, and with practically unlimited powers of investing the syndicate's capital.

With the ranch formally organized, Craig sailed home to Canada and set out for the North West. In 1882 the Canadian Pacific Railway had not yet reached the range country, so Craig, leaving his family temporarily in Ontario, journeyed west by railway through Chicago, Kansas City, and Salt Lake City, then north by narrow-gauge railway to Silver Bow (Butte), Montana. He took a stagecoach to Helena where he arranged a loan of $2,000 to enable him to purchase a team and supplies for the trip north to his lease in Canada. Negotiation for the loan with Samuel Hauser, the president and founder of the Bank of Montana, took only 15 minutes. Craig signed no promissory note—the bank simply accepted his word.

The trip from Helena to the Oxley lease was a long and lonely one, but one which Craig would make often. On his arrival at Fort Macleod he bought a mower and horse-drawn rake, and then continued north for another 30 miles to the Leavings of Willow Creek. (The term "leavings" was used where a trail on the plains left water and trees, and warned travellers to stock up on supplies and wood before moving out onto the prairie.) A former buffalo hunter and whisky trader, Henry Kountz, had built a rude cabin at the Leavings; Craig acquired the building and Kountz's squatters' rights for $1,500, and hired a man as ranch cook. Kountz's cabin at the Leavings became the first headquarters for the Oxley Ranche.

Meanwhile, Staveley Hill and his son Henry had left England to visit Canada and the new ranch. The two Englishmen travelled west on the new railway to the end-of-steel at Swift Current where they changed to wagons which they had bought at Regina. (Hill described the country around Regina as "an absolute flat, with no wood and no water, and not very promising land; and as a friend observed, you would have to take advantage of the convexity of the earth if you wanted to get out of sight.")

After visiting Fort Walsh the Hills and their guides and drivers crossed southern Alberta to the St. Mary River and then drove north to old Fort Whoop-Up. At this point they got lost. Craig, who had arranged to meet them at Fort Macleod, became quite upset when they failed to appear, especially when a rumour began to circulate that they had been murdered. After a week or so the Hills managed to get their bearings and meet Craig, and then head for their ranch. On their way the Oxley party watched in confident anticipation as a herd of four thousand cattle passed them on the trail, destined for the Cochrane Ranche on the Bow River. This was Hill's first view of a large band of cattle and he was very impressed. A day or so later he had a long conversation with Orr, the Montana rancher who was supervising the Cochrane drive with his partner, Poindexter.

After a couple of days at the Leavings, the Hills, Craig, and several others started out to inspect the Oxley lease. Hill reckoned the eastern boundary of their range to be about eighteen miles west of their buildings at the Leavings, and the block of which they had the lease about nine miles by eighteen miles in length, consisting of land which had not yet been surveyed or inspected, and "upon which in all probability no white man had ever yet set foot."

The excursion seemed fated for trouble right from the start. Kountz, thinking it was a hunting trip, took along very little food, expecting that the party would shoot some game. There was, however, very little game to be found. On September 28 the same snowstorm which blocked the Cochrane cattle at Fish Creek struck the Oxley party near the Chain Lakes in the Porcupine Hills. The Hills and Craig were stuck in their camp. Kountz was sent for help but did not return for so many days that the rest of the group decided to try to get out on their own. After several days they struggled out to safety, shaken and hungry, but with enough experiences to fill a dozen pages in Hill's book of travels.

The expedition was a disaster in another way. Hill and Craig were distressed to discover that the Oxley lease was so far up into the foothills and Rocky Mountains as to be quite unsuitable for cattle (though, in the words of the Macleod *Gazette*, "admirably adapted to the raising of grizzly bears, mountain sheep and goats"). They looked longingly at the Porcupine Hills with their gentle, grassy slopes and nearby plains, both watered by Willow Creek and its tributaries. But it was impossible to know whether these far more desirable lands had already been granted to another company. Hill determined to take possession of the valley bottom around the Leavings on Willow Creek, about one thousand acres, and trust to the chance of obtaining a lease from the government of the surrounding land, or if it was already granted, of buying out the leaseholders.

Having made his decision regarding the land, Hill marked out a location for Craig to build a house and planned various improvements, including the construction of a sawmill back in the timber of the Porcupine Hills. He and Craig also purchased, for $70 a head, some horses which had just been driven in from British Columbia. The Hills and Craig then headed south for Montana to look for stock for the ranch and to catch the train at Billings for the Hills' return trip east.

On November 2, 1882 the Oxley party camped near Dupuyer Creek in northern Montana where they learned of a local rancher with a band of cattle for sale. Although the herd was scattered over the range for a hundred miles and mixed with other cattle, Hill and Craig nevertheless decided to buy the whole operation for $115,000. The rancher pocketed Hill's cheque for the amount, loaded his blankets on a packhorse and rode away, leaving Hill and Craig in possession of the ranch.

As was the practice at the time, purchase was made by "book count," a system which left open many avenues for abuse and quite possibly defeated numerous inexperienced (and a few experienced) cattle investors. The book count simply indicated how many cattle *should* be in a herd, providing that they could all be found. There was a certain logic in the system, of course, for it was obviously impossible to round up scattered cattle for inspection by every prospective buyer. Furthermore, there were certain easily ascertained facts which allowed a fairly good estimate of the number of cattle on hand—for example, how many cattle had been placed on the range, how long they had been out and the annual sale of steers or any other cattle. It was possible to assume an annual increase of a herd of range cattle at 25 to 30 percent, depending on the severity of the winter and spring. A spring branding of 500 calves would usually represent a herd of about two thousand head.

Craig and the Hills left their newly acquired ranch in the care of a foreman and continued southeast, following a trail along Muddy Creek and the

Teton River to Fort Benton, where they were the first registered guests in the beautiful new Grand Union Hotel. They crossed the Missouri River at Fort Benton and started across the Shonkin range on the south side of the river. Here they met with a Mr. Kingsbury and his ranching partner, Lepeley. Kingsbury had previously offered his cattle to Craig, an offer the Oxley manager had declined. On this occasion, Kingsbury offered his herd to the Oxley a second time, but as the price had increased, Craig again turned him down.

The Oxley party moved on to Garden Land and U-Bet, then to Billings on the Yellowstone River where the Hills boarded their train. Before he left, Staveley Hill sat down with Craig to discuss the ranch's future and calculate the cost of operating the business. As manager, Craig felt confident that the venture was well underway. After seeing the Hills off on their train, he set out on his own journey of five hundred miles across the lonely plains. Fortunately, he managed to find suitable and safe company, and except for a short stop at Dupuyer again, where he bought 160 horses, the journey was uneventful.

Hill travelled east on the Northern Pacific Railroad to St. Paul, and then through Chicago, Detroit, and Toronto to Ottawa. In Ottawa he discovered that the lands in the neighbourhood of the Leavings had indeed already been granted. Willow Creek, in fact, was the boundary between the lease of the St. Clair Ranche Company on the north, and that of the Collingwood Ranche Company on the south. Hill's syndicate was trespassing on both sides of Willow Creek.

Fortunately, both ranching companies were willing to part with their leases for a sufficient price, and so after some negotiations the Oxley syndicate acquired both leases, covering some 80,000 acres. Shortly afterward, a third and smaller lease was assigned to the Oxley by Fred Watcher. These new leases were registered in Staveley Hill's own name so that the syndicate could retain the original Oxley lease of 100,000 acres as well. The Oxley now had one of the finest tracts of grazing land in the North West.

After Hill returned to England the original syndicate was reorganized and incorporated as a private company, called the Oxley Ranche (Limited), with increased capital and a board of directors consisting of Hill and his wife, Lathom and his wife, Baird and his wife and, to make up the necessary seven directors, Colonel Villiers, Lathom's brother-in-law.

Upon his return from Montana, Craig remained at the Leavings for only a week, long enough to get some work underway on the buildings and corrals, before heading back south to look for more cattle. He bought another 1000 head along Dupuyer Creek from O.G. Cooper, and a further 300 from Frank Bain on the Shonkin range. Copies of the agreements to purchase were forwarded to Hill in England; the terms called for delivery of the cattle and payment in four months—April 1883. Altogether the Oxley now had about 3,500 head of cattle in Montana, all to be driven north to the company's lease in the spring.

When the weather warmed up after the winter, Craig floated logs down Willow Creek to the Leavings, set his cowboys to work putting up corrals and buildings, and then went south to take charge of the cattle in Montana. The foreman on the Dupuyer ranch remained there to attend the roundup on the Teton range while Craig went down to the Shonkin range to help with the roundup there.

Payment for Bain's and Cooper's cattle was now due, but when Craig arrived in Fort Benton, he was dismayed to discover that no funds had been sent over by Hill. He sent an urgent cable to England requesting speedy action and pointing out that Montana stockmen were not agreeable to giving credit.

No answer arrived from England. Craig's only alternative was to arrange another loan. He consulted the I.G. Baker Company, which advanced him the amount necessary to pay for the cattle and the men on the drive at the usual rate of interest—one percent per month, added monthly. The Oxley manager was confident that such an unhappy financial arrangement would be necessary only temporarily, but he was also upset that the first year's purchase had to be done through a firm of American bankers and merchants.

Craig took Bain's and Cooper's cattle and started them north, moving about 10 to 12 miles a day. The season was early and there was plenty of grass and water along the route to keep the animals in good condition. The drive was a pleasant, if demanding, diversion after the discomfiture and pressures caused by the payment difficulty. Craig could even take a certain detached amusement when, having arrived at the Blackfoot reservation in northern Montana, the Indian agent charged the Oxley outfit a transit toll of ten cents per head of cattle. Craig would not speculate on the amount of the toll which the Indians actually received, but as the distance around the reserve was considerable, he figured the cost was worth the savings in time and effort.

The Oxley cowboys rested the herd for two days on the St. Mary River in southern Alberta and then pushed on to Willow Creek in late July. As with the Cochrane drive, a wagon followed behind the herd, picking up the calves which were dropped along the way, but unlike the Cochrane affair, nearly all the calves were saved. The herd arrived on the Oxley range safely and in good shape. Cows with calves were cut out of the herd, the calves were branded and returned to graze with the rest of the herd. Craig paid off the cowboys on the drive with the money he had borrowed in Montana, but was again disappointed to find that there was no money from Hill waiting for him at Fort Macleod.

The Leavings was a major stopping place for the stagecoach between Fort Macleod and Calgary; on August 11 the driver delivered a letter to the Oxley from Hill, who asked that Craig meet him and Lathom in Calgary when they arrived by train on August 30. The message brought a sense of relief to the hard-pressed manager; hopefully, Hill's visit would give him an opportunity to settle the difficulties over the money. Except for the money problem the ranch was making progress, and in honour of the visit by the two directors, Craig dispatched some men to the hills to cut timber with which to build additional rooms on the original log shack, and he even put up a flagpole. Lathom and Hill arrived in Calgary on the first through passenger train from Winnipeg; Craig drove a team and wagon from the Leavings to meet them.

During the following days Lathom and Hill inspected the lease and cattle. Lathom was both impressed and pleased with the condition and quality of the ranch and livestock. Hill, on the other hand, felt that the quality of the range cattle should be improved. Lathom realistically warned that keeping them at their present grade would be achievement enough on the unfenced range.

Hill, Lathom, and Craig also discussed possible expansion of the operation and concluded that the additional cost of grazing four thousand to five thousand more head would be relatively insignificant. They decided to consider buying Kingsbury's and Lepeley's cattle in Montana, since all the stock they needed could then be bought at one time. Hill directed Craig to write and ask the two ranchers to meet the Oxley directors in Helena on October 5 to discuss the sale if they were interested. Craig agreed to write, but pointed out that there was no time for the Montanans to reply to his letter.

Since the question of money, and especially the loan from the I.G. Baker Company, was becoming pressing and embarrassing, Craig suggested that Hill and Lathom go over the ranch accounts with him. Hill proposed instead that they defer the matter of the accounts and that Craig come along to Helena to assist in the purchase of the cattle. They could discuss the accounts then. With their plans settled, the two Englishmen left for a tour through the Kootenay country in British Columbia, leaving Craig frustrated but still hopeful.

By the beginning of October the three men had arrived in Helena, though Hill had been in town several days before Craig and apparently spoke with Kingsbury. When Craig arrived and met with Hill, he was dumbfounded when the Englishman said, "We don't want to buy his cattle. How did he know we were to be here?"

Craig protested. He reminded Hill that it was he who had instructed

Craig to write and arrange the meeting, and that there was no point in Craig travelling all the way from the Leavings to simply discuss the ranch's accounts, business which could have been settled earlier at the Oxley. Craig finally persuaded Hill that they should talk again with Kingsbury and Lepeley. Hill agreed to do so, though he continued to refuse to commit himself to a purchase.

Kingsbury made a proposal to Hill, who said he had to discuss it with the other shareholders and that they needed time to consider. As soon as a decision was reached, it would be cabled to Kingsbury, at Kingsbury's expense. This arrangement seemed satisfactory to both parties for the time being, and so the matter rested. (So far as Craig could learn, no answer was ever sent.)

Craig then went over the Oxley's accounts with Lathom. The ranch owed creditors $15,000, an amount which had been charged to Craig personally. Upon hearing of these debts Lathom exploded in anger; "Borrowing money from shop-keepers to carry on our ranching!" He turned to Hill and demanded, "Have you kept Craig out here doing our business, buying cattle with money borrowed from shop-keepers?" Hill looked at his manager with the utmost coolness and replied, "Craig, you ought not to have done this. You should have let me know all about the business and being out of funds."

Craig then produced copies of the letters which he had sent Hill, and indicated to Lathom that he had in fact kept Hill informed. The managing director, without acknowledging Craig's evidence, did however agree to send out the required amount when he returned to England. No, Lathom insisted, the money must be paid before they left Helena. And then, just to make the situation worse, a telegraph message arrived from the I.G. Baker Company for Craig, demanding that the balance due them be paid into the company's account in Helena the next day.

Staveley Hill left Craig and Lathom to visit the local bankers and negotiate a loan to cover the ranch's liabilities. An hour later he advised the other two that the loan had been arranged, and that Craig could obtain the money the next morning when the banks reopened for business. Lathom insisted that Craig write to him personally and provide a six-month statement of the ranch's probable expenses, plus ten per cent for safety. There was to be no more borrowing. Hill and Lathom thereupon boarded their train, which was "tolerably punctual (coming in within three or four hours of its time)."

Craig was reasonably satisfied with the results of the directors' visit, at least until the next morning when he went to the bank to withdraw the money which Hill had arranged. He was astounded to find that Hill had merely given the bank a draft for £100, and nothing more. As the Oxley Ranche still owed its creditors over $15,000, Craig had to arrange another personal loan to cover its liabilities; there was nothing else he could do if the ranch was to continue operations.

Having settled affairs in Montana, John Craig, instead of returning directly to the Leavings, travelled east to meet his family in Winnipeg. He had left his wife and four children in Ontario the previous year, planning to have them join him when he was settled in the new country and had a suitable house ready. Craig took the Northern Pacific Railroad to Minnesota, then went north to Winnipeg. From there the Craigs rode the Canadian Pacific Railway to Moose Jaw, but the ride was so disagreeable and uncomfortable that Craig decided that his family would go no farther under such conditions. Women and children had not travelled on the railway yet, and facilities were indeed primitive, dirty, and crowded.

Craig left his family in one of the ramshackle hotels which had sprung up along the new railway and set out to find better transportation. The hotel provided Mrs. Craig and the children with such a steady diet of hash that years afterwards they referred to any tiresome food as "Moose Jaw hash." Eventually the CPR crew managed to supply a more comfortable car for the Craigs, and the family finally arrived safely in Calgary.

Craig was happy to have his family with him, and their arrival seemed to signal a change in his fortunes. While they were in Calgary getting ready to drive to the Oxley, Craig met Capt. John Stewart. Stewart had just recently begun ranching near Pincher Creek in the southern part of Alberta, and planned to tender for the government beef contract for the Indian agencies for the next year. Even though the cattle were not needed for eight months, Stewart concluded a deal with Craig to buy 250 Oxley steers at $60 a head. The total purchase price, $15,000, was to be paid in cash and deposited with the I.G. Baker Company branch in Calgary within 15 days. Such a transaction—cash down for future delivery, and top price as well—was very unusual. But then unusual practices seemed characteristic of the Oxley Ranche, and this one helped Craig out of his embarrassing situation.

The winter of 1883–84 passed uneventfully for the Oxley Ranche. Craig had the satisfaction of knowing that the debts were paid off and there was even some cash on hand from various cattle sales. The company held 200,000 acres of land, three thousand cattle and three hundred horses.

The spring of 1884 brought fine weather and a letter from Staveley Hill in London directing Craig to increase the herd by an immediate purchase of breeding stock. The instructions urged speed, so that the cattle would be on the Oxley range by August, and have time to recover from the drive and become accustomed to their new ground by winter. The letter included no money; the cattle were to be purchased on credit.

The Oxley manager could hardly believe that the directors expected him to purchase cattle on credit. They had assured Craig that there was plenty of money among them when they formed the ranching syndicate. Besides, it was common knowledge even in the remote country of Montana and the Canadian North West that Lord Latham had recently purchased a single cow at a Shorthorn sale in New York for $30,000. Furthermore, it was simply not the custom on the range to expect ranchers to sell their herds on credit, and then drive the cattle out of the country. When cattle were sold on the range it was always for cash. To sell to outside and then to drive the cattle 250 miles clear out of the country without paying for them was simply asking too much.

Nevertheless, Craig dutifully went south again to look for cattle on the terms outlined by Hill. Everywhere he was greeted with refusals, but he hung on. Eventually, after showing a number of Montana ranchers Hill's letter of instructions and emphasizing the directors' exalted positions, Craig persuaded three young men to sell their cattle on Hill's terms. Frank Farmer of Choteau offered to sell 400 head, and two other ranchers, William Ralston and E.D. Hastie, offered 850 and 1350 head respectively.

Craig gave the three men bank drafts on Hill's account for 8 percent of the whole amount due, payable at sight, and the remaining balance in 60 and 90 days, terms which were even better than those Hill outlined in the letter. Craig then returned to the Oxley Ranche to get ready to receive the additional cattle.

Soon after he arrived at the Leavings, an urgent message called him back to Montana. When the drafts on Hill had been presented, they had been refused; Hill would not pay the eight per cent. The three ranchers thereupon took steps to set aside the sale and seize the cattle. The foreman Craig had left in charge of the cowboys, their horses, and all the cattle—were all under the sheriff's charge until the Oxley Ranche paid up.

The Montana cattlemen by this time had become very suspicious of Craig and the Oxley Ranche. The cowboys still herding the company's cattle made their disapproval of the whole mess known by demanding assurances that their wages would be paid. They were convinced that Craig had acted without due authority, and could not really believe that such illustrious directors would refuse to pay such a paltry amount.

Craig decided the best thing would be to meet with the three young ranchers. They, of course, were bitter about the situation and doubtful about an operation that would authorize its manager to purchase cattle on such unusual terms and then not meet the first payment. After some lengthy and heated discussions Craig persuaded the three men to accompany him to Fort Benton where he cabled Hill in London. For once the busy managing director replied promptly, advising Craig and the three Montanans that the deposit was on its way. Farmer, Hastie, and Ralston accepted Hill's cable as evidence of the company's intent to pay, even though they remained skeptical about future payments.

They did, however, agree to let the cattle go. A new agreement was drawn up on August 26, 1884 on the same basis as the original agreement, and the three men dropped legal action against the Oxley Ranche.

At the end of August the cattle started north. The herd had been detained for 30 days and had trampled and grazed off all the nearby grass. Craig also estimated that because of the delay, the company had lost about five hundred head through strays and stampedes.

Craig hurried back to the Oxley and drove into Calgary to meet Hill, who arrived by train on September 18. Craig, ever the optimist, was pleased to see the managing director. The cowboys would arrive with the cattle soon and would need to be paid. Surely Hill would supply the money which the ranch so desperately needed.

As he stepped down from the train, Hill insisted that they leave directly for the ranch. Craig reminded him that there were claims against the Oxley in Calgary, and that the sheriff would surely follow them if they left without paying these debts. Hill paid off the accounts, and he and Craig left for the Leavings, arriving just in time to see the herd from Montana come in, one month later than expected.

Staveley Hill remained at the Oxley for almost a month this time, talking happily with the cowboys (still unpaid), taking pictures, one of which showed the Honourable Member of Parliament seated on a horse and was later published in a London magazine with the caption "An MP with a safe seat," and generally enjoying the role of gentleman rancher. Much to Craig's consternation, however, Hill refused to discuss the company's finances.

Hill remained at the Oxley for the fall roundup, after which he and Craig went to Fort Macleod where their bookkeeper, Mr. Black, made up the cowboys' time for wages. Most of the cowboys had not been paid for months; while some of them were almost beating down the door, Hill calmly advised Craig that he did not have money enough to pay all of them.

As fortune would have it, Mr. Black happened to have a packet of his own money in the safe. He offered to make Hill a loan on the condition that it would be repaid just as soon as Hill reached Calgary several days hence. The Englishman was delighted at this happy turn of events, took the whole amount, paid off the cowboys and kept the rest for any eventualities which might arise. (Hill paid off the loan ten months later.)

With the cowboys' wages settled, Craig drove the managing director to

Calgary. However, claims by other creditors remained outstanding, but Hill repeatedly assured Craig that he would arrange for funds on his way home.

Although the cowboys at Fort Macleod had been paid their wages, the hands who had remained at the Oxley had not received theirs and were becoming very bitter. To solve the problem, Craig drove a herd of cattle to Medicine Hat and sold it to a buyer from Winnipeg. As he rather wistfully remarked later, the cattle were sold for part cash and part drafts for one, two, and three months, all of which were promptly honoured on their due dates.

Just as he resolved one crisis in Medicine Hat, however, Craig suddenly faced another before he even left the town; he received a message that the drafts given to Ralston, Hastie, and Farmer had been dishonoured again—and he had just sold some of their cattle to pay other debts! Craig then wrote to Lord Lathom, outlining the desperate situation with creditors. Lathom apparently passed the letter to Hill, who denied the seriousness of the predicament and blamed the problem on inadequate banking facilities and communications in the North West.

The fall passed into winter without a change in the situation. The creditors in Montana grew more insistent in their demands for payment, but Craig had no money to give to them. Hill in London responded to Craig's reports with letters of a peculiarly social nature and messages to the three ranchers in Montana promising payment at an early date and trusting that the unavoidable delays did not cause them any serious inconvenience.

In late January 1885 Frank Farmer, in a state of mental anguish at not receiving payment, left his ranch near Choteau and started for the Oxley on Willow Creek to try to collect his money. A fierce storm overtook him on January 26. He wandered off the trail and died alone on the frozen plains. The young rancher's plans had all come to nothing; with the proceeds of the sale he had planned to take his family east again. There was considerable anger and indignation among Montana cattlemen over the Oxley Ranche's continuing financial delinquencies which had led to such a tragic consequence. The people of Choteau also felt Farmer's loss deeply; the Fort Benton River *Press* reported that "it was a strange scene to witness the weather-beaten frontiersmen, hardy ranchmen and reckless cowboys overcome with grief at the sight of their old friend Frank lying cold in death's embrace ... In Frank Farmer Choteau has lost one of her best citizens, a good neighbour, a kind friend, a man ever-ready to sacrifice his own personal interests where the good of the community was at stake."

Soon after word of Farmer's death reached the Leavings, Craig received more bad news. The I.G. Baker Company filed against the Oxley Ranche a $27,000-claim for the purchase of a large herd of cattle the previous year.

Hastie, Ralston, and the executors of Farmer's estate filed similar suits and all four cases were heard in court at Fort Macleod. The court found in favour of the plaintiffs in each case and the sheriff, S.E. Chapleau, prepared to seize Oxley property and advertise it for sale.

Some of the Oxley Ranche cowboys, having completely lost confidence in Craig and the company, promptly quit when the sale notices were posted. In lieu of wages still owed them, Craig could only offer them promissory notes. When the bailiff and two deputies arrived to seize the company's saddle horses, Craig discovered that the bailiff's two assistants were former Oxley cowboys who were greatly relishing the turn of events. Craig rushed a cable off to Lathom and letters to each of the other directors, informing them of the seizure of the ranch's assets and the imminent liquidation of the company's operations.

On May 6, one day before the sheriff's sale was scheduled to take place, Craig received a cable from London, dated May 5, directing him to draw $75,000 on a New York bank. He now had reason to believe that the ranch was saved. Along with the company's counsel, C.C. McCaul, Fort Macleod District Deputy Sheriff D.J. Campbell, E.D. Hastie, and William Ralston, Craig set out for Calgary where he received the money and finally settled the cases—or at least most of them. Farmer's claims were left unsettled.

Earlier in the spring Craig had requested permission from the directors to proceed to London to discuss the company's affairs in the North West, but had received no answer and so remained at the Leavings on Willow Creek. The latest crisis, however, seemed to rouse the London directors, who sent out Hill's nephew, Stanley Pinhorne, with a secret power of attorney. Pinhorne arrived at the ranch in late May 1885, though he had been in the neighbourhood since the early part of the month. Craig did not know all the circumstances of his visit, but, having seen Pinhorne previously in company with Hill, welcomed him to the Oxley. Pinhorne explained that he was on a visit and would probably return to England in a few months' time.

Spring was always a busy time on the ranch, what with the roundup and branding. Craig was therefore hardly in a frame of mind to cope with a new crisis when a messenger arrived with a telegram from the manager of the Oxley's ranch in Dupuyer Creek. The sheriff of Choteau County had seized the Oxley's cattle and horses and planned to sell them if the balance of the debt to Frank Farmer's estate was not paid promptly. Craig showed the telegram to Pinhorne, who offered to go to Montana and settle the matter for the Oxley. Surely, Pinhorne reasoned, as he hurried south to Fort Benton with a companion, he would be able to obtain the necessary money from his uncle.

Pinhorne cabled Staveley Hill from Fort Benton, but there was no reply. Unable to do anything more, he returned to Willow Creek where he reported the dismal results of his trip—he had received nothing from London and the cattle remained in the possession of the sheriff. Craig was amazed that London seemed to acquiesce in the seizure and sale of the company's property and to believe that the sheriff in Montana would look after the Oxley's interests.

In August the sheriff of Choteau County advertised the sale of the Oxley cattle at Grass Lake corral, and this time there was no eleventh-hour rescue. Two hundred and eighteen head of cattle were sold for about $8,000, and nine horses for $400. Craig was outraged at these numbers and amounts. By his count, the Oxley had close to a thousand head in Montana. His foreman, however, pointed out that, given the Oxley's reputation with the Montana cattlemen, it was hardly surprising that so many cattle had disappeared in the roundup for the sale.

Despite the notoriety the Oxley Ranche was gaining in the North West and Montana, the business and ranching community around Fort Macleod continued to express confidence in John Craig personally. Indeed, a petition was circulated asking Craig to accept the nomination as representative of the Macleod district in the territorial council in Regina. Among those signing the requisition were C.C. McCaul, solicitor; John D. Higinbotham, Lethbridge druggist; Harry Taylor, proprietor of the Macleod Hotel; C.E.D. Wood, publisher of the Macleod *Gazette*; and Edward H. Maunsell, William F. Cochrane, Walter Huckvale, and F. C. Inderwick, all prominent ranchers. The document expressed faith in Craig's integrity, knowledge of the legislative requirements of the North West Territories, and his suitability as the best man to represent the farming, ranching, and commercial interests of the community. Craig declined the nomination, explaining that "certain conditions connected with my business engagements render me unable to become a candidate ..."

During the summer, too, the Macleod *Gazette* printed a story on Staveley Hill's book *From Home to Home*, which had just been published. The *Gazette* explained that "several of the inhabitants of Macleod and vicinity are immortalized, and will be handed down to history through the pages of Mr. Hill's book. We have to acknowledge, with many thanks, the receipt of one of the volumes direct from Mr. Hill himself, a compliment which we appreciate and shall not forget. It may gratify him to know that, since it was discovered that we are in possession of the book, there has been a perfect stampede for it."

Shortly after his return from Montana to the Oxley Ranche, Pinhorne gave Craig a letter from the directors in London with instructions to sell some steers and transmit the receipts of the sale to Hill. Pinhorne demanded that

Craig carry out the instructions, but Craig refused so long as there were creditors in Montana and the North West still to be paid.

Craig's refusal, perhaps coupled with his recent purchase of some unusually poor stock which no one else would buy, infuriated Pinhorne. He showed
Craig his power of attorney and rode out to the cowboys' camp where he told
the Oxley hands that he was now acting as manager and they would take their
orders from him. As well, he took possession of the ranch's books and placed
a notice of his action in the Macleod *Gazette*.

Craig refused to yield his position as manager and hurried off to Calgary
to seek legal assistance. There he obtained a writ by which all the assets of the
Oxley Ranche were redelivered to him by the sheriff of the Macleod district.
Soon afterward, however, C.C. McCaul, acting for the Oxley Ranche, succeeded in having the writ set aside and obtained an injunction restraining
Craig from interfering with the company's business. All the company's assets,
except the manager's house which was still occupied by Craig, and a large field
surrounding it, were then turned over to Pinhorne.

The whole confusing mess spilled out in the pages of the *Gazette*. On
October 6, 1885 the newspaper carried two notices from Craig, in which he
claimed the right of management and accused Pinhorne of acting under a
pretended power of attorney. The same issue also carried two notices from
Pinhorne, one advertising the sale of Oxley horses under his name and the
second proclaiming his power of attorney and right of management of the
Oxley. C.C. McCaul also took the unusual step of explaining his position to
the community; he took his instructions from Pinhorne, whom he recognized
as having "the full power and authority of the company ..." And finally, on
October 13, Hill got into the act with a notice that Craig was "absolutely dismissed from the service of the Oxley Ranche (Limited)."

Even before the battle of the notices in the *Gazette*, Craig had received
a telegram from Lathom requesting him to travel to London immediately.
Shortly afterward, a letter from Hill also arrived telling Craig to report to
London, but to leave the books and records with Pinhorne, who would
forward them to the directors at a later date. In late October Craig published a notice in the *Gazette* that he would shortly leave for London on the
company's business.

If Craig expected to settle the business of the ranch quickly, he was
sorely disappointed. In London he met several times with various directors,
though they never managed to be together all at one time. The first meeting included Craig, Lathom, Baird, and Villiers; the second meeting, only
Craig, Lathom and Hill. The questions were sharp and accusatory. Why were
returns not forthcoming? How many cattle were there on the range? Baird

demanded to know what had happened to the £60,000 he had sent. Craig could only fall back on the ranch records for evidence and exact information; but though he had requested Pinhorne to forward the records or copies to London, they never arrived.

At the second meeting Hill insisted that his Canadian manager tell the directors the number of cattle on the ranch property. When Craig gave him, from memory, the number of cattle purchased and calves branded, Hill turned to Lathom and said that they had over eleven thousand head. They certainly did not, Craig protested; they had not deducted the ranch's sales or the sheriff's sales, which would leave about seventy-five hundred head.

To protect his own interests, which seemed increasingly threatened, Craig hired a solicitor. At a third meeting of the directors and Craig, Hill demanded that Craig's counsel leave the room—which he did—and threatened to sue Craig for mismanagement. When the solicitor requested details of the suit so that he could prepare a defence, he received no reply. Three times after this series of meetings with the directors Craig attempted, without success, to meet privately with Lathom. Finally, after a month of fruitless waiting to conclude the affair, Craig sailed home to Canada.

After Craig's departure from the Oxley, Pinhorne became the official manager and hired James Patterson as foreman. (Patterson also retained his position as foreman at the Walrond Ranche.) But trouble continued to plague the Oxley operation. Just prior to his resignation (or firing), Craig had sold some Oxley cattle to Angus Sparrow of the High River-Calgary district. Sparrow was a major cattle buyer, and when he came to take delivery after the change in management at the Oxley, Pinhorne argued that the selling price was too low, and consequently refused to let the cattle go. The dispute dragged on for some days, and the ranchers in the cattle country found their sympathies sharply divided. The Willow Creek cattlemen stood behind Pinhorne, while the High River people backed Sparrow.

Sparrow returned to the High River area, gathered some of his friends together and rode back to the Oxley to take his cattle. Pinhorne and some of his neighbours loaded their guns and rode out to meet the High River men; Pinhorne threatened to shoot the first man who took a single animal. The situation was extremely tense and range war seemed imminent. In the end, George Emerson, the patriarch of the range, managed to defuse the situation and avert violence. Pinhorne kept his cattle, but there were bitter feelings among the High River men as they rode home.

Craig, meanwhile, returned to the North West and took up ranching with his son on Meadow Creek, just to the south of the Oxley Ranche. (Ironically, Craig's postal address was New Oxley, NWT; the ranch was designated a post office and Pinhorne postmaster in 1891.) He continued to be active in the affairs of the ranching community as president of the first Macleod fall fair and chairman of the South West Stock Growers' Association.

When the southern stockmen met in April 1886 to organize a new stock association, it was moved that Craig, as chairman of the old one, take the chair. Another rancher moved, seconded by Pinhorne, that a different person assume the position. In the discussion which followed, the majority agreed that Craig had the chair by right until new elections were held, whereupon Pinhorne and his friends left the meeting in a body. Craig referred to a "conflict of opinion," but would say nothing more and carried on with the meeting.

The directors of the Oxley now undertook a reorganization of the ranch, and in the spring of 1886 issued a prospectus in London offering shares in the New Oxley (Canada) Ranch Company, the capital of which was £120,000 in 10,000 shares of £12 each. The prospectus further stated that "the business of this ranch having been proved by its conduct by the private company to be a highly lucrative and successful one, it has now been arranged to transfer it to a public company, so as to enable the different interests to be determined and the affairs of the private company closed."

The Oxley's former manager believed that the reorganization was simply a fraudulent promotion by which Hill intended to unload a business worth about £54,000 (Craig's estimate) upon an unsuspecting public for £110,000. Craig also claimed later that the new company never paid a dividend on its capital.

But Craig soon had troubles of his own with which to contend. In August 1885 he had made a homestead entry under the provisions of the Dominion Lands Act for the quarter section of land on the Oxley lease on which the building and house he had occupied as manager were situated, having sworn that the improvements were his own, not the Oxley's. The land agent at Calgary had issued a certificate of entry, under the terms of which Craig was by law entitled "to take, occupy, and cultivate the land entered for, and to hold possession of the same to the exclusion of any other persons whatsoever."

According to regulations, however, when lands were already leased, the applicant for a homestead entry had to produce the written consent of the leaseholder before the land agent could grant him entry. The agent at Calgary had thought that Craig's position as manager of the Oxley Ranche justified dispensing with any written consent and issued the certificate. To further complicate matters, the leases of the new lands had not yet been fully assigned to the Oxley Ranche. Nevertheless, Craig retained possession of the quarter section within the Oxley's lease, even after his dismissal from the company.

In 1887 the New Oxley (Canada) Ranch Company instituted proceedings against Craig, claiming that he obtained the property by fraud. Craig, on the other hand, claimed title by prior occupation. Further, he sought to establish a consent by the company to his homesteading when it had agreed to build and make improvements for him personally in consideration of his bringing out his wife and family, and entertaining visitors to the ranch as well as guests of the company.

Both sides filed numerous affidavits, and the proceedings before the Dominion Lands Board dragged on into the autumn of 1887, when the case was closed and all papers submitted for a decision to the minister of the interior, Thomas White. In February 1888 White ruled on the matter and the two parties were informally notified that the entry would be set aside on payment by the New Oxley of actual cash spent by Craig privately in additional improvements. Before a formal decision was announced, however, White died. It was some months after the appointment of his successor that the parties were notified that though no objection had been made on either side to the jurisdiction of the minister of the interior, and both parties had fully submitted their evidence, the minister was advised by the Department of Justice that his power to set aside the entry was doubtful. Furthermore, even though the evidence clearly indicated fraud, affidavit evidence was not sufficient, and the matter should be decided by the courts.

On November 5, 1889 then, the New Oxley Ranch filed a bill, claiming that the entry by Craig should be set aside as obtained by fraud, and granted in error and improvidence by the Crown, and that all lands and improvements held by the defendant should be delivered up to them.

Craig answered that he was a squatter on the lands prior to the granting of any lease, and as such had the first right to them. He further claimed that the Oxley Ranche had always recognized the land as his homestead, that he had their consent and also the consent of the St. Clair Ranche Company to his homestead, and that by a special agreement with the Oxley company the improvements were to his private property.

On July 3, 1889 the case came up for trial before Justice Macleod. C.C. McCaul and Frederick Haultain represented the New Oxley, and Mr. Galliher, the defendant. The examination of witnesses occupied two days. Staveley Hill travelled from England expressly for the trial; other witnesses included Pinhorne; Sheriff (formerly deputy sheriff) D.J. Campbell of the Fort Macleod district; Mr. Black, former bookkeeper for the Oxley; and Mr. Greenwood, former teamster for the ranch. In addition, commissions were read giving the evidence of R.G. Kirby, the agent who took Craig's entry, and that of Solomon White, one of the original members of the St. Clair Ranche

Company. Craig's wife also testified, as did his son F.W. Craig, and Henry Kountz, the squatter whose rights Craig had originally purchased.

The trial subsequently moved from Fort Macleod to Lethbridge and it was there on July 30, 1890 that Justice Macleod handed down his judgement: that the homestead entry be cancelled, and that the New Oxley (Canada) Ranch Company was entitled to the possession of the land in question and that the defendant must deliver up possession thereof to the New Oxley.

The ranch continued to be managed by Stanley Pinhorne through these years, assisted by the capable Jim Patterson. Pinhorne, who was 32 at the time of his arrival at the Oxley, had acquired some livestock experience in England before crossing to Canada, and as the New Oxley was one of the premier ranches of the North West, its progress and the travels of its manager were dutifully noted in the Macleod *Gazette*.

Pinhorne was a popular man among some of his ranching neighbours and was active in the stock associations, sharing the leadership of the Willow Creek–Mosquito Creek roundup areas with Charlie Sharples. When E. Wilmot introduced polo to the southern range country, Pinhorne became an enthusiastic member of the Fort Macleod team.

Yet there was a tragic streak in the man as well. Caught as he was in the struggle between his uncle, Staveley Hill, and Craig, burdened with the responsibility of running an enormous ranch, and perhaps trapped by the loneliness of a single man's life on the range, Pinhorne became a heavy drinker. In the fall of 1892, when he stopped by to visit his friend and neighbour Charlie Sharples, he struck Sharples as being profoundly depressed. By the time he left for home, however, Pinhorne seemed to be in a happier and more optimistic frame of mind and in September he even hosted a gathering of the stockmen.

But on Sunday morning, October 2, 1892, Pinhorne was found dead in his bed with a bullet hole in his head and a discharged pistol in his hand. His apparent suicide was a shock to the community. On October 13, 1892 a poem appeared anonymously in the Macleod *Gazette*:

> By thine own deed? And this is then the ending
> Of a strong life, if ever life was strong.
> Bravest of all, if haply too unbending,
> Dead in thy prime, who might have lived so long.
>
> Well read withal, a happy combination
> Of sport and letters, fair to criticize,
> One who had seen full many a distant nation,
> Who spoke the truth, nor tolerated lies.

Going or gone the old set disappeareth,
Room must be made for generations new,
Railroads are spreading, and the country neareth
Civilization, and her curses too.

Far stretched the ranges, wild the lonely land was,
In days gone by, in days forever past,
But, cautiously, the wide progressive hand was
Reaching to grasp the Western wilds at last.

And thou has plucked aside the awful curtain,
Knowing at length what all of us shall know;
Beyond is mist, and Death alone is certain,
Thou has but gone where all alike must go.

Staveley Hill, who was visiting the southern United States, went to Fort Macleod upon receiving news of Pinhorne's death. He was at a loss to explain the suicide, since there was no evidence of any kind of trouble. The ranch seemed to be in a satisfactory state, and at the time of Hill's and Pinhorne's last meeting, Pinhorne had seemed happy and had even made plans for a visit to England.

Jim Patterson had left the ranch in 1889, and the operation obviously required capable and experienced management. Hill announced that the company planned to appoint Arthur R. Springett to the manager's position. Springett arrived in Fort Macleod in mid-October.

The ranch's new manager had left the range country only the previous December after many years as Indian agent at the Peigan Reserve near Fort Macleod. A tall, thin man with fine, blond hair, he could speak with the Indians in their own language (they called him Ab-see-cum, meaning white crane.) Springett had been given a rousing tribute and farewell by the ranching community when he resigned as Indian agent in 1891. Colonel Macleod had chaired the occasion, assisted by D.W. Davis, member of Parliament for Alberta; the large number of guests had included North-West Mounted Police Supt. Sam Steele, William F. Cochrane, and Stanley Pinhorne.

Springett then returned east to marry Evelyn Galt, daughter of Sir Alexander T. Galt, Father of Confederation and developer of the coal mines in Lethbridge.

Arthur Springett managed the New Oxley until 1903, when William Roper Hull purchased the whole operation from the English shareholders for about $250,000. At the time of the sale the ranch consisted of about three thousand acres of deeded land, several thousand head of cattle, a large

number of horses, and numerous buildings and implements. The holdings of
the Oxley underwent a number of changes, and ownership passed through
several hands until it was purchased by George Lane's family in the 1920s.

John Craig ranched at Meadow Creek until 1909, when he sold the
property and moved to the Cypress Hills, south of Gull Lake, Saskatchewan,
where his son had established his own ranching operation. When his wife
died in 1911, Craig returned east to live with one of his daughters until his
death in 1929.

Alexander Staveley Hill visited the Oxley Ranch several times after
Craig's departure. After 1895 he divided most of his time among his homes at
Oxley Manor, Kensington, and London. He died on 28 June 1905, leaving the
bulk of his estate to his son Henry, and gifts of cash to his faithful servants.

Chapter Five

THE NORTH WEST CATTLE COMPANY (BAR U)

While the Cochrane and the Oxley ranches staggered from crisis to crisis, another large ranching venture got underway—one which developed far more smoothly, managing always to land on its feet, no matter what the situation, and which gained great fame in Canada and abroad. This was the North West Cattle Company, operator of the famous Bar U Ranch.

William Winder, one of the original North-West Mounted Police, who came west in 1873 and whose family home was in the Eastern Townships of Quebec, retired from the police force in 1881 when his enlistment expired. During his service with the Mounted Police in the North West Territories he had watched and helped protect the fledgling cattle industry in southern Alberta, and after careful consideration of the prospects, decided to begin ranching himself.

When he returned east to organize his venture, Winder visited his wife's father, Charles Stimson, a successful Quebec businessman, and her brother, Fred Stimson, who managed the family farm in Compton County. His enthusiasm convinced the Stimsons that they should have a ranch of their own in the North West, following the example of the Cochrane operation which was, of course, also based in Montreal and Compton County. However, the Stimsons were unable to finance such a venture on their own, and they put the proposition to two other members of the Montreal business community, Sir Hugh and Andrew Allan.

At that time, Sir Hugh Allan was one of the wealthiest men in Canada. He was born in 1810 at Saltcoats on the east coast of Scotland (and after which, at the request of the Allans, Saltcoats, Saskatchewan, was named). His father was the master of a brig operating out of the River Clyde. Hugh Allan arrived in Canada in 1826 and worked for a few years with a dry goods firm in Montreal. In 1831, Allan joined a shipbuilding firm, and by 1835 had become a partner in the business. When the head of the firm died in 1839, Allan and the other surviving partner reorganized the business, which subsequently developed into a great shipping line, the Montreal Ocean Steamship Company, or simply the Allan Line, with Hugh as its head.

In the early 1850s Allan obtained a contract from the government of Canada to establish a line of screw steamers on the St. Lawrence River, and then another contract to carry the royal mail between Montreal and Liverpool. The company received an additional boost when its ships were hired to carry troops during the Crimean War and later, in 1874, to South Africa. The initial trans-Atlantic service was on a weekly basis and soon the line's passenger and freight services became renowned the world over. Thousands of immigrants gained their first view of Canada from the decks of Allan ships.

Besides heading the steamship company, Allan also had interests in the Merchants' Bank of Canada, communications, manufacturing, and insurance. In 1871 he was knighted for his services to Canadian commerce, and to mark his success and status he built a huge mansion on the lower slopes of Mount Royal in Montreal. (Ravenscrag, as he named it, is now part of the Royal Victoria Hospital.) His younger brother Andrew joined him in the business; his mansion stood only a short distance away, at the head of Peel Street, also on lower Mount Royal.

Sir Hugh Allan had little regard for the public, press, or politicians. He always believed the last two groups could be easily bought, and so it came as something of a surprise when the two combined to bring his good name crashing down, at least temporarily. In 1872 the Conservative government of Sir John A. Macdonald awarded Allan a contract to build a Canadian Pacific Railway. When it came out in the House of Commons and the press that Sir Hugh had made very large contributions to the Macdonald campaign funds, the resulting uproar brought down the Conservative government in the following year. (Eventually, a new Canadian Pacific Railway syndicate was formed and the project completed, but without Allan's participation. However, Canadian Pacific purchased the Allan Line and its agencies for about $8,500,000 in 1909; the amalgamation was completed in 1917, and the Allan Line Steamship Company disappeared as a legal entity in 1931.)

When, in 1881, the Stimsons laid their plans before Sir Hugh and Andrew Allan, the two brothers expressed interest in a North West ranch, and suggested that Fred Stimson travel to Alberta, scout the country and select a suitable location. So, with the arrival of spring, Stimson took the usual route to the Canadian North West by train to Chicago, then west to the Missouri River, up the river to Fort Benton and by trail from Fort Benton to Fort Macleod. He rode over the country between the Bow River and the international boundary, making a careful study of the various localities, their advantages, the available grass and feed, the shelter, and supplies of water and timber. When he returned to Montreal later in the summer, he recommended to his father and the Allans that they obtain a lease in the district south of the Highwood River, extending over the plains and foothills between the Calgary–Fort Macleod trail and the front ranges of the Rockies.

The Allans moved promptly on Stimson's suggestions and formed the North West Cattle Company, which received its letters of patent on March 20, 1882. The company's capital was originally set at $150,000, divided into 1,500 shares of $100 each. Sir Hugh Allan subscribed 396 shares. The Allan family retained 1311 shares and the Stimsons, 289. (Charles Stimson also invested in the ranching venture of his son-in-law, William Winder.) A meeting of the directors in August 1884 enacted a bylaw which increased the capital to $300,000.

The directors appointed Fred Stimson manager of their ranch and gave him instructions to take the necessary steps to complete the establishment of operations in Alberta. In the fall of 1881 Stimson took the train to Chicago and visited the stockyards there to look over the cattle coming to market from the western ranges and to choose appropriate bulls for the range. While in Chicago he chanced to meet a young Illinois farm boy named Herb Millar, and in his characteristic way waxed so enthusiastically over the ranching propects in the North West that Millar "boned" him for a job right on the spot. Stimson obliged him and put Millar in charge of 21 purebred bulls he had bought for delivery to the Bar U range the next spring. Millar was to care for them over the winter, then take them to Fort Benton.

Early spring 1882 found Fred Stimson at Spitzie Crossing on the Highwood River, locating the new ranch and establishing a centre of operations. He stopped in at the log cabin headquarters of George Emerson and Tom Lynch and made a deal with Emerson to help run the lines of the lease and locate the range. Then he made arrangements with Lynch to meet in Helena later in the spring in order to select the foundation herd for the ranch. In addition he contracted with Jim Minesinger, a Montana frontiersman who ran a few head of cattle near the crossing, to put up a log building just west of Emerson's and Lynch's cabin for the ranch's headquarters.

As soon as navigation resumed on the Missouri River in the spring, Herb Millar started out on his journey with Stimson's bulls. He was only 20 years old, and his experience and knowledge of the world and cattle had been pretty well confined to his father's modest farm. Stimson, though, had assured Millar that he would learn everything he needed to know along the way. First, he arranged to ship the bulls to Bismarck, Dakota Territory, over the

Northern Pacific Railroad, which was then pushing its way slowly westward through the northern United States. At Bismarck Millar loaded the cattle on the stern-wheeler *Black Hills* for the trip to Fort Benton. Millar and the cattle arrived without incident at Fort Benton where Millar turned the bulls over to the outfit driving the Cochrane herd north, and proceeded to prepare for his own trip to the Highwood. Following Stimson's instructions, he bought a wagon, filled it with supplies and hitched it to a northbound bull train.

Great bull trains transported much of the freight on the dry plains of southern Alberta and the northern United States, while the Red River cart dominated transportation in the wetter and softer country farther north. A bull train consisted of eight or so span, or pairs, of oxen yoked together, pulling three freight wagons which were linked together by sturdy chains. The lead wagon carried about three tons of cargo, the second, half as much, and the last wagon held the camp equipment as well as some cargo. Each team was driven by a bull-whacker, who walked alongside the team and handled a heavy rawhide whip with a fifteen-foot lash and a "popper" which cracked like a rifle. The train boss rode horseback and kept a constant check on the trail and the teams in the train.

The pace was slow, about 12 miles a day. On one occasion James Walker inquired for his mail at Fort Macleod and was informed that it had been sent north by bull train to Calgary two weeks previously. Riding north, Walker caught up with the train, took his mail, and was told by the bull-whacker that he expected to be in Calgary shortly, in about ten days.

Miller walked beside his wagon all the way from Fort Benton to Fort Macleod where he looked around for another bull train going north to the Highwood River and Calgary. The boss of one bull train assured him that there was no problem pulling his wagon—he had lots of power—but the bull-whackers had just gone on strike, a "laydown" strike as Millar called it. The boss then mulled over the situation for a while and suggested that perhaps if Millar would drive the bulls, he could haul his wagon to the Highwood at no cost.

Now Millar knew nothing about driving a bull-team, but the boss told him that there was really nothing to it and that he could teach Millar everything about it in ten minutes. The train boss led Millar to the bulls, showed him how to adjust their yokes and harness, how to hook the oxen to the long draw chain which ran through the yoke rings from the wheel wagon to the lead team, and cheerfully finished the lesson with "There kid, that's all there is to it. Let's go!" He shouted a sharp command to the oxen to get moving, and Millar suddenly found himself in the great brotherhood of bull-whackers, a group whose reputation for slowness was exceeded only by their colourful use of the language.

The bull-teams did not respond to polite commands and showed a marked tendency to remain standing still when so addressed. William Pearce, an early arrival in the range country, delighted in the story of a driver, accompanied by a missionary, being unable to extricate his team from a mud-hole owing to the fact that his working style was cramped by the clergyman's presence. "Having vainly expostulated with his team in a language and tone wholly new to them, and the whip having proved equally useless, he asked his passenger to choose between the physical inconvenience of an extra night or so on the trail or the aesthetic pain of listening to his stream of expletives." The missionary "wisely" chose the latter course. And on another occasion, Ed Higinbotham took his father, from Ontario, on a drive near Fort Macleod and drew his attention to a bull-team pulling a hay wagon across the Oldman River. "Here is something you will not see in the east," Higinbotham proudly told his father. Then, while they watched, the heavy chain connecting the team and the wagon suddenly snapped. The oxen walked leisurely out of the water and stood quietly on the river bank. The bull-whacker also emerged; throwing first his whip on the ground, then his dripping coat, vest and hat, he fell to his knees and let loose such a succession of hair-raising blasphemies that the elder Higinbotham cried out, "Drive on at once, Ed, or the ground will surely open and swallow us up."

Eventually Millar reached the Highwood River. He bade farewell to his companion, unhitched his wagon, walked over to the rising quarters of the ranch, introduced himself, and started in to help.

When the 21 bulls arrived at the ranch, they were the subject of jokes in the district, and many oldtimers thought Stimson must be quite a rancher to have so many bulls and not a single cow, but then maybe they did things differently in the east. However, Stimson was not idle, and during the summer he met Lynch in Helena to look for additional cattle. Demand for stocker cattle was high everywhere, and so were prices. Stimson and Lynch suspected that they might be able to purchase cattle cheaper in Idaho than in Montana, and headed for the Lost River country in the southeastern region of Idaho Territory.

Stockmen on the plains east of the Rockies had long known that there was a great pool of good cattle in Oregon, Idaho, and Washington for which the owners did not have sufficient markets, but the trail across the Great Divide was considered too gruelling for the cattle. By the 1880s, however, the price of even these cattle had increased with both demand from the growing cities of Seattle and Portland and the discovery by some enterprising Montanan ranchers that cattle could be driven over the mountain passes after all without much loss and with considerable profit. For their part, Stimson and Lynch were very pleased to find that cattle could be purchased in Idaho at

$19 a head—fully $6 cheaper than in Montana—and so bought 3,000 head and 75 horses in the Lost River country. Once the transaction was completed, Stimson headed back to the Highwood, leaving Lynch in charge of the drive north.

Lynch, after scouring the area for good cowboys, hired Ab Cottrell of American Falls as foreman for the drive and range operations in Canada. Then he asked a cowboy named Bill Moodie to join the outfit. Moodie agreed on condition that Lynch also hire his friend John Ware, who had just completed a long, hard drive from Texas with him. Lynch at first demurred when he met Ware, who was black (about one in every six American cowboys was black), but finally agreed to take him on as the cook's helper and night herder. As soon as he had put together a crew of eight men, Lynch lost little time in starting the cattle north towards Montana and then Alberta.

Cattle being trailed from Idaho crossed the Great Divide into Montana by the Targhee Pass, or more commonly by the Monida Pass. The first route dropped down to the south fork of the Madison River, then followed it north towards Bozeman if the cattle were heading for the eastern ranges of Montana, or towards the forks of the Missouri and Helena if they were moving to the northern ranges. The route over the Monida Pass followed the Beaverhead and Jefferson river valleys until it, too, headed north to Helena.

John Ware had been assigned for the drive an old plug of a horse with an appropriately decrepit bridle and saddle. As the outfit moved north Ware grew tired of his inferior position and one day respectfully approached Lynch and requested "a little better saddle and a little worse horse." The other men, overhearing this appeal and always looking for an opportunity for some fun and excitement, took the matter in hand and agreed that Ware's wish should be granted. After looking over the available horses, they picked out the toughest, meanest animal they could find, managed to saddle it, and then led it to Ware. It certainly looked better and more lively than his present mount, and Ware swung up into the saddle.

The horse exploded into action, pitching and twisting like a mad demon. But Ware stayed in the saddle, and the cowboys stood in astonished silence as the horse gradually quit bucking and submitted to the black cowboy's firm control. The other men knew good riding when they saw it, and they had surely seen it that day. Ware was soon promoted from night duty to day duty and given a position of responsibility near the head of the herd.

Ware impressed Lynch even more as the drive moved north of Helena towards the Marias River. Lynch suspected that some of the cattle were missing and detailed Ware to try to find them. Several hours later, Ware rode back to the outfit, driving before him the missing cattle and leading behind his horse at the end of his lariat, two very nervous rustlers. They had reason to tremble, for they knew the rough justice that western cattlemen dispensed. Lynch relieved the rustlers of their horses and guns, delivered a stern reprimand and some sage advice designed to prolong the pair's lives, and let them go.

As the cattle moved out of the mountains and onto the plains, the herd took on the classic appearance of the western cattle drive. In front of the herd rode Lynch with the chuckwagon near at hand. As trail boss he kept his eyes open for hazards and watering holes, and circled the herd frequently, ensuring that everything was all right. The boss controlled his men through hand signals, an idea borrowed from the Indians, and by movements of his hat. Near the end of the day he searched out a bed ground where the cattle could graze and settle down for the night. If the trail was heavily used, the bed ground was established a short distance off the trail where grass was more abundant.

Behind the boss trailed the cattle, strung out in a long, winding line. During the first days on a drive there was usually much confusion among the cattle, and they were pressed forward 20 miles or so a day in order to trail-break them and get them away from their home range. The rapid pace also tired them so that they would bed down at night rather than wander or mill about. After the first few days, when the cattle were trail broken, the pace was slackened. By that time, too, the animals had more or less sorted themselves into the order that they would usually maintain throughout the drive. Often a particular steer or bull showed a certain capacity for leadership on the trail, and the rest of the cattle followed his lead. Lynch, for example, had a rangy, temperamental old one-horned steer called Old Yellow, who was so useful in this way that he ended his life comfortably on the range rather than on the dinner table.

On either side of the lead was a pair of riders called pointers, who directed the cattle along the route. A second pair of riders farther back was called the swing, and a third set near the end of the herd, the flank. Bringing up the rear were several drag men and they constituted the low end of the cowboys' scale. Drag men choked on the dust raised by thousands of hooves, chased after strays, and constantly pushed forward the slower animals in the herd.

With a mixed herd during a spring drive, a special wagon often followed picking up newly born calves, though some ranchers did not believe that the expense and time the extra wagon entailed were worth it and either killed the calves or simply gave them away. On spring drives it seemed that every morning there were a few more new calves on the bed ground.

Trailing cattle was hard on the horses as well as the men. Few horses had the capacity for such hard work day after day, and a herd of spare horses, called the remuda, was driven along with the cattle. The cowboy in charge of the remuda, the horse wrangler, trailed them alongside the cattle, behind the chuckwagon but out of the dust raised by the herd. The wrangler was often a young and adventurous boy starting, after drag men, close to the bottom of the cow country hierarchy.

A cattle drive was not just a continuous forward movement. After an early breakfast the riders caught their saddle horses for the day and moved the herd off the bed ground to graze for a couple of hours. Then there followed a period of steady driving, until about noon, when there was another two- or three-hour break for rest and grazing. Finally, another period of driving lasted until it was time to stop for the night. With this sort of routine, 12 to 13 miles a day was considered good progress, and the cattle remained in good condition and lost little weight.

Towards evening the trail boss indicated the bed ground, with a sweep of his hand or hat, and the pointers rode out in front and stopped the cattle. The rest of the herd was drawn up into a compact group and all cattle were put onto the bed ground before sunset, when the night herders took up their watch.

Rustlers, such as the ones Ware and Lynch had dealt with, were only one of the many hazards on the trail. One constant fear was a stampede, especially during the first week or so, after which the danger seemed to lessen. But some cowboys always slept with a saddle horse nearby, just in case. A brilliant flash of lightning, an ear-splitting clap of thunder, or perhaps a strange, lurking fear could throw a herd into panic and cause them to stampede. Philip S. Long described a stampede in *The Great Canadian Range:*

> The men were silent as they rode around the restless cattle ... A faint noise crackled along the ground; the sheet lightning grew ever lighter and more frequent. The low rumbling of thunder could be heard—as if the elements were growling before they sprang ... Every animal was on its feet and moving; there was none bedded down on this night.
>
> A blinding flash lit up the entire herd and the riders, followed by an earsplitting crash that rocked the earth ... chaos ruled the range. The thunder of thousands of hooves shook the ground.

The usual plan for controlling a stampede was to circle the cattle and throw the leaders back into the drags. Sometimes a rider would fire his six-shooter beside the heads of the leaders or wave his rope or slicker to make them turn, for if the cattle could not be stopped or guided, they would run blindly until they were exhausted and spread all over the range, which meant a long day rounding them up again.

Lynch moved his outfit across the shallow Marias River, the international boundary, and then across the St. Mary River. Early in September they arrived at Fort Macleod where Stimson met them and delightedly watched his herd roll past. There was a wild celebration at the Macleod Hotel that night, prompting the correspondent for the Benton *Weekly Record* to report in the Fort Macleod Personals column that "vice has seceded from the beef herds and is now in town." The Macleod *Gazette* also approvingly noted that

> the herd of this company [the North West Cattle Company] passed through here ... en route to their range on High River .... It consisted of 3,000 head of the best grade cattle in Idaho, among which are 70 pedigreed cows and 10 thoroughbred bulls. Several of our leading officials and stockmen visited the herd and were surprised at the good condition of the cattle after so long a drive. The number of calves was conspicuous to everyone. This is evidently one of the most successful drives ever made to this country and Capt. Stimson is to be congratulated on having secured the services of such an experienced stockman as Tom Lynch. This enterprise has our best wishes.

The leaves on the cottonwoods along the prairie streams had turned gold and fresh snow sparkled on the distant peaks of the Rockies as Stimson's cattle passed along the eastern fringe of the Porcupine Hills. Finally, on September 25, the cattle splashed across the Highwood River and bedded down near the new headquarters of the North West Cattle Company. They had travelled seven hundred miles, and at last Stimson had some cows for his bulls. (The bulls had been reduced to 20; much to Stimson's outrage, Jim Minesinger had killed a bull for meat when supplies were running low. But Stimson was a forgiving man, and Minesinger continued to work for him.)

Lynch paid off the cowboys from the south, except for a few who he hired for the ranch. Among those who stayed were John Ware and Bill Moodie. Stimson's cattle soon settled down on their new range, obviously satisfied with the abundance of good grass and the warmth of early fall days. Only a few days after the arrival of the North West cattle, the great Cochrane herd with Poindexter and Orr passed across the Highwood River on its way to its range at Big Hill.

Suddenly, at the end of September, the bright warm days disappeared and a fierce storm blew in from the north, bringing strong winds and heavy snow. For eight days it snowed, dumping almost two feet on the ground. While the Cochrane cattle were stuck at Fish Creek, the North West cattle, unaccustomed to such weather, turned their tails to the north wind and began to drift south. Fortunately, the weather was not extremely cold, but the storm was still bad enough to keep the cattle on their feet, looking for grass and shelter. The Highwood River was so low that it presented no barrier to the drifting cattle; although the cowboys tried to stop them, the cattle simply scattered and moved around them, making it even more difficult to keep track of the herd. Finally, the cattle were allowed to drift south.

The storm was followed by a chinook that cleared the snow from the range south of the Highwood, and everyone on the ranch was soon out looking for the cattle. The sense of urgency was compounded by John Ware's absence, and the cowboys were afraid that he might have become lost and perished in the storm when he went out to check on the herd.

After several days of hard riding, Stimson's cowboys managed to round up most of the cattle, which had drifted as far as the north bank of the Oldman River where the deep-flowing waters had held them up. And there with the cattle was John Ware, trying his best to keep them together while allowing them to drift.

Stimson left the herd on the Oldman range for the winter, and assigned two cowboys to stay with the cattle to prevent them from crossing the river when it froze over. The wisdom of leaving the cattle in the south was proven in the spring, when the North West Cattle Company compared its relatively slight winter losses with the terrible losses the Cochrane operations took on the Bow River. In April 1883 Stimson ordered an early roundup to count the company's stock and move them back to the Highwood range.

By 1883 the country along the Highwood was becoming more settled, something the ranchers did not appreciate. Homesteaders were moving into the area, taking up the good land and starting to break the range in preparation for farming. Consequently, a number of ranchers decided to move farther west towards the foothills where, in any case, there was more water and shelter than on the plains.

Stimson, too decided to shift his operations farther west and picked out a site on Pekisko Creek. He set Minesinger and the cowboys to work again, hauling spruce from the foothills and cutting cottonwoods along the creek for new buildings. The new headquarters nestled in a sheltered valley on the banks of the creek, with a spectacular panorama of foothills and mountains to the west.

About this time Ab Cottrell told Stimson that he wanted to return home to American Falls, and that Stimson should start looking for a new foreman. Knowing that there were plenty of good hands in the cattle business south of the boundary, Stimson wrote to the Montana Stock Growers' Association and asked them to recommend a good man to run his range operations. The association promptly suggested George Lane, a native of Des Moines, Iowa, who had been in the territory for some time.

Lane, born in 1856, had travelled west to Montana while very young. His father was a prospector there and with several others had discovered the famous Alder Gulch gold strike. George Lane spent some time with his father in Virginia City, and then for three years did some cowpunching, freighting, Indian fighting, and scouting for the u.s. Army during the Indian wars of the 1870s. After the Indian campaigns drew to a close, Lane went back to cattle, and having heard about the cowman's paradise north of the border, went to see for himself. He rode over the Canadian range, taking note of the country and considering its potential. Lane was free when the request from Stimson came. He accepted the offer and headed north in the spring of 1884. Stimson met him at Fort Macleod and they joined the general roundup then in progress.

Lane was a cattleman to his fingertips. There was nothing haphazard about his operations; he planned very carefully and carried out his plans to the last detail. His efficiency and skill were quickly recognized, and for many years he was elected captain of the annual general roundup in southern Alberta. One of the first changes he made in the North West Cattle Company operations was to scrap the ranch's original brand, the Double Circle, one circle inside the other. This brand tended to blotch and proved wholly unsatisfactory. Lane chose instead the Bar U ($\overline{U}$), and ever afterwards the operations of the North West Cattle Company became known as the Bar U, one of the most famous brands in the cattle country.

So many cowboys who worked at various times for the Bar U became well-known or successful ranchers in their own right that the Bar U was often called the school for cowboys. If the school had a director it was Herb Millar, the same adventurous youth who brought in Stimson's first bulls. Millar arrived just as the ranch was getting underway and maintained a close working relationship with it until his retirement 53 years later.

Probably the most famous cowboy who worked for the Bar U was Harry Longbaugh, described by Fred Ings (who rode with him briefly) as "a thoroughly likeable fellow, a general favourite with everyone, a splendid rider and a top notch cow hand." Longbaugh had come north after some brushes with the law in the United States. He briefly worked for the Bar U, then returned to Montana where he again got into trouble. "He had not been long gone from our range when we heard that he had joined up with the notorious Currie gang and with them had blown up an express car in Montana, getting about $60,000," Ings remembered. Longbaugh eventually made for South America with a companion, where according to Ings,

at last, their doings became so outrageous that the troops were ordered
out against them;

They were followed to their hold-out where a real battle took place
… They kept up the fight as long as their ammunition lasted, and when
they had but a cartridge apiece, they nodded to one another and each
raised his gun against his pal and shot.

Longbaugh was, of course, the Sundance Kid, and his companion,
Butch Cassidy.

None of the Bar U cowboys, however, contributed as much to the folk-
lore of the range country as did their manager Fred Stimson, whose bons mots
on every subject under the sun, on and off the range, were repeated throughout southern Alberta, though most people acknowledged that they were best
told by Stimson himself. Stimson was the driving force behind the Bar U in its
early days. A distinguished-looking man, large and well built, he was equally
home on the range or in the drawing rooms of Montreal. He had a low voice
and a carefully cultivated drawl which led many people to think that he was
from the American midwest. His bright eyes sparkled when he sprung his
stories upon unsuspecting visitors.

On one occasion the Crown was prosecuting a man accused of mis-
branding one of the Bar U's cattle. The accused was defended by the famous
Calgary lawyer Paddy Nolan, whose own reputation for humour and good
living equalled Stimson's. The Bar U manager was an important witness in
the case, and Nolan tried hard to discredit his evidence. The exchange between the two men in court provides insights into each of them.

Mr. Nolan: Your name is Frederick Stimson, I believe.
Mr. Stimson: It is, sir.
Mr. Nolan: You spend most of your time riding the range, do you not?
Mr. Stimson: No, sir, I spend most of my time in bed.
Mr. Nolan: You are very short-sighted, I believe, Mr. Stimson
Mr. Stimson: No, sir, I am not.
Mr. Nolan: Then why do you wear glasses [actually, a monocle]?
Mr. Stimson: Oh, just for effect.
Mr. Nolan: Now, Mr. Stimson, you claim that my client misbranded one
              of your cattle?
Mr. Stimson: I do, sir.
Mr. Nolan: Please describe the animal in the court.
Mr. Stimson: Well, it was an ordinary, everyday steer with a leg on each
              corner.

Mr. Nolan: [disgusted at not making any headway with the witness] I be-
               lieve, Mr. Stimson, that you regard yourself as something of a
               smart aleck.
Mr. Stimson: I am also informed that you do a little smart alecking your-
               self.
Mr. Nolan: That will do, Mr. Stimson. Your Lordship, I am through with
               the witness.

In the course of another case arising from a horse being struck and killed
by a train on the CPR right-of-way, Stimson remarked that any horse which
could not outrun a CPR train was no good anyway, and deserved to be killed.

One day, Stimson and a number of other southern Alberta worthies
were relaxing in the rotunda of the Alberta Hotel in Calgary, talking as usual
of the open range, outlaws, roundups, and steers. The company included Gilbert E. Goddard of the Bow River Horse Ranche, Pat Burns, William Roper
Hull—and Paddy Nolan snoozing in the comfort of a big leather-covered
chair.

Watching the group, and looking with obvious disdain upon what they
considered vulgar surroundings, were two young Englishmen, dressed in correct English riding costume and, in very audible voices, trying to impress the
locals with accounts of hunting in England with proper gentlemen and for
real game.

Stimson coolly appraised the two boasters and called out to a friend,
E.H. Hodder, who was sitting some distance away. At once, other talk ceased.
The company knew from experience that Stimson was about to say some-
thing.

"You remember, Hodder, last year when I took a consignment of five
hundred fat steers to Liverpool, I did some visiting in England before I
returned?"

"Well," Stimson went on, "as soon as the steers were disposed of, I made
a little journey up to London and registered at the Cecil Hotel, intending to
engage in a little diversion. However, by some means or other, the Old Lady
of Windsor [Queen Victoria] found out that I was in town, and she sent for
me and insisted that I take up my quarters at the Castle.

"It was an honour, of course, but exceedingly stuffy, and there was
nothing much to do. They didn't even allow cards to be played in the Castle,
but the Old Lady was quite friendly and her daughter, Miss Beatrice, was
particularly so.

"There was a sort of pavilion on the grounds; and on occasion I used
to go there and sit around with Miss Beatrice and taught her to play euchre

which she learned with great aptitude. One evening, when we were going to the pavilion, the Old Lady herself announced that she would accompany us, which she did, attended by a gigantic footman.

"We passed an exceedingly pleasant evening, and the Old Lady took quite a fancy to the game. However, about nine o'clock, she stood up and said, 'It is my bedtime, Mr. Stimson, and I must go home. I will leave my daughter in your charge.' And she departed with her footman and umbrella because it had commenced to rain.

"Miss Beatrice and I passed an exceedingly delightful evening. The time went rapidly and after playing several games, we suddenly heard the clock in the tower of the Castle strike midnight. Miss Beatrice stood up and said, 'Oh, Mr. Stimson, it's midnight. Whatever will Ma say!'

"She quickly put on her wraps, and I escorted her to the portals of the Castle. The great building seemed wrapped in slumber. Not a light glimmered and the front door was locked. I attempted to ring the bell, but the only result was to pull about one hundred yards of wire out of the place that had been prepared for it and there wasn't an answering tinkle. I then walked up to the door and produced my six-shooter—the one, you know, Hodder, with which I killed the rustler—and with the butt of it, I banged on the door which gave forth a hollow reverberation.

"For a minute there was no response, and then the window over our heads was thrown open, and somebody called out, 'Who's there?'

" 'It's me, Ma,' said Miss Beatrice, with a fine disregard for grammar.

" 'Yes, indeed, I know that, Miss,' responded the voice. 'But who have you got with you?'

" 'Oh, it's only old Fred Stimson from Pekisko.'

" 'All right,' said the voice. 'Just wait for a minute until I put my Crown on and then I will come down and let you in!' "

As Stimson's friends broke up in laughter, the two Englishmen snorted and left the room—to the immense amusement and satisfaction of the company.

Despite the fact that Stimson's wife Mary disliked life on an isolated ranch and consequently spent much time visiting and staying with friends in High River, the Bar U became noted for its hospitality and was a favourite destination for travellers from eastern Canada and England. Stimson's son Bryce also lived on the ranch, as did Stimson's niece, Nellie Bowen, who very capably managed the household. Stimson extended his hospitality to the Indians in the neighbourhood and got on very well with them. He was one of the few ranchers fluent in the Blackfoot language and was an avid collector of native handicrafts and artifacts.

One of the early employees of the Bar U was a Mrs. Bedingfeld, the widow of an English officer who had been stationed in India. When her husband died, she and her son Frank sailed to the United States where they spent a few months in Iowa, then moved north to Canada in 1884. Mrs. Bedingfield was a very aristocratic-looking and well-bred woman, and though she did not get on very well with the cowboys, she enjoyed life on the Alberta range. After working for a brief time as housekeeper at the Bar U, she established her own ranch just a short distance to the west. Eventually, the Bedingfeld ranch eclipsed even the Bar U in fame.

Under Stimson's and Lane's management, the Bar U prospered. The original range of the North West Cattle Company consisted of two leases; the first granted to the company on September 21, 1882 and consisting of 59,000 acres, and the second given to Fred Stimson and covering 55,000 acres. In 1886 the Bar U purchased the 44,000-acre lease of the Mount Head Ranche located on the south fork of the Highwood River, an operation established in 1884 with English capital. The principal shareholder of the Mount Head, Thomas Todd Milbourne of Brighton, England, was a major shareholder in the North West Cattle Company as well. Stimson turned the Mount Head Ranche headquarters, well situated in a sheltered valley, into a feed camp for the Bar U cattle.

The Bar U suffered the usual setbacks from weather, prices, and other hazards, but always managed to recover and gain in strength. For many years the ranch rewarded its owners with gratifying dividends of 19 percent on invested capital.

George Lane, like many other cowboys and foremen in the range country, developed his own interests and ambitions beyond the Bar U. As he accumulated experience and capital, he devoted more time to buying and selling cattle on his own, finally leaving the Bar U entirely. In 1892 he acquired the Flying E ranch on Willow Creek, and later the YT on the Little Bow River, which he built up as a horse ranch. The YT eventually covered 40,000 acres of deeded and leased land. During this period, too, Lane worked with Pat Burns, the rising king of the meat-packing industry in the North West. Burns at various times held contracts to supply beef to the southern Alberta Indians, and George Lane worked with him on some of these contracts.

The North West Cattle Company underwent some profound changes as well. Sir Hugh Allan died in 1883, and his brother, Andrew, in 1901. The Allan interests then came under the management of Andrew's son Sir Hugh Montague Allan, who later became famous for his sponsorship of the Allan Cup for amateur hockey. In January 1902 Allan and the directors of the North West Cattle Company sold the company's property, cattle, and other assets to a company organized by George Lane.

When Lane had determined that the Bar U might be available, he travelled to Montreal to negotiate a deal with the Allan interests. He was given three days to finance the purchase. To meet the deadline, he brought in the meat-packing firm of Gordon, Ironsides, and Fares, and formed a new company—Lane, Gordon, Ironsides, and Fares—to take over the Bar U. The transaction involved 18,000 acres of deeded land, various range leases, 500 horses, 1,000 tons of hay and extensive buildings. The deal, valued at $250,000, was the largest ranch transaction in the North West to that date.

The Calgary *Herald* commented:

There is a touch of romance in the deal, inasmuch as Mr. Lane originally came to Alberta to work for this very outfit. He struck the country with exactly $100 and started to work for the Bar U outfit for $100 a month … he has by his own unaided efforts become one of the most wealthy and substantial men in Alberta. From a plain cowboy he has risen to be one of the largest, if not the largest, cattle ranche owner in Western Canada.

Another commentary on the sale of the Bar U came from Charlie Millar, the younger brother of Herb Millar, and appeared in the Calgary *Eye Opener*:

The shades of night were falling fast
And the Bar U ranche was reached at last
For the YT boss had a telegram
That knocked from the roost the great I AM
Who said "Goddimit!"

The great I AM did cry and moan
So he lifted his foot and kicked a stone
And dear little somebody made an awful fuss
When she left the ranch with the poor old cuss
Who always said "Goddimit!"

It lifted a load from the cowboys' heart
When they saw the old fellow ready to start,
For he docked their wages on a stormy day,
And when they kicked you would hear him say
"Goddimit!"

The Nitchies will miss their bread and jam
Since they lost their friend the great I AM,
For he's gone to the East perhaps to stay,
And no more the cowboys will hear him say
"Goddimit!"

The Great I AM is now no more
And old George Lane will take the floor,
He'll tell the cowboys what to do,
And shake them up with a
"Goddamyou!"

In March 1902 a special general meeting of the shareholders of the North West Cattle Company was held at the firm's office in Montreal in order to ratify the directors' action and to consider the advisability of winding up the affairs of the company, the voluntary surrender of its charter, and the distribution of its assets. A resolution was passed at the meeting authorizing the directors to take steps to wind up the company and surrender the charter.

Then, on 5 April, officers of the North West Cattle Company presented a petition to the Superior Court of the District of Montreal asking for authority to appoint H. Montague Allan, president of the company, as liquidator. According to the affidavit submitted by E. W. Riley, treasurer of the company, the firm's assets included approximately $233,000 in cash while liabilities amounted to no more than $5,000. The petition was granted.

The sale of the Bar U by the company's directors had been strongly opposed by Stimson—he claimed that the sale had been made at a sacrifice of over $100,000—and he also objected to all the other proceedings on the grounds that the shareholders and creditors of the company had not been properly consulted. (Stimson was not only a shareholder, but also a creditor—the company owing him $1,000 of his annual salary.) The former manager of the Bar U therefore presented a petition to the court to have the proceedings taken by the North West Cattle Company set aside, particularly the appointment of the liquidator, as he had been appointed without any notice to the shareholders or creditors of the company. The superior court decided against Stimson, however, and judgement was given against his petition.

Stimson appealed the judgement; the court of appeal unanimously reversed the opinion of the superior court and decided that Stimson's objections had merit, and that H. Montague Allan could not be appointed liquidator of the company unless a previous notice had been given to the shareholders and creditors, who were entitled to have an opportunity to object to the appointment. The court further declared Allan's appointment illegal, ousted him from the position of liquidator, and set aside all proceedings which he had taken since his appointment. Costs of both courts were given in favour of Stimson.

Stimson remained in Montreal, but soon became involved in another ranching venture, this one backed by Sir William van Horne, president of the CPR, who had large financial interests in a Mexican estate. After some years in Mexico Stimson returned to Montreal where he died suddenly on January 15, 1912, and western Canada lost one of it most colourful pioneer cattlemen.

The newly acquired Bar U was obviously the feather in George Lane's hat, but he did not rest there. He acquired a large farm at Namaka east of Calgary, where he put 14,000 acres into grain and feed production. In their continuing search for new and profitable lines of ranching, Lane and George Emerson travelled to Mexico where they purchased 10,000 stocker cattle in 1902 and brought them back to Alberta. This was a rather controversial move among the members of the ranching community in view of the generally poor quality of the animals. The shipment brought the Bar U herds up to eighteen thousand head, and by the fall of 1906 they exceeded forty thousand head. Then disaster struck. A terrible winter in 1906–7 left half the Bar U livestock dead, with the imported Mexican cattle suffering especially high losses. Ever the optimist, Lane rebounded with new plans for recovery and expansion.

Lane, with his keen eye for trends and development in the North West and the opportunities they presented, became interested in raising horses. In 1898 he stocked his YT ranch with a herd of horses he purchased in Dillon, Montana. The herd included a few registered Percherons which became the nucleus of the famous Bar U herd. However, W.H. Fares, Lane's partner in the YT, was reluctant to get into horse ranching on a large scale. In the late 1890s the west was hardly booming. Depression was in the air, and prospects for quick recovery looked poor at best. Lane perceived, on the other hand, that days of the open range were limited and that settlers would eventually pour into the country. The cry was already being heard that the future of the North West lay in wheat farming, and all those farmers were going to need power for their plows and power meant horses.

Confident that his assessment was correct, Lane began to develop a herd of the finest registered Percherons. These large and powerful horses were excellent for field work and therefore right for a growing market. Through careful breeding and management, Lane built up his herd into one of the most notable in the world. As their reputation spread, they began to take prizes and awards everywhere, and Lane could look with satisfaction on both the quality of his work and the profit it provided for the Bar U.

The years after the First World War were hard ones for the cattlemen on the plains. The cattle market collapsed and many operators were driven out of business. Lane's partners in the Bar U—Gordon, Ironsides, and Fares—ran into financial difficulties as well, and many people expected that the meat-packing company's bankers would take over the Bar U. This possibility moved Lane to buy out his partners in 1920, leaving him in sole possession of the ranch. While the purchase left him with a heavy debt load, he at least had kept the Bar U out of the bankers' hands. (Herb Millar advised him at one point to let the banks take over the ranch; they would not know what to do with it and would then be ready to dispose of it on favourable terms. Lane had not followed that advice, preferring not to risk losing the ranch.)

As one of the great successes of early Alberta ranching, Lane was well known and respected throughout the range country. One early pioneer recalled that there was absolutely no pretentiousness to the man; he was always natural, though sometimes breezy to the point of brusqueness. He drove himself hard and expected no less from his employees and business associates. A display of temper from the "old man" was taken seriously.

Respect for Lane, however, was often tinged with controversy. A. Ernest Cross of the a7 ranch ran some cattle on the Bar U at one time with Lane and when it was time to round them up was bluntly advised that he would simply have to await Lane's leisure. Cross thereupon offered the Bar U riders five dollars more in wages than Lane was paying them and they promptly changed employers. Lane was suitably impressed, and after that he and Cross became good friends.

While many people in the range country may have had some misgivings about the sweep and mode of Lane's operations, they could not help admiring his mettle in one particular situation. In 1902 the Bar U gathered some twelve hundred head of beef for shipment via the CPR from Claresholm to market in Chicago. However, Lane and the CPR could not come to an agreement on rates for hauling the livestock. When word finally arrived from the Montreal headquarters of the CPR after Lane had held the herd for a week at Claresholm, and it was not in his favour, the Bar U boss made arrangements with the Great Northern Railway in the United States to ship the cattle on its line from Browning, Montana. This meant trailing the herd two hundred miles south, but Lane was not about to be held hostage by the CPR. When it came to cattle, Lane knew what he wanted and usually got it through patience and sheer persistence. Cattle were almost sacred to him, and some people claimed it was sacrilegious to spit or laugh within ten feet of his steers.

In 1885 Lane had married Elizabeth Sexsmith, born in the Gatineau valley, Quebec, and whose family arrived in the North West in 1883—one of the first in the High River district. The Lanes raised eight children and carried on the tradition of the Bar U's hospitality to friends and strangers from many walks of life. One of the most notable visitors was Edward, Prince of Wales, who was a guest at the ranch in 1919. Even with royalty, Lane retained his informality and air of frontier democracy. One morning when the prince and the Lanes set out on a tour of the range, the prince suggested that he should drive the carriage in which the women were riding. Lane definitely had other ideas and replied, "No, Prince, you stay on horseback. My daughter will do the driving." For Lane, the future king of England was just "the Prince" and he introduced him as such: "Bill, meet the Prince: Prince, meet Bill."

The prince enjoyed the foothills country and indicated that he would like to buy property in the area. When Frank Bedingfeld advised Lane in 1919 that their ranch was up for sale, Lane purchased it on behalf of the Prince of Wales. The Bedingfeld ranch was renamed the EP (Edward Prince) Ranch, the name it has retained since. The prince visited his ranch several times, though the ranching community was probably more impressed with their new neighbour than the prince was with the prospect of living on the range.

During the 1920s Lane wintered in California, but always returned to Alberta range country to oversee the spring operations at the Bar U. And when he died at the ranch in 1925, the Calgary *Herald* noted his passing on the front page and lamented the loss of yet another of the early pioneers.

The Bar U story did not end with George Lane. The range was purchased in 1926 by Pat Burns and became the finest gem in the crown of western Canada's newly acknowledged cattle king.

After Burns' death in 1937 the Bar U was operated by P. Burns Ranches until 1950, when the deeded land and lease was sold in parcels; neighbouring ranches purchased much of the land.

Chapter Six

EXPANSION AND CONSOLIDATION

B y their sheer size and the prominence of their owners, as well as their much-publicized early trials—the Oxley, Bar U, and Cochrane ranches dominated the early Alberta range. During the 1880s many other ranches were established, while some of the very early cattlemen consolidated their existing enterprises.

There were many small ranches, founded and operated by a single person or family. Other ranches were started as partnerships or companies with distant shareholders. Some ranches existed for only a few months or a year—just long enough for a speculator to make his profit. Others are still in existence today. Practically all of them add an interesting story to the history of the cattle kingdom.

The Military Colonization Company Ranche

One of the more exotic ranching ventures in Alberta was that of Maj.-Gen. Thomas Bland Strange and his Military Colonization Company Ranche, commonly known as the MCC. The MCC Ranche suffered continually from poor financing and the erratic management of its founder. But even in a country which was never lacking in unusual characters and enterprises, its very idea was unique.

Thomas Bland Strange was born in Meerut, India. He was the son of Col. H.F. Strange and his wife, the daughter of Maj. N. Bland. Educated at Edinburgh Academy and then the Royal Military Academy in Woolwich, England, he later took a commission in the Royal Artillery and served during the 1857 Indian Mutiny where he participated in the siege and capture of Lucknow.

Strange's service then took him to Canada with the British garrison at

Quebec. In 1868, when the British government decided to eliminate their North American garrisons, the government of the new Dominion of Canada organized two batteries, one at Quebec and the other at Kingston, Ontario.

In 1871 Strange entered the service of the Dominion as commander of artillery at the Fortress of Quebec, and later, at Kingston. In 1881, after 30 years in the Imperial and Dominion service, he was entitled to a military pension, but was advised by the government in London that it would not be paid to him so long as he remained in active service. Since there seemed little to be gained by continuing in the military, Strange resigned. He was placed on the reserve of officers and given the rank of major-general. But he was not ready to fade quietly away to some retirement villa in the south of France.

Instead, an idea which he had harboured for many years began to take shape.

Some years before, Strange and a fellow officer, Major Hennell, had been sent west to report upon the best terminus, from a military viewpoint, for the Canadian Pacific Railway. In their travels the two men noted the excellent ranching prospects offered by the western plains in America. And, of course, by the early 1880s the great cattle boom in the United States was starting its giddy climb.

After his retirement from the military in 1881, Strange travelled west to look over the land with the idea of setting up his own ranch. In Montana he joined up with a young Englishman who had been on a sheep station in Australia and was considering just such an enterprise in the North West. The major-general and his young companion eventually settled upon some land along the Bow River below Calgary. However, as Strange wrote in his memoirs,

> ... just at this juncture came the ordinance of the Canadian Government, forbidding sheep to be raised north of the Bow River, which was to be reserved for cattle on the advice of a certain ranching senator [Cochrane], who subsequently changed his mind and took his cattle south, when this monstrous restriction was withdrawn—too late for me—but it decided my wavering Australian companion to leave me, for he understood nothing but sheep.

Strange's companion may have relished the prospect of a Canadian winter even less. As it was, however, the major-general paid back his companion's investment with a wagon, team and store of provisions. Then he set to work to occupy his choice of land and hired two Blackfoot Indians from the nearby reserve to help him build a log shack. While the men cut trees from a wooded island in the Bow River and fashioned a crude house, their wives cut poles and grass for the roof and chinked the cabin with mud. Strange also hired the capable son of former Manitoba Lt.-Gov. Alexander Morris to help him.

Strange applied to the Dominion government for a lease of 90,000 acres in a strip some 24 miles long and 6 miles wide along the north side of the Bow River. On the eastern end the lease adjoined the Blackfoot Reserve. The river formed a natural boundary which not only kept the cattle from drifting south, but under its north bank also provided shelter from storms. Strange compared his location favourably with that of Stimson and the cowboys from the Bar U who frequently spent much time and effort retrieving their cattle from the southern ranges after winter storms. The major-general also learned from the Indians that the river, when frozen, served as a convenient highway to Calgary.

The size of his projected operation was far beyond Strange's financial means, and so he invited various friends, principally officers in Canada, England, and India, to invest with him and establish the Military Colonization Company Ranche. Its purpose was to breed horses for the British army and to provide land for the officer-shareholders when they retired from the military. He wrote to Moreton Frewen as well, inviting him to join the venture, but received in reply a "sneering letter that he [Frewen] did not intend to run cattle up the North Pole." He was, however, successful with some of his other petitions and the MCC Ranche was duly established. The original lease for the ranch had been given to Strange, who subsequently assigned it to the MCC.

When many of the initial shareholders in the company left Canada, Strange's application for a corporate charter fell through, and he was forced to return east in order to submit a new application, or lose the lease. At the beginning of his journey, two young Mounted Police on their way to Cypress Hills invited Strange to accompany them. They were overcome by a sudden blizzard and fully expected to die on the prairie, when a survey party with carts chanced upon them. Both parties then struggled to the Cypress Hills, where Major-General Strange rested for a while before continuing to the end of the CPR line near Swift Current. He then boarded an eastbound train.

From his temporary quarters in Kingston, Strange prevailed upon Sir Alexander Galt, a prominent businessman and public figure, to place his new application before the Privy Council. As he put it to Galt,

> It is most important to avoid further delay as we can do nothing until we are a body corporate and I am waiting to start west and begin operations ... I write you a line to explain matters to you that you may help if need be to get it [the charter application] passed in council ... I venture

to think I at least deserve some consideration from the gov't for the past [and] in the effort to develop the N.W. in the future and I have not hitherto lacked encouragement having obtained a grazing lease.

Strange estimated the cost of establishing the ranch at $75,000. He paid most of the initial expenses, purchased many of the shares in the MCC, and managed to raise $35,000 by the sale of remaining shares to various officers. But he felt that he also should have one or two Canadian businessmen in the company, and was quite relieved when Alexander Gunn of Kingston offered to purchase some of the stock. Gunn was a prosperous grocer, "a prince of the trade" according to a contemporary, but for Strange he had one obvious disadvantage. In the election of 1878 Gunn had offered himself as a Liberal candidate and was elected, defeating no less a personage than Sir John A. Macdonald in the prime minister's own "pocket borough." The major-general hastened to write to Macdonald, who had been elected in two other constituencies and before whom [as minister of the interior] the application for a charter would be laid, that Gunn was a

... good solid businessman whatever he may be in politics—Business is one thing, politics is another—I write to tell you believing *you* will have no sort of feeling in the matter. Rather the contrary [you] will feel your position strengthened when your political opponents take advantage of the measures you take for the prosperity and opening up of the country ... when they also benefit by the grazing lease system their mouths will be shut on the point.

Whatever Macdonald's feelings may have been, Strange obtained his charter, secured his lease, and returned to the North West, accompanied by his younger son Aleck. They travelled as far as they could on the still unfinished CPR, then by horses and wagons, and joined forces with E. Wilmot, who was on his way to establish the Alberta Ranche, and Lord Boyle, who was heading for his homestead near Pincher Creek. Once settled in at the MCC headquarters, Strange purchased 100 brood mares and 3 stallions in the United States, placed them on his range, hired a few cowboys, and looked forward to a prosperous future.

As the major-general made plans to bring his family to the North West, it was clear that the original log shack built at the mouth of Home Coulee was wholly inadequate. His elder son Harry had already joined the ranch, after working for a time with the Dominion Survey. Strange drew up some house plans and sketches and sent them east where they were turned into a prefab-

ricated house—right down to the window sills. The house was then shipped
in pieces to the North West and assembled like a puzzle on the site by Strange
and his sons. The men were still working on the roof when the cold weather
arrived, making the job "extremely trying and provocative of profanity, especially when the hammers land on the thumb."

The two-story, nine-room, terra cotta coloured house was christened
Strangmuir, and attracted much attention from the nearby Indians and their
chief, Crowfoot. The Stranges occasionally played host to the Blackfoot leader
and observed that "Crowfoot's table manners were those of the gentleman he
was. He would gulp down gallons of tea, and then cool himself with the fan
provided by one of the ladies of the house." Indians of lesser rank and native
women were not allowed to enter the house as easily as their chief, however;
they had to content themselves with peering in at the windows.

Strange's Irish cook had her own opinions about the neighbours and occasional guests. She was, in the major-general's words, "a thorough aristocrat
like all her race when 'niggurs' are concerned" and it distressed her to "think
that the 'loikes of her should be cookin' Christian mate for durty haythen in
paint and blankets.' "

The cook may simply have reflected her employer's attitude towards
Indians, for in spite of his hospitality to Crowfoot, Strange distrusted and
disliked the native people and constantly complained that they ran off his
horses, stole his cattle, and burned his range. He denounced the Mounted
Police for doing nothing to protect his property and punish the Indians. (He
did, however, have kind words for Insp. Sam Steele, who later spent several
pleasant weekends with the Strange family.) Major-General Strange then
visited the Blackfoot Reserve, saw some of the leading men and told them
that he had come among them as a friend, but if they chose to make him an
enemy, they would find him a different man.

As part of his campaign to attract investors to his enterprise Strange
advertised in the British newspapers for men of means and good character to
become shareholders in the company. Subscribers were required to pay $1,000
cash for shares and to work for the ranch at $50 per month. If they wished,
they could also take a homestead on land adjacent to the MCC lease and
begin ranching for themselves, drawing on the resources of the parent ranch.
Among those who answered the advertisements was a young man, Robert
Newbolt, whose father had been governor of St. Helena from 1877 to 1880.
Newbolt outfitted himself with complete English riding regalia in the latest
style and equipment of the best quality. He booked passage to Canada on the
Allan steamship *Parisian*, and after landing at Quebec made his way to Kings-
ton where he met the major-general. Strange took one look at Newbolt's new

riding gear and forbade him to take it west. The Englishman disposed of his outfit at a nearby riding academy—at half of its original cost, much to his dismay.

Major Hennell, Strange's old travelling companion in the west, was now an officer of the Bombay army. He also purchased a share in the MCC and spent a few months on the ranch in 1886, helping with accounts and making plans to settle there; however, before he could establish himself, he was ordered to rejoin his regiment in Burma. Another shareholder, Charles Hawkes, settled on a site upstream from Strangmuir, and built a log cabin near the river which quickly became known as the Hawkes' Nest. The "nest" eventually sailed off on the crest of the rampaging river in full flood, but fortunately, Mr. Hawkes was not in residence at the time. Another shareholder, Col. Arthur Goldfinch, established a small operation still farther upstream called the Horsetrack Ranche. A Mr. Pruen and Strange's two sons took homesteads on the southern fringe of the MCC lease, so that after a few years there were a number of cabins scattered along the southern boundary.

The rebellion of 1885 caused Strange to look with even more suspicion on his Indian neighbours. He promptly fortified his house by cutting loopholes on the second floor, moved his family into Calgary and set about to organize a force of armed men to protect his ranch and stock. In April, however, he was directed by the minister of militia, Adolphe Caron, and the commander of the militia, Gen. Frederick B. Middleton, to take charge of military operations in the Alberta district. At first, Strange found it impossible to organize anything or anybody. The mayor of Calgary forbade recruiting in the town because it would take able-bodied men from the district. "I have had a terrible time fighting the greed and selfishness of the people here," Strange wrote to his friend Henri Joly in Quebec. "Of all the cowardly rascals I ever dealt with the Calgary people are the worst. No patriotism, nothing but trying to cheat gov't into paying enormous sums for transport." While he may have somewhat overstated the case, there might well have been some justification for his frustrations and suspicions. But then Strange accused some of his white neighbours of burning the grass on his ranch, compared the courage of "the thugs calling themselves men in Calgary" unfavourably with that of his "poor, little wife," and declared the CPR "full of Fenians" (Irish sympathizers with a strong anti-British feeling). In spite of having succeeded in offending just about everyone, the major-general did manage to pull together a force and finally departed for Edmonton on 20 April. In contrast to his low opinion of Calgary men, Strange was extremely pleased with and complimentary towards the cowboys (including some Americans) who served under him. He also got along very well with the two battalions of French-Canadians which were given to him. (Middleton distrusted them, particularly as he was preparing to move against the Métis at Batoche in the Saskatchewan district.)

Major-General Strange left Lt.-Col. Osborne Smith of the Ninety-first Winnipeg Light Infantry in command at Calgary with orders that the Blackfoot were to be strictly confined to their reserve and no nonsense tolerated, orders which infuriated Lieutenant-Governor Dewdney, who was trying to keep the Indians quiet. Some of Strange's troops were sent to Gleichen where the CPR parties had refused to work without military protection. When a party of Blackfoot had attempted to run off some of Strange's own horses, one of the Indians was shot by the major-general's stablehands. Apparently, Strange had given orders for his sentries to shoot on sight any Indian seen running off horses. These orders prompted Dewdney to call upon the minister of militia to intervene and direct Strange to deal with native people only through government-appointed agents.

When the hostilities ended, Strange returned to his ranch to find the range once again burned over. He promptly accused the Indians of taking this vengeance because he had led troops against their people. But other difficulties were piling up for him as well.

The increasingly shaky financial foundation of the MCC led to a serious deterioration of Strange's relations with the directors of the company. Letter after letter travelled east, filled with complaints about the lack of funds for running expenses and accusations that the directors, in particular Alexander Gunn (who was also vice-president of the company), were letting him down.

Strange cited Gunn's interests in the troubled Mount Royal Ranche west of Calgary as evidence of betrayal of his obligations to the MCC. Gunn was both a shareholder and a director of the Mount Royal, despite Strange's protests that its manager, Edward A. Baynes, was a "rascal" and untrustworthy, remarks which caused Baynes to threaten Strange with a lawsuit for libel. In addition, Gunn had invested more money in the Mount Royal than he had in the MCC, and Strange was fearful that Gunn's association with the Mount Royal would destroy investors' confidence in his own company.

As it was, the MCC found itself in trouble with various creditors, Strange wrote that "horse and cattle thieves, cattle speculators and creditors gather round what is considered a shaky ranche like wolves round a dying animal and leave nothing but well-picked bones to the shareholders." He insisted that he was keeping close account of the ranch's business, but that the directors were simply not doing enough to raise additional capital by selling the rest of the authorized stock. The shareholders and directors did appear rather reluctant to purchase additional stock themselves—after all, this was the apogee of the cattle boom and yet no dividends had been paid. Strange insisted that their reluctance to invest was forcing the company to drift, and he pointed out that the Mount Royal Ranche had been sold recently "for next to nothing."

More difficulties piled up for Strange. There was news that the British government had stopped his pension on the ground that he had violated regulations by serving with the Dominion forces during the rebellion. Furthermore, he was expected to refund all monies he had received from the date of his resuming active service. In addition, Strange became involved in a messy controversy over the awarding of honours and decorations to officers in the rebellion.

The conflict between Strange and the other MCC directors developed into a personal feud between the major-general and Gunn. While Strange hoped that Gunn, in the course of his forthcoming visit to England, would place the remaining $25,000 in shares with investors there, at the same time he expressed total lack of confidence in Gunn as a businessman. Gunn held a mortgage on part of the MCC herd; Strange speculated that Gunn was perhaps trying to break up the company, since he would be the only one to get his money back in the event of failure. Strange's suspicion was that Gunn, having pushed the ranch to disaster, could then purchase the whole enterprise himself.

In 1886 the MCC made a profit of $16,000 from the sale of horses and cattle, but there were no dividends after the company paid off its various debts. Then the ranch foreman quit, thinking the MCC was a sinking concern. Since the beginning, Strange had worked as president and managing director of the company without pay. When the question of a salary came up, he declared that he would be willing to give up his position as managing director if the company would give him the house, Strangmuir, on his homestead in lieu of salary. But he wanted to remain as president of the MCC and move to Calgary where he could continue to oversee and protect his interests and those of the absent shareholders. Although such a move would be desirable, it would require that he build a house in the town and keep a pair of horses in order to maintain contact with the ranch. He would also require a man to take care of the horses.

Strange was confident that the MCC would eventually be profitable— "it seems a pity with a war in the future (sooner or later) to give up the horse business"—even though the company seemed to be heading for disaster. When Sir John Lister-Kaye offered to take over the MCC in exchange for shares in his new venture, Strange pointedly turned him down.

New problems plagued the already beleaguered Strange; he broke his leg and was unable to do much work or riding. Although he bathed it regularly in the hot springs at the newly established national park in Banff, the leg continued to give him trouble.

A letter arrived from Mr. McIvor, secretary of the MCC, demanding that Strange explain certain derogatory statements allegedly made by him about Mr. Gunn, the vice-president. Apparently, the wife of one of the shareholders had stated publicly that Strange said he had been robbed by Gunn. Strange denied that the woman had "any authority to make such a statement" and could not understand "her purpose in saying such a thing."

The Military Colonization Company Ranche seemed to go from one storm to another, with no haven in sight. Strange looked into possible amalgamation with the Sheep Creek Ranche Company (Quorn) and cabled an offer to its principal shareholder, C.W. Martin, proposing that the MCC herd consisting of 2000 head of cattle and 400 horses be combined with the Quorn's livestock. The two operations would share expenses and grazing lands and John J. Barter of the Quorn would serve as manager of the combined herd. Martin appeared amenable to the offer, but wanted to change the terms somewhat to a shared-expense basis for three years for the cattle, and a charge of five dollars per head per year for the horses.

Martin's terms were not favourably received by Strange; he felt that the horses and cattle should be treated on the same basis. Unfortunately, there was also a mix-up in the telegrams between Strange and Martin. Martin's reply was sent to Gleichen while Strange was in Kingston and, of course, the major-general was unable to consider Martin's counterproposal and reply in time. Martin then sent another telegram to Strange, advising the major-general that he was dealing with gentlemen and should conduct himself accordingly. The proposed amalgamation collapsed.

At a general meeting of the MCC in 1887, the shareholders present re-elected the board of directors, which then proceeded to replace Major-General Strange with Alexander Gunn as president. The board also appointed a new ranch manager, S.S. Rogers, who had been manager of a stock farm belonging to one of the directors. Rogers was described by W. Manly, another director, as "a rough fellow, a very rough fellow, but for the purpose of a ranche in difficulties the right man." Rogers was to join the spring roundup on behalf of the MCC, take inventory of the company's cattle and make a valuation of them as well as the ranch's other assets.

Both Strange and Rogers travelled to the North West Territories after the meeting, Rogers to the ranch and Strange to Calgary. Almost immediately, there was friction between the two men. Strange disagreed with Rogers' valuation of the MCC's cattle, protesting that it was much too low. Rogers admitted that he had taken everything below actual value, but he had done exactly what any prudent merchant should—value his goods at, or slightly below, cost with no intention of selling them at those rates. (Rogers also moved the ranch headquarters to the western end of the lease and, according to Strange, threatened to turn his son Aleck out of the home place.) But the manager had the full support of the directors, who were satisfied that a forced sale would not realize a dollar beyond his valuation, and that a possible buyer would adopt just the same mode of valuation, leaving himself a wide margin of safety.

Except for Aleck, Major-General Strange was quite alone now. His wife and daughters had returned to England so that the girls might attend school there, and Harry went off to India. Having been humiliated by the directors of his own company and by the government of Canada, which refused to properly recognize his military services, Strange remained in Calgary and attempted to recover his losses. At one time, he considered selling his collection of curios, acquired during his many years abroad, to a rich American businessman. He tried to meet various promissory notes by selling lots in Calgary. In spite of his misfortunes, he could at least take comfort in the knowledge that he had stayed in the North West to do what he could to save the MCC.

With its new management, the ranch did appear to make some progress towards clearing its debt and establishing a more solid foundation. Perhaps the directors also paid more attention to its affairs, particularly after heavy losses of cattle in the disasterous winter of 1886–87. One director confessed

> the day for couleur-de-rose Reports and Prospectus to captivate capital for ranching investment is gone forever, and I venture to assert that there is no thorough businessman who has been connected with ventures of the sort in our North West [who] will be found ready today to admit that until the last two or three years he had been "living in a fool's paradise."

The shareholders and directors were ready to dump the MCC when an offer once again arrived from Sir John Lister-Kaye. Although the offer was accepted this time, it is debatable whether the ranch had passed into more capable hands. The MCC disappeared as a separate entity and became part of the Lister-Kaye's ambitious ranching-farming enterprise.

As he prepared to leave Canada in 1889, Strange's prospects brightened somewhat. For one thing, his pension from the British government was restored, giving him some financial security. He returned to England and shortly thereafter met Hiram Maxim, the American-born inventor of a new type of automatic gun. Maxim suggested that Strange write a manual on the tactical use of the gun and help market the weapon abroad. The project appealed to Strange, and after spending a few weeks in the Maxim-Nordenfelt workshop, he embarked on an extended tour of Hawaii, Australia, New Zealand and the Far East. He eventually retired to England and died there on July 9, 1925.

The McIntyre Ranch

One of the most durable of the early ranches in southern Alberta was the McIntyre Ranch. Its founder, William H. McIntyre, was born in Grime County, Texas, in 1848. His father had been soldier in the American army during the Mexican War. When the war was over and the soldiers were given scrip for land, McIntyre's father used his to take up land north of Houston. He then traded horses and mules for scrip belonging to other soldiers until he had acquired a substantial amount of good land. He died in 1849, leaving three sons. William, aged only one year, was the youngest.

McIntyre's mother remarried, the family converted to Mormonism and shortly afterward moved to Salt Lake City, Utah. The eldest McIntyre boy worked for a rancher in that territory for a time, but was killed by Indians while he and a companion were looking for stray cattle. Later, William and the second-oldest son, Samuel, began hauling freight with mule teams between California and Salt Lake City and, occasionally, as far north as Virginia City in Montana.

In 1870 Samuel and William travelled back to Texas to sell the land which their father had left them. With the money from the land sale, the two brothers started buying cattle and by April of 1871 they had between six and seven thousand longhorns which they drove north along the old Chisholm Trail. The drive took eight months, but the cattle arrived in Utah in excellent shape, fat and sleek. Samuel and William ranged their herd about one hundred miles south of Salt Lake City for the winter and sold them the next spring at $24 a head. Since they had bought the stock at $3.75 a head in Texas, the two brothers had a good profit to show for their first venture into the cattle business.

The McIntyres prospered for several years and then lost practically all of their cattle during the winter of 1886–87. To complicate matters, sheep were moving into Utah, and the good cattle range was being "barked"—grazed off—by the sheep and spoiled for the cattle.

When a friend told the McIntyres that there was good land with plenty of trees and few settlers near Cardston in southern Alberta, William McIntyre set out to investigate. He first visited the area in 1891 and then returned several times during the following years to observe how the cattle and horses on the Canadian range came through the northern winters. McIntyre was impressed with what he saw, and decided to establish an operation on the Milk River Ridge about twenty-four miles east of Cardston. McIntyre bought the land from the Alberta Railway and Irrigation Company in 1894. He located his headquarters at the foot of the Milk River Ridge, on a level spot between the two branches of Pot Hole Creek, a sporadic little stream that could flow like a river during the spring, but which usually dried up, except for a few deep holes, during the summer. He shipped in a small herd of purebred black Galloway cattle and some Shorthorn cows and bulls from Utah. Later, he also brought in cattle from Manitoba and Oregon under contract. The McIntyre brand was IHL. (Some suggested the brand meant "I have lost," hardly appropriate for what was a very successful venture.)

McIntyre's first land purchase, 23,000 acres, was followed by two additional purchases, bringing the ranch to about 64,000 acres of deeded land. He immediately began to fence part of his range in order that farming operations to provide feed for the cattle and horses could get underway. The fence corners were marked with piled-up buffalo skulls. Since the remains of the great herds were still abundantly scattered across the land, skulls were easy to find and, because of their whiteness, were clearly visible from a considerable distance.

The McIntyres continued to maintain extensive ranching interests in Utah, and William travelled frequently between Alberta and the United States, drawing many of his cowboys and foremen to Alberta from Utah. From 1903 to 1911, John Kenny, a Utah man, was foreman on the Milk River Ridge operation. Kenny was not only very energetic, he was also impatient; he often cursed because winter daylight on the northern range came so late he could not get on with his work. Anyone who worked for Kenny never sat at the table very long either, because the foreman did not tolerate any small talk at mealtimes. It was a continual race among the men to see who could gulp down his meal fastest and get out of the house first.

Later, the McIntyres leased another 80,000 acres for summer pastures between the international boundary and the north fork of the Milk River, driving the cattle back to their home range on the ridge in late November. This lease was thrown open for homesteading in 1912. They also expanded their own grain operations, not only for feed, but also for the help that grain provided in pulling the ranch through severe winters.

About 1900, Jesse Knight of Provo, Utah, acquired one and a half townships of land immediately west of the McIntyre ranch and started the Bar K2. Knight also purchased a large block of land from the Alberta Railway and

Irrigation Company. He introduced sugar beets as a crop in southern Alberta, and built and operated a sugar factory to process the beets. This venture failed and the factory was later dismantled and shipped to the United States. When Jesse Knight died, his son Raymond (after whom the town is named) operated the Bar K2. In 1936 the extensive Knight operation passed into bankers' hands and was later acquired by the McIntyre Ranch.

The McIntyre Ranch is no longer owned by the McIntyre family, but remains one of the largest and most successful ranches in southern Alberta.

The Alberta Ranche

In spite of the Marquess of Lorne's wish to be a rancher in southern Alberta, he never managed to do so, but during his tour of the west in 1881, several members of his party were sufficiently impressed with the beauty and potential of the country that they did return. At the conclusion of the Governor General's tour, Sir Francis De Winton, Lorne's aide-de-camp, hurried back to England and formed the Alberta Ranche Company. He then returned to Canada and negotiated leases with the Dominion government.

Besides De Winton, the ranch's shareholders included H.J. Hanson, E. Wilmot, the Honourable J. Boyle, and Richard Duthie. Duthie, a native of Quebec, became involved in the venture while working as a canoeman for Princess Louise, whose husband, Lord Lorne, was salmon fishing in the Cascapedia area of Quebec. At the urging of De Winton, Duthie travelled west and hired on with the Cochrane Ranche, and then moved to the Alberta Ranche as manager when the leases were granted.

The company first purchased the Brecon Ranch near Calgary and brought in a herd of sheep from Montana. In 1884 it also bought property from Mose LeGrandeur, one of the early settlers near Pincher Creek, and leased an additional 28,000 acres in that area to raise cattle. The company briefly operated both ranches, but eventually sold the Brecon, possibly because of the cattlemen's distaste for sheep. The Alberta Ranche continued operations for 18 years, and then closed down, selling its 3,000 head of cattle to Edward Maunsell.

The Glengarry Ranch

One of the choicest ranches was the Glengarry, known by its brand, the "44." The ranch was established by Allan Ban Macdonald in 1885 and derived its name from Macdonald's home in Glengarry, Ontario. Macdonald was originally a merchant who moved to Emerson, Manitoba, in the early

1880s where he contracted to furnish supplies for the CPR as it moved its line westward. He followed the railway as far as Revelstoke in British Columbia and then returned east to organize his ranching company with most of the investors coming from Glengarry County.

In 1889, William Mackenzie and Donald Mann, railway contractors and later the promoters of the Canadian Northern Railway, purchased the Glengarry from its original owners, but retained Macdonald as manager, a position he held until the ranch was again sold in 1910. Macdonald then was appointed superintendent of Banff National Park, and in 1913 he retired to Fort Macleod.

The Glengarry's location was ideal in that it was set well into the Porcupine Hills west of Claresholm. This area was not considered good farming land; consequently, it was not threatened by settlers as were many of the other early ranches. A report in the Macleod *Gazette* in 1903 noted that the entire ranch, 18,000 acres, was surrounded by a substantial fence and that two sections and three quarter sections were fenced separately into pastures and farming lands where crops were grown to feed the ranch's cattle. A particularly favourable feature was the ranch's 12 miles of frontage on Trout Creek, a stream which not only provided water for the cattle, but also afforded some of the best fishing in the country. In addition there were several springs on the property, so that lack of water was seldom a problem, even during dry periods. The Glengarry managed to have all its land in one compact block as well.

Macdonald put up a number of substantial buildings; two large cattle sheds, a frame barn on sandstone foundations whose loft could hold 50 tons of hay, a spacious and comfortable house constructed of British Columbia lumber for the manager, bunkhouses, a granary, blacksmith shop, chicken house, and storehouse. "Mr. Macdonald, being a careful and systematic manager, has everything on the ranche in apple pie order," the Macleod *Gazette* reported. The cattle numbered somewhat over thirty-five hundred and were very high-grade Shorthorns and Herefords. The Glengarry also kept about seventy horses and "two extra fine teams which in the open market would command almost record figures."

Pat Burns purchased the Glengarry Ranch in 1922, but it is now owned and operated independently.

The Winder Ranche

In 1879 Supt. William Winder of the North-West Mounted Police returned on leave from Fort Macleod to his family home at Lennoxville, Quebec. His visit had far-reaching effects for the ranching industry in Alberta. Winder was already deeply involved in the developing cattle industry in western Canada, and the stock-raisers of Compton County proved to be a receptive audience for his stories of the vast ranges and the opportunities they presented. Winder was typical of a number of men who helped expand the Alberta Cattle industry, tying together the NWMP, the stockmen of the Eastern Townships and the business community of Montreal.

Winder, one of the first officers in the NWMP, received his commission in 1873 together with the task of recruiting for the force in the Eastern Townships. When, in the summer of 1874, the police prepared to leave Lower Fort Garry, Winder took command of C troop (artillery) for the march west. The next year he was placed in charge of Fort Macleod and oversaw improvements to the police's headquarters and to the system of patrols. Despite the rude conditions of the fort, his wife Julie joined him in time for Christmas 1876, and in September 1877 both he and Julie signed Treaty No. 7 as witnesses and the next day took part in the payment of treaty monies and gifts to the Blackfoot Indians.

By the late 1870s Winder, in association with Insp. Albert Shurtliff of the police, was buying cattle and placing them on the open range. He took part in the small roundup of 1879, but later that year took his leave and travelled east to raise capital and organize his ranching venture.

The Winder Ranche Company was established in May 1880, though it was not until 1883 that it finally secured its lease of 50,000 acres along Willow Creek west of Claresholm. Shareholders in that company included Winder; John L. Gibb, a Quebec City merchant; J.M Lemoine, a Compton stockman; George Barry and Charles Stimson, both Montreal merchants; W. M. Ramsay, a "gentleman" of Montreal; and Charlie Sharples of Quebec City. Stimson discovered that a group of Halifax merchants, with the support of Sir Charles Tupper, were negotiating for the same lease the Winder Ranche Company had its eye on, and so he urged the deputy minister of the interior, A.M. Burgess, to act quickly on the company's request. The Winder Ranche did succeed in obtaining the desired lease, while the Halifax group took a lease somewhat farther south.

William Winder was considered by his fellow ranchers to be a progressive cattleman. He purchased 1,200 head of mixed cattle from a ranch on Trout Creek, and 75 head of Oregon mares as the foundation for a breeding herd. These horses were bred to produce choice remounts for the North-West Mounted Police, the company's major market, and later for the army during the Boer War.

In 1882 Charlie Sharples moved to the ranch as the manager. He came from a long-established family in Quebec City which had built a fortune in the timber trade by supplying lumber for the British navy and commerce. The Sharples' stately home, Broadgreen, sat at the top of the cliffs above the coves at Quebec where the great timber booms were held until shipment overseas.

Charlie Sharples carried on a family tradition of fine horsemanship, a fact which was proven in a famous episode recounted by Insp. Sam Steele of the NWMP. Sharples took some horses to Fort Macleod to sell to the Mounted Police. He put the horses up in a stable near the Oldman River. While Sharples was showing one of the horses to the police commissioner, the animal bucked fiercely towards the river bank, a perpendicular drop of about forty feet. The frightened horse was sidling and fighting against the rider until at last there appeared to be nothing for it to do but go over the edge, sideways. But Sharples would have none of that—he turned the horse sharply towards the bank, gave it his spurs and flew out into space. Everyone watching the struggle rushed to the bank to see what had become of horse and rider. All were mightily surprised to see Sharples still firmly in the saddle, with the horse swimming towards the opposite bank.

Winder died in 1885 after a fall and Charlie Sharples continued to manage the ranch for its investors. As the ranch did not have freehold title to its land, it had little defence against the settlers pushing into the district. Consequently, Sharples sold the stock—some three thousand cattle and seven hundred horses—to a neighbour, John Nelson of the Quarter Circle N Ranch, and dissolved the company in 1892. Sharples filed a homestead on the quarter section containing the ranch buildings, and was surprised to get four deeds instead of one; through an error, his quarter section took a piece out of each quarter in the section. Later he managed to acquire the rest of the section.

Among Sharple's neighbours were the Oxley Ranche, whose manager, Stanley Pinhorne, was a frequent visitor, and the Glengarry Ranch. Sharples married Barbara Macdonald, the daughter of the Glengarry's founder and manager. In later years he acted as justice of the peace for the Willow Creek area as well as brand inspector. He died in 1909, but the ranch continues to be operated by the Sharples family.

The Walrond Ranche

Another of the "big ranches" which were established in southern Alberta in the early 1880s was the Walrond. The Walrond Ranche Company was organized in 1883 by Dominion Veterinarian Dr. Duncan McEachran, one of the original shareholders of the Cochrane Ranche. The Walrond's success was due largely to his persistence and optimistic vision of the future of the range country. The capital for the ranch, however, came mostly from England, in particular from Sir John Walrond of Brooke Street, Middlesex. When the company was organized, Lord Clinton of London was elected president by the directors and McEachran was appointed general manager. The ranch was headquartered in London, as were very many of the North American ranches at that time.

The Walrond acquired several leases, which together gave it a range of approximately two hundred and sixty thousand acres along the north fork of the Oldman River and stretching east into the Porcupine Hills. McEachran centred his operations just above the junction of Callum Creek and the Oldman River, on a wide slope facing the Livingstone Range of the Rocky Mountains. There he built a ranch house of logs, which eventually boasted a unique double roof—an inner roof of poles and sod and an outer roof of rafters, boards and shingles.

The Walrond purchased its first cattle—3,125 head at $32 dollars a head—from the Judith Cattle Company of Montana, and paid in cash with a cheque for $100,000. Additional stock was bought near Bismarck, Dakota Territory, and from various outfits near Fort Benton and points south of the Missouri River. All these cattle were driven north in the summer of 1883 by Jim Patterson, an experienced cattleman. McEachran also purchased a number of fine saddle horses—some in Montana, some from the Garnett brothers on the south fork of the Oldman River, and others from Charlie Sharples on Willow Creek. He then set up horse camps and corrals on Beaver Creek, Sharples Creek, and the north fork of the Oldman River.

Sir John Walrond died in April 1889 in Cannes where he retired for his health. In 1897 some of the original shareholders in the company decided to withdraw their capital; in December of that year the Walrond Ranche was reorganized and incorporated as the New Walrond Ranche with McEachran as both president and manager. The New Walrond bought the old company's lease and other assets, mostly buildings and cattle, for £49,000. Among the assets was a government contract to supply the nearby Peigan Indians with beef, a contract valued at about £600 per month. In 1889, under this contract, the Walrond delivered 208 cows and 277 steers for slaughter at eight cents per pound, dressed. The original lease included a mere 160 acres of deeded land, though by 1905 this had grown to 37,500 acres.

At the time of the reorganization, the New Walrond estimated its herd at 12,300 head, including 25 range bulls, though no actual count had been taken since 1890. The company had been writing off five per cent of its book annually for losses, which was considerably less than the actual losses, as was later discovered. After the reorganization McEachran immediately set out to upgrade the stock by purchasing 54 Shorthorn and 17 Galloway bulls and reducing the herd to 7,600 head. The annual cost of operation was estimated at between $10,000 and $12,000, while the gross return was approximately $50,000.

There was little doubt of McEachran's earnest interest in the successful development of ranching in the North West Territories, but his position as shareholder and Dominion veterinarian, combined with his abrasive personality, caused tremendous resentment among the homesteaders in southwestern Alberta. Furthermore, his prolonged feud with settlers did nothing to enhance his standing, even in the ranching community. However, he did have some excellent cattlemen working for him. The first foreman was G.W. Frields, generally known as "Doc" Frields, since he was also a veterinary surgeon. Frields gained his experience on the American ranges and came to the Walrond from the Fort Benton area. One of his activities was considered peculiar by the people in the Fort Macleod area—he rode nothing but pacers, and kept a string of eight on the Walrond for his own use.

Jim Patterson, who drove the first Walrond herd north from Montana, succeeded Frields as foreman in 1884. He had been recommended to McEachran by the Montana Stock Growers' Association. Born in Waco, Texas, Patterson was a veteran of numerous drives over the old Chisholm Trail, and he knew the western ranges from the Rio Grande to the South Saskatchewan River. In 1893 he left the Walrond to start his own ranch on the south slope of the Cypress Hills, and later was appointed brand inspector at Winnipeg.

Patterson was also a proficient gunman. One Sunday morning he and McEachran were riding in the Porcupine Hills when a blue grouse flew up into the jack pines. "How would you like one for breakfast, Doc?" Patterson asked. McEachran said he would and Patterson rode his horse into the bush. Presently there were two shots and Patterson came out of the trees carrying the headless grouse. When McEachran twitted Patterson for having taken two shots, the manager insisted that the doctor come and see why. The first shot was necessary to cut off a small branch so that the second shot would take the head off and not blast the bird to pieces. All this was done while Patterson was sitting in the saddle!

R.G. Mathews, Secretary of the Western Stock Growers' Association, also recalled a Sunday in Patterson's company. Patterson was not a churchgoing man, but Mathews persuaded him to accompany him to church in Fort Macleod on this one occasion. Patterson sat nervously through the service until the collection plate came around, at which point he stood up and pulled out of his pocket a rough-looking piece of rock which he deposited in the plate, explaining in a loud voice, "Saskatchewan gold, the pure McCoy." Smiling, he took his seat again.

Apart from the bitter feud between McEachran and the settlers, the Walrond was the setting for several other notable armed clashes. One incident involved John Lamarr, a cowboy who joined the ranch in 1886 and later became foreman. A quarrel developed between Lamarr and Gilbert McKay, a nearby rancher; McKay felt that he had been wronged by Lamarr and accused the Walrond man of intercepting his correspondence. One day McKay worked himself into a rage, saddled up and rode over to the Walrond ranch house where he called for Lamarr to come out so that he could kill him.

Lamarr stepped from the house, unarmed. McKay demanded that he go back inside and get his gun. At first Lamarr refused, the exchange of words grew more heated and Lamarr finally lost his temper, stormed inside, and strapped on his six-gun. As he strode back onto the verandah, McKay drew his revolver, but Lamarr beat him to the draw and fired twice, wounding McKay in the arm. The Walrond cowboys, watching the show from the sidelines, ran up to McKay and applied first aid, while Lamarr rode to Fort Macleod and gave himself up to the Mounted Police.

Even though the Walrond suffered the inevitable setbacks compounded by the ongoing dispute between McEachran and the settlers, it was a successful operation. Its roundup outfits, cattle, and cowboys established an enviable reputation and were considered among the finest in the cattle country. The Calgary *Herald* reported that the Walrond paid dividends of 30 percent on invested capital during the 1880s.

The winter of 1906 was disastrous for the ranch when over five thousand head of cattle were lost. In the summer of 1908 the Walrond disposed of all its cattle to Pat Burns for $26.50 a head, with calves added free of charge. The horses on the ranch were also sold, and the land leased first to William Roper Hull, and later, to Pat Burns. The company held back about one thousand acres, however, to pasture some Clydesdales. The Walrond finally disappeared as a separate entity in 1946 when the last of the ranch lands were sold to John Miller of Las Vegas. Some of the original range has since been assembled as the Waldron [*sic*] Grazing Co-op.

The Quorn Ranch

There was nothing commonplace about the Quorn Ranch except, perhaps, its dissolution. The Quorn had a spectacular beginning, flourished for a few years and then broke up, leaving behind a wealth of stories and legends for oldtimers to pass on and amuse a younger generation. More importantly, new blood for the livestock of southern Alberta was part of the Quorn's legacy.

The Quorn was organized during the height of the cattle boom of 1885–86 by a syndicate of Englishmen who had a common interest in fine horses and fox-hunting. The ranch was named after the Quorn Hunt Club, one of numerous hunt clubs in Leicestershire, England. The shareholders proposed to specialize in remounts for the British cavalry by raising one or two crosses of thoroughbreds with native American mares. Although there were to be cattle on the ranch, the focus was to be on horses, at least initially.

There was plenty of capital for the venture and the ranch obtained a lease of 66,000 acres southwest of Calgary. The Quorn extended southward from the Sheep River to Tongue Creek, and west from Cameron Coulee to points which were never accurately identified—not that the exact location mattered anyway, since cattle seldom observed the boundaries of unfenced leases.

At first, the ranch was managed by C.W. Martin, a major shareholder and the man who had organized the operation in England. Martin attempted to oversee the ranch by travelling from England to the Quorn for the summer and returning to his home in the fall, but this arrangement soon proved unsatisfactory. The directors then hired John J. Barter, a tall, lean Irishman who had worked for the Hudson's Bay company for many years and was familiar with the North West. Barter set to work fencing the east boundary of the lease, running the fence from the Big Rock to the Sheep River. The Big Rock, one of the largest glacial erratics known, was a prominent landmark in the district (and from which the town Okotoks, meaning big stone, derives its name). The Big Rock marked the entrance to the Quorn property, and the road from Calgary to the ranch became known as the Barter Trail.

Early in 1886 Tom Lynch brought in a herd of 500 horses for the Quorn, mostly mares from the south. They were placed in the charge of the famous black cowboy John Ware, who had left the Bar U and hired on with the Quorn. At the same time, a fine set of buildings was going up, forming a little colony of houses, barns, and corrals about eight miles west of Okotoks. At considerable expense, lumber for the buildings was hauled from Calgary, and spruce logs for the corrals, from the foothills.

The bunkhouse and cookhouse were built close together, while the manager's house was placed a little apart and the barns and corrals to the west. The breaking stable held ten horses, each horse having a separate stall, with passageways between the stalls to facilitate handling. Another barn, the stud barn, contained loose box stalls, with numbers made of coyote feet nailed into place on each door.

In the same year some English thoroughbreds together with 15 Irish Hunter mares, as well as several stallions, were brought over. Many of those horses had been raced, and though most of them could no longer compete, they were still suitable for breeding. News of their arrival spread quickly through the ranching community, and Fred Stimson and his friends lost little time in hurrying over to the Quorn to look over the new arrivals.

In 1886 the Quorn also imported 300 head of yearling steers and heifers from Manitoba and Ontario, but these cattle did not take to the prairie grass. "I don't think they like our company very well," John Ware commented, and Barter thought that the cattle might get all the way back to Ontario by Christmas if they didn't settle down and stop their wandering. But the cattle never did adjust to their new range and most perished in the severe winter which followed their arrival.

Over the years the Quorn continued to import fine horses, some from Montana, others from England. The ranch's horse brands were I and V. One of the most notable imports was Eagle Plume, widely considered the best of the Quorn's stallions and famous throughout the North West. Another import, Acrostic, had won the Ascot in England. The Quorn brought out some heavier horses of the coach-type as well. One of them, Ballyminnock, half-Clydesdale and half-Shire, purebred on each side, provided the foundation of the excellent draft horses in the Okotoks–Sheep River district.

In addition to bringing fine horses into the district, the Quorn imported many cattle, and its herd numbered 1,500 head at the ranch's peak. The operation's cattle brand was Z on the right ribs. Much to the Quorn's distress, the Q brand they would have liked to use was owned by John Quirk, an early settler in the High River district, who later moved into the Sheep River area west of the Quorn.

In 1889 one of the Quorn shareholders, Walter Gordon Cumming, brought out a herd of Purebred Polled Angus cattle—91 heifers and 6 bulls—from his own herd in Scotland. Later that year, J.D. McGregor, proprietor of the Glencarrock Farm at Brandon, Manitoba, brought some two thousand cattle to fatten on the Quorn range. McGregor was anxious to improve his stock and offered to buy Cumming's purebreds on the spot. He was turned down, but he remained interested in the Cumming stock. He eventually purchased the herd and took it back to Brandon where it won many awards and tremendous fame.

Quality was an obsession with the owners of the Quorn, one which extended even to the ranch's dogs, specially imported long-legged hunting hounds. Although the gentleman owners and visitors to the Quorn could not count on finding any foxes in the vicinity, coyotes were considered an acceptable substitute. Hunting seemed to be an absolute necessity for the amusement of the many visitors. Each spring a wagon from Calgary deposited at the ranch a load of the English directors' younger sons and friends. They all came west to "do" a season on the range and learn about ranching—preferably in the comfort of a good chair on the manager's verandah. Entertaining these visitors in the elaborate fashion to which they were accustomed was a drain on the ranch's resources and did little to contribute to the success of the operation. Other problems soon became apparent, in particular the poor communications between England and Alberta. (The Quorn might have learned from the Oxley experience.) Despite the good stock which it imported and bred, the Quorn never managed to break into the English market, even though a couple of buyers for the British army were impressed with the Quorn's horses.

In 1892 the Quorn shipped 100 horses to England, but when they reached Liverpool, the expected deal fell through and they had to be sold at a loss. Nor were the ranch's horses really suitable as Mounted Police remounts; the police required animals which could take the tiring work of patrol in rough terrain day after day, and the Quorn's horses were highly bred racers. Eventually, many of the fine Quorn horses were offered for sale on the local market and used for such plebeian tasks as construction.

John Barter died of typhoid in 1892, and though the Quorn suffered from the loss, the operation was already in decline. E.J. Swann, one of the English directors, settled in at the ranch, hoping to reverse its fortunes, but he failed. The combined problems of extravagance in its operations and its failure to develop markets finally led to the Quorn's demise in 1906. Swann held a sale of household goods and the local ranchers gradually bought up the stock, thus effectively marking the end of an unusual and remarkable ranching venture.

The Stewart Ranche

The Stewart Ranche at Pincher Creek was established in 1881 by Capt. John Stewart, a member of a prominent Ottawa family, who were a part of the Ottawa lumber aristocracy, a position which was further consolidated when Stewart married into the Shead family, whose fortune derived from the same source. In 1878, at the request of Sir John A. Macdonald, Stewart organized the Princess Louise Dragoon Guards to escort visiting royalty and to serve at the opening of Parliament.

Stewart's sergeant major in the guards was John Herron, one of the original North-West Mounted Police, who marched west with the first contingent in 1874 and returned to eastern Canada after taking his discharge in 1878. Herron was enthusiastic about the ranching possibilities in southern Alberta, and when he returned to the North West in 1881 to prepare for Lord Lorne's visit, he negotiated the takeover of the NWMP Remount Station at Pincher Creek; this became the foundation of the Stewart Ranche. (The farm had been established in 1878 by Insp. Albert Shurtliff for growing feed and breeding remounts for the police. Some of the police at the farm stayed in the district and began ranching as well.) Jim Christie, one of the early cattle traders in southern Alberta, joined Stewart and Herron in their ranching venture, as did Stewart's brother Macleod, a director of the Edmonton and Saskatchewan Land Company.

Visitors to the Stewart Ranche were always impressed by the extensive buildings and stables for the horses. By 1886 Stewart was running about twenty-five hundred cattle and three hundred horses on his 50,000-acre lease.

Apart from his activities as a rancher and a Calgary businessman—he had interests in real estate, mining, and transportation—Stewart played a major role in the ranching country during the Riel Rebellion of 1885. Although the southern Alberta range was distant from the centre of the rebellion in Saskatchewan, the proximity of large numbers of Indians on the Blackfoot Reserve east of Calgary, the Blood Reserve southeast of Fort Macleod, and the Peigan Reserve northeast of Pincher Creek, as well as the Sarcee Reserve west of Calgary, was a source of concern among the ranchers and settlers.

In early 1885, as the news from Saskatchewan grew more troubling, some families moved into Fort Macleod, though reports in eastern Canada that women and children were flocking to the safety of the fort were vehemently denied by the Macleod *Gazette*. The newspaper observed that the only refugees were "two or three ladies whose husbands were obliged to be away from home a great deal, but with the exception of these ladies of the Macleod district are staying quietly at home."

Nevertheless, there was an air of tense expectation in the area. In a letter dated April 6, 1885 William F. Cochrane wrote,

> there is a great deal of uneasiness about the Indians, who it is expected may break out any day ... Dunlop was at Stand Off Friday and thought it looked a serious threat he hurried home and I went immediately into town and got some rifles and ammunition, as we were not in very good shape for any trouble.

John Stewart had hurried off to Ottawa in March, met with Adolphe Caron, the minister of militia, and proposed the raising of a body of volunteers in the Fort Macleod district to supplement the police force already there. Stewart received his answer within a few days—permission to recruit four troops of mounted men to be called the Rocky Mountain Rangers. Stewart immediately returned to southern Alberta and set about organizing his force.

He quickly recruited 114 men, whom he organized into three troops of rangers. Each man provided most of his own supplies; the government supplied saddles and carbines. Most of the rangers were cowboys from the area and they were an enthusiastic lot. When Stewart held his first drill on April 18, he discovered that the discipline of the range did not necessarily carry over into the military. One ranger called out casually to his commander during drill. "Hold on, Cap, till I cinch my horse."

On April 29 the Rocky Mountain Rangers rode down the main street of Fort Macleod, and the large crowd gave them a rousing sendoff with a long-drawn-out tiger yell. John Higinbotham described the rangers as "armed to the teeth with Winchesters, and waist and cross-belts jammed full of cartridges … they would make it extremely unhealthy for several times their number of rebel half-breeds or Indians, should occasion require."

The rangers' assignment was to guard the telegraph line under construction from Coal Banks, near Lethbridge, to Fort Macleod, and the property and work crews of the North West Coal Company, which was building a narrow-gauge railway between Lethbridge and Dunmore, near Medicine Hat. When the Rocky Mountain Rangers arrived in Lethbridge, Stewart divided them into two groups, sending one north to patrol the area east of High River, and the second, the Number One troop, east to Medicine Hat. Stewart himself, remained with the latter.

Stewart's troop consisted of 42 officers and men. It included Kootenai Brown, who left his mountain refuge near Waterton Lakes to act as scout, Lord Boyle, and, as a second lieutenant, the Honourable Henry J. Boyle. Stewart established his headquarters at Medicine Hat and dispatched patrols north towards the Red Deer River, east along the Canadian Pacific Railway to meet police patrols from Maple Creek and the Cypress Hills, and west to join up with patrols from Fort Macleod. His intention was to seal off any reinforcements or supplies for the rebels which might come north from Montana. Together with the Mounted Police Stewart set up a complete chain of patrols and communications across the range country, from the Rockies to the Cypress Hills and then on to the Manitoba border.

Fort Macleod was reinforced with two companies of troops from the Ninth Battalion Quebec Voltigeurs. On May 22 the telegraph line finally reached the community from Lethbridge, and on May 31 it brought alarming news: a ranger had exchanged shots with Indians 30 miles west of Medicine

Hat. The police also received reports from their scouts that Indians were gathering east of Lethbridge. The people at Fort Macleod prepared for the worst.

Superintendent Cotton of the Mounted Police set out from Fort Macleod with a strong force, but though there was evidence that Indians had been in the vicinity, the police did not actually come upon any parties. In fact, the Indians involved in the earlier report had promptly fled south after the exchange of shots, and Cotton concluded that American Indians may have accidentally strayed across the poorly marked boundary and stumbled into the rangers.

With the capture of Batoche and the arrest of Louis Riel in mid-May, the rebellion effectively ended, but as the news took several days to reach Fort Macleod, the people of the area remained in suspense for some time longer. The Rocky Mountain Rangers returned on July 8 and were greeted with a salute from the fort's police cannon. The next day, drawn up in a line opposite the post office, they heard an address of appreciation by William Black, secretary of the South West Stock Growers' Association, and ten days later the rangers were paid off and disbanded.

At the end of July the townspeople and the police held a grand banquet and ball in honour of the rangers. At the dinner Stewart spoke of the performance of his men, regretted that his troops were not involved in any action, but went on to say that "in this district a body of Mounted men could be raised superior to ANY CAVALRY IN THE DOMINION," and challenged the Eastern press to take up his statement and deny it.

There was considerable dissatisfaction on the part of the rangers over the pay received and the hasty and haphazard disbandment of the force, and Stewart pressed these grievances to Ottawa. As a result of his efforts, each volunteer received entitlement to 320 acres of land, or $80 in scrip. Most of the rangers chose the land.

With the conclusion of the rebellion, Stewart returned to his cattle and business interests. John Herron managed the ranch until 1888, when it was sold and the land divided. As well, he operated his own ranch nearby for many years and was elected to Parliament as a Conservative member in 1904 and again in 1908.

TOP LEFT AND FACING PAGE: These photographs of Frederick Inderwick and his wife, who ran the North Fork, or Inderwick, Ranch in the Pincher Creek area, were taken in the 1880s.
(GLENBOW ARCHIVES: NA–1365–1, NA–1365–2)

BOTTOM LEFT : John Roderick Craig and his wife at the Oakley Ranch in the 1890s. Cairns of bleached cattle skulls were commonly used as markers on the range because of their visibility.
(GLENBOW ARCHIVES: NA–1238–3)

This 1890 photo of a cowboy and his horse in front of a log house in south-ern Alberta reflects much of the gritty reality of the cowboy's life on the range. (GLENBOW ARCHIVES: NA–1906–14)

The Fred Stimson house and outbuildings on the Bar U Ranch, Pekisko, Alberta, as they appeared in 1895. (GLENBOW ARCHIVES: NA–1459–22)

Dipping cattle on the Circle Ranch near Queenstown, Alberta.
(GLENBOW ARCHIVES: NA–761–4)

146

Horses in corrals on the McHugh brothers' ranch, also known as the H2 Ranch, Arrowwood, Alberta, 1906.
(GLENBOW ARCHIVES: NA–761–2)

Branding a cow on the Deer Creek Ranch in the Milk River area, 1912.
(GLENBOW ARCHIVES: NA–774–7)

A rare photograph of John Ware, the legendary black cowboy, taken before 1902 when he went to Duchess.

(GLENBOW ARCHIVES: NA–101–37)

Fred Stimson, manager of the North West Cattle Company's Bar U Ranch.

(GLENBOW ARCHIVES: NA–117–1)

An 1888 photograph of the strong voice of the cattle kingdom: C.E.D. Wood, publisher of the Macleod *Gazette*.

(GLENBOW ARCHIVES: NA–659–73)

George Emerson started
out as a freighter for the
Hudson's Bay Company
in Alberta and in 1879
began ranching with Tom
Lynch on the north side
of the Highwood River.
Four years later, they
moved their ranch west
to the middle fork of the
Highwood.
(GLENBOW ARCHIVES:

NA–3627–19)

The well-known veterinar-
ian, Dr. Duncan McNab
McEachran.
(PUBLIC ARCHIVES CANADA
PA–C–32880)

A cowboy having his shave on the Milk River roundup.
(GLENBOW ARCHIVES: NA–777–21)

Cowboy Bob Evans riding a bronc on the 1912 Milk River roundup, the beginning of the twilight years for the cattle kingdom of Alberta.
(GLENBOW ARCHIVES: NA–777–14)

A roundup camp on the Milk River in 1912. (GLENBOW ARCHIVES: NA–777–6)

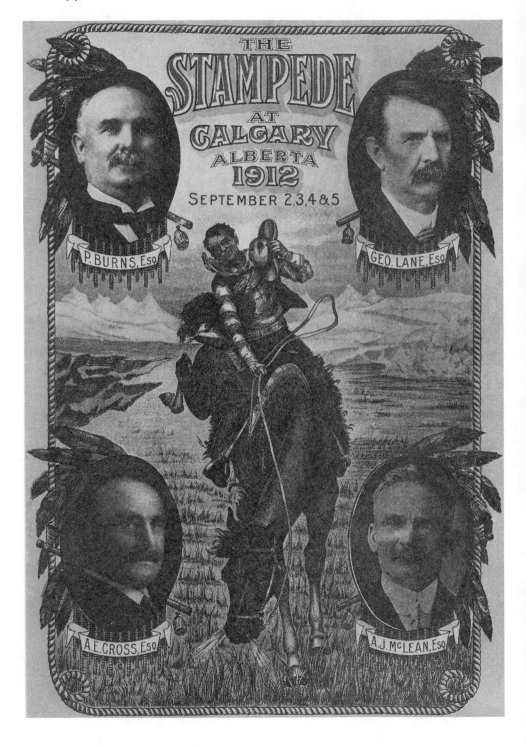

ABOVE: Tom Three Persons and a young admirer. Three Persons' thrilling and triumphant ride on the great bucker Cyclone was the highlight of the first Calgary Stampede in 1912. (GLENBOW ARCHIVES: NA–1137–1)

FACING PAGE: This program cover for the 1912 Stampede shows four of the prime movers of the Stampede in the early days rather uncharacteristically adorned in Indian headdress. (GLENBOW ARCHIVES: NA–604–1)

Chapter Seven

HAZARDS TO EARLY RANCHING

The Oxley Ranche people have been making it interesting for the wolves and coyotes this fall. They have killed something like twenty altogether, about a third of them being big gray wolves. Let the good work go on on every ranche in the coutry [sic].

Macleod *Gazette,* November 9, 1886

Wolves were very numerous while the great bison herds still roamed the plains, but with the disappearance of the herds the wolves began to leave the open prairies and retreat to the Cypress Hills and the foothills of the Rocky Mountains. The appearance of cattle on the plains, however, meant new prey, and the wolves moved back down onto the plains. At first, the ranchers considered them little more than a nuisance, but gradually they became a serious menace.

Some ranchers referred to them as timber wolves, while others called them grey wolves. Much of southern Alberta and Saskatchewan was the range of the Great Plains wolf, the buffalo-killer of earlier times, and the Montana grey wolf. Most ranchers, though, cared less about identifying the species than the damage they caused to their herds.

A full-grown wolf in good health and strength could do hundreds of dollars damage to a herd in a year. A.E. Cross, in the Porcupine Hills west of Nanton, estimated that he lost 10 to 24 colts out of a herd of 200 to 250 horses to wolves each year. Stockmen frequently petitioned the North West Council to pass legislation granting a bounty for wolf skins, but they were continually turned down. It fell on individual ranchers to bear the cost of the battle against the wolves.

Although ranchers were frequently able to shoot coyotes with rifles and even six-shooters at times, wolves were too cunning to come within rifle range very often. Various methods were tried to control the wolves, but early attempts were largely unco-ordinated and generally unsuccessful.

T.B. Long, who ranched in southern Saskatchewan, described the wolf as

> a deadly fighter who never took hold with his teeth. He fought with a snapping, turning and twisting of his mighty jaws and razor sharp fangs, that could slash and cut like a knife. He never held on to a hold but would only dart in and slash. He was active and quick and with a darting side sweep he could cut in behind a full grown cow and, with one slash, cut the ham strings in her hind legs, thus putting her legs out of commission. Then it was only a matter of seconds until one of the pack would dart in and open up her jugular vein as she lay helpless on the ground.

One rancher imported six Russian wolfhounds and turned them loose on a wolf. The wolf and hounds soon outdistanced the riders and disappeared. Eventually, however, the men came upon the bloody scene where the hounds had caught up with the wolf. Four of the hounds lay dead, their throats slashed. The fifth hound lay dying nearby, its belly torn open and guts hanging out; the sixth also lay nearby, its front legs severed. The astonished riders sadly shot the two survivors.

Ranchers sometimes placed rewards on the heads of certain well known and particularly destructive wolves. One such, in the Porcupine Hills, was a big, white female with a black-tipped tail. Several ranchers posted rewards totalling $75, and this prompted two cowboys to go after her. They succeeded in catching her with ropes and then dragged her over the ground until she was dead. However, they were disappointed in the reward, for only Stanley Pinhorne of the Oxley Ranche paid up his share—$25.

In 1891 the Alberta Stock Growers' Association took the matter of wolf bounties into its own hands, and offered a reward for every skin brought in. Even though in response many cowboys and Indians devoted much time to hunting down the animals, two years later wolves were still a serious problem. Ranchers' losses to the killers almost crippled some of the small operators; one rancher claimed to have killed 50 wolves in one year.

In 1896 the newly organized Western Stock Growers' Association offered a bounty of ten dollars for every female wolf killed, and later upped it to $15 for females, $5 for males, $3 for cubs and lesser amounts for coyotes (the latter bounty payable only to half-breeds and Indians). In 1901 the association also petitioned the Dominion government to return to it a portion of the revenue raised through the association's rental of grazing leases to ranchers to cover the payments for wolf and coyote bounties. From 1897 to 1902 the association paid out a total of $12,078 on 2,254 wolves.

As settlement on the plains advanced, however, and through the concerted efforts of the settlers and ranchers and the system of bounties, the wolf problem receded and eventually virtually disappeared.

> The large companies are making ample preparation for the winter in the way of hay ... Every cowman in the country should put up enough hay on his range to feed weak stock through any bad storm ... Hay may not be an absolute necessity, but it is a wise precaution against unnecessary loss which those stockmen who wish to reap the greatest possible profit from their business should not neglect. Put up plenty of hay, gentlemen, and you will sleep better during the cold and stormy nights of the winter.
>
> Macleod *Gazette*, August 4, 1885

One of the great attractions of the southern Alberta range was the mildness of the winters, which allowed ranchers to leave their cattle on the prairie and in the hills where the animals could graze all winter without having to be fed hay. Since the snowfall was usually light and the chinook winds dependable, the range was generally clear enough that stockmen did not have to put up hay; and most of them did not. During the first decade of the range cattle industry there had not been a bad winter. As a result, the *Gazette's* advice was not considered by most ranchers to be terribly prescient.

In the fall of 1886 the *Gazette* reported a prediction by an old-time cowman that the coming winter would be mild, since a good winter always followed a dry summer. An uncommonly dry summer and high winds had indeed left the range parched and the amount of good feed reduced. In November the cattlemen welcomed a timely snowfall which not only averted the danger of fires, but just barely covered the ground so that the cattle could still rustle feed.

Just before Christmas 1886 the temperature in the range country plunged, ushering in a cold spell which did not let up until early March. In early January a severe storm swept over the country, making travel difficult and causing ranchers some anxiety. Although the cattle had gone into the bad weather in good condition, a month of hard weather would undoubtedly run them down badly. If, after that, the spring was a hard one, there would be heavy losses.

By early February 1887 ranchers' hopes began to fade as the cold weather hung on. Although relatively few cattle had died, the weather left many in weakened condition, especially those imported from the east. Perhaps to reassure its eastern and British readers, who had money invested in the cattle industry, the Macleod *Gazette* speculated that the worst was over and that losses would probably be no higher than average. The newspaper further advised its readers to "hang around the stove, and be sure to keep up a good time."

As cold weather dragged on, cattle began to die. Stock in the Porcupine Hills managed to do fairly well; the hills were blown clear of snow and the animals were able to get at the grass. Reports from the Cochrane range were also encouraging. But elsewhere the news was almost uniformly bad. The snow along the north fork of the Oldman River and in the Pincher Creek district was 18 inches to 2 feet deep. An occasional short-lived chinook raised hopes, but they were always dashed as the Arctic weather once again clamped down on the country. Even worse, the warm spells melted the surface snow, which then froze and formed a heavy crust of ice which prevented stock from reaching the grass underneath.

The cattle drifted along before the storms, and storms seemed to follow each other in such rapid succession that cowboys had no chance to gather up strays before another storm caught the animals and pushed them on again. A large number of the High River cattle drifted south into the Fort Macleod district.

In Lethbridge feed of all kinds ran out and by the middle of February there was not a pound of grain to be had in town. Although there was a large store of feed at Dunmore, near Medicine Hat, the railway to Lethbridge was so frequently blocked by drifts that it was many days before the feed could be shipped and unloaded at Lethbridge. The price of hay in some districts went to $40 a ton, but even if a rancher could afford to pay the price, there was little for sale. Many starving cattle sought shelter in the coulees and well-treed river bottoms where they browsed on the willows and shrubs, the brittle twigs often puncturing their stomachs. Other cattle wandered into the settlements and around ranch buildings, and as John Higinbotham later wrote of this winter, "the bellowing, especially during still, frosty nights was pitiable."

"The Indians say that we are to have fifty days of this cold," the *Gazette* noted on February 15, 1887. "Wheather [sic] they mean the time stated about two months ago or that there is going to be fifty days more of it, it was not ascertained, but it is to be hoped that it is the former."

The situation was no better farther east. The Maple Creek district was also covered with two feet of snow, and a traveller on the railway between Dunmore and Lethbridge said that as far as the eye could see there was not a bare spot of ground on either side of the track. The cattle he observed were skin poor and scarcely able to drag one foot after another, sinking as they did up to their bellies in snow with each step. Some animals simply died standing up. Trains had to stop several times for cattle which often gathered ahead of the engines; even the shrill whistle could not make them move off the track back into the deep snow. As a consequence some were run over.

In early March the cold weather finally broke, and as the warm winds took away the snow and cleared the ranges, they also exposed hundreds of dead cattle, some strewn across the prairie, others piled on top of each other in coulee bottoms, pressed against buildings and fences. Sadly, the stockmen surveyed the damage. A.E. Cross of the a7 estimated his loss at about sixty percent of a herd of 500; the Glengarry Ranch lost about six hundred head; and Walter Skrine on Mosquito Creek, about seventy percent of his herd. Tom Lynch had imported about two hundred and ninety eastern cattle the previous fall; only 80 survived the winter. One outfit near Wood Mountain had driven in 6,000 head from the United States in 1886; it took back 2,000 the following spring. Average losses were about twenty-five percent in the Calgary district, fifty percent in the Medicine Hat district, twenty to twenty-five percent around Pincher Creek, and fifty to sixty percent in the High River-Oldman area.

Those ranches with hay fared somewhat better, and some smaller stockmen who had kept their herds close together and moved them around to wherever there was bare range also suffered relatively light losses. Horses came through the winter quite well; unlike cattle, they were able to paw through the snow and ice to feed underneath. The lessons of the disaster were noted and progressive ranchers began to change some of their practices accordingly; putting up a good supply of hay became standard procedure.

One of the most destructive elements which plagued the early ranchers was prairie fires. Early spring and late fall were the worst times for fires, when the grass was usually tinder dry and the ranges clear of snow. Prairie fires may have been impressive when seen from a distance, but they terrified people travelling and living on the range. The fires, fanned by the slightest breezes, could change direction quickly, race across the plains and threaten areas previously thought safe.

In his book *Manitoba and the Great North West*, John Macoun described a prairie fire which overtook him and his party while on the plains in 1877.

> The lurid glare in the heavens kept increasing as the shadows of evening fell, and darkness had not settled over the prairie before we saw long tongues of flame thrown up against the sky from a distant ridge; these disappeared and the bright glare only remained. A few minutes passed

and a nearer ridge was reached and a long line of fire was seen to cross it and disappear …

A few minutes more and the fire had passed the last ridge, and with the speed of a fast horse it bore down upon us. As it came near us the whirling smoke and flames seemed to take the forms of living things that were in terrible agony and added largely to the sublimity of the spectacle. When it reached our oasis it swept past on either side, and a few gulps of smoke accompanied with a strong, hot wind were the only discomforts it caused us. When it was past we saw that it kept an even front, and wherever the grass was long and thick the flames continued for some time after the first rush had passed.

In 1884 the Military Colonization Company range was destroyed by a fire which swept over the entire lease, and it was necessary to move hundreds of cattle and horses to an unburned district. Shortly afterwards, F. W. Godsal's range near Pincher Creek was also swept clean. Each fall many ranchers lost to fires their winter range, stacks of hay which had been put up during the summer, and buildings and livestock.

On occasion fires even threatened towns. On October 29, 1887 a prairie fire was observed burning very fiercely to the southwest of Fort Macleod, and a party of police under Sergeant Hetherington was sent out to try to extinguish or divert it. After fighting the flames for six hours in the face of a very strong wind, Hetherington and his men succeeded in driving the fire into the Waterton River, where it apparently remained smouldering in the timber. On the evening of October 31, under the influence of a strong southwesterly wind, it started up again and rapidly approached Fort Macleod.

Every available man in the detachment was mounted. All the horse blankets were soaked with water and placed in a wagon. The police, accompanied by a large contingent of merchants and others from the town, worked across a front of several miles. They finally succeeded in completely putting out the fire, which was discovered to have been started by a shooting party near Pincher Creek. The group later drove into the village and one of them gave evidence before Captain Scobie, justice of the peace, against their cook, who was arraigned that evening. The cook pleaded guilty and was fined $50. The fire, however, had destroyed the grass on a range some sixty-eight miles long and, in some places, fifteen miles wide.

Railways added to the problem, as sparks from their smokestacks and wheels set the grass ablaze. In the spring of 1892 a train running south from Calgary to Fort Macleod started a fire which the police and nearby ranchers and settlers managed to put out in about four hours. Major-General Strange of the Military Colonization Ranch probably articulated the fear and frustration of many cattlemen when he wrote:

> The one terror that never leaves me is the fear of fire—CPR burning the range. I fear gov't will do nothing. Sir John is under the thumb of the CPR … After the first fire two years ago I used every means in my power to get up a petition to parliament. I sent it in. Sir John was to [sic] busy … Said nothing could be done. I have now started another petition, wrote to every one I could think of, wrote to the papers, began legal proceedings against the CPR but gave it up because our lawyer advised me to, saying the CPR employes [sic] were perjuring themselves for fear of dismissal and it was no use.

In 1892 another very serious fire started in the vicinity of Gleichen where the drought had left the grass extremely dry. For three days the fire ravaged the range, burning over the country lying between the Bow and Little Bow rivers. This was the range of the Circle Ranch, and manager Howell Harris and his roundup crew still happened to be in the area. They killed 14 of their animals, cut the carcasses in half, and snaked them along the ground to smother the advancing line of fire. But the roots of the grass were also dry and held fire long after the blades were consumed; consequently, the slightest wind fanned the smouldering roots into flame, and fires kept breaking out all over the place when it was thought they had been extinguished. The ground itself seemed to be on fire, and Harris reported that 28 horses had their feet badly burned.

In 1901 the same area was swept again when a cowboy lit his pipe and accidentally dropped the match on the grass. The fire spread extremely quickly and killed scores of cattle. Many more animals were horribly maimed, their hoofs burned off or their eyes burned out, and they crawled away to die in hidden places along valley bottoms. When the fire finally burned itself out, riders covered the range and shot as many of these crippled animals as they could find. Losses ran into the thousands of dollars.

The Canadian Northwest Territories Stock Association included the hazard of fires in its bylaws of 1886:

> That in case of a prairie fire it shall be incumbent upon every member of this Association, resident within a distance of fifteen miles from the starting point or place where the fire may be burning, or any member receiving notification that his assistance is required, to immediately turn out to such fire and shall also, with all possible haste, inform his nearest

neighbours of the fact of the fire, and render all assistance in his power towards extinguishing it. Any member neglecting to observe the above provision shall be liable to a fine not exceeding ($50) fifty dollars, by and in the descetion [sic] of the committee, unless such member shall give satisfactory reasons to the committee for such neglect.

And in 1888 stockmen petitioned the federal government:

... that in any charter granted to any railway company for building a road through any portion of the province [sic] of Alberta a clause be inserted to compel the said railroad company to make and maintain in an efficient manner, a fireguard on either side of the track, and we your petitioners humbly suggest that such fireguard should consist of two furrows plowed on either side of the track at a distance of three hundred yards, and the prairie between the track and the furrows burned off at least once a year, as early in the fall as possible.

However, prairie fires continued to pose a severe threat to ranchers until settlers began to break up the range. Crops, plowed fields, and roads all presented barriers to fires, besides eliminating the grass on which the fires—and the cattle—thrived.

Although some of the early ranching companies, such as the Cochrane Ranche, the Quorn, and the Bar U, paid careful attention to the quality of their breeding stock, particularly the bulls, the open range system was hardly conducive to controlling and maintaining high quality herds, especially when many other cattlemen showed little interest in careful breeding practices. The animals wandered, mixed, and bred at will on the unfenced range, and within a few years the general quality of cattle on the North West ranges deteriorated considerably. In 1885 the Cochrane Ranche strung a fence for 25 miles from the Oldman River to the Porcupine Hills to enclose its southern lease in order to keep out scrubby range bulls and to guard against further deterioration of its stock. But the fence had only a brief existence: some settlers simply cut their way through the wire, then discovered that the posts made good fuel.

In addition to the problems of the open range system, there was much debate over the respective merits of various breeds. Commissioner Herchmer of the North-West Mounted Police noted in 1898 that the class of cattle on the range was certainly not as good as formerly and attributed the decline to the reduction of good Shorthorn bulls and the indiscriminate use of Herefords and Angus. Herchmer further maintained that the best ranchers were moving back to Shorthorns, but that many of the smaller ranchers had too few bulls and so relied on the enterprise of their neighbours on the open range to provide new blood. (According to Herchmer, the best steers in the North West came from Battleford, Carrot River, Yorkton, and the Touchwood Hills, where operations were small and the stockmen fed hay to their cattle all winter and paid more attention to the breeding herds.)

Various stock associations recognized the need for greater care in breeding, and in 1901, in co-operation with the government of the North West Territories, they organized an auction of good stock at Calgary. Sixty-four head—bulls, cows, and heifers—were sold. Most were Shorthorns, three were Aberdeen Angus and none were Herefords. The average price for the animals was $84. The second Calgary sale, in 1902, attracted much more interest and also brought higher prices. Two hundred and twenty head were sold at an average price of $95.81. The stock associations and the territorial government paid the freight on animals shipped to the sale as well as delivery costs to the buyers' nearest railway station.

The Calgary Bull Sale developed into an annual event and was credited with much of the subsequent improvement in the cattle of the North West. Herchmer commented favourably on the changes in his 1903 report, noting also that a large number of worthless bulls had been disposed of. Still, he felt there were "many very indifferent specimens on the prairies which, ranging at will, destroy the efforts of the few to improve their cattle."

Every owner of the range cows was presumed to have bulls in proportion; some ranchers ran 1 bull to 25 cows, and some, 1 to 50. Still others continued to carry no bulls and take their chances with their neighbours'. The Macleod *Gazette* sternly noted that "the men who sin in this way should surely be able to realize the fact that, when they trust to their neighbours' bulls, their own calf crop will be short in pretty much the same portion as the man's who supplied the bulls."

In some parts of the range country there was a "bull ordinance" which prohibited any bulls running at large on the range between April 1 and July 1 in order that ranchers could be reasonably sure that calving did not begin before the arrival of spring. On July 1 the bulls were turned loose and the range cows bred during the following months. R.G. Mathews of the Western Stock Growers' Association admitted that this method of breeding seemed rather haphazard, and that the percentage of dry cows in some years was alarming. But he pointed out that it was the only feasible method on the range, and there were years when the percentage of calves to cows was astonishingly high, considering the circumstances. "It is no uncommon thing for a rancher to get seventy-five per cent of calves, and it sometimes goes even higher, and I know of one instance where one got ninety-eight out of one hundred and three cows," Mathews reported in *Farming World*.

Gradually, however, breeding practices changed, and ranchers began to heed the benefits of better stock. Some cattlemen also began to keep their cows fenced in much of the year, rather than have them on the open range. They also fed them through the winter, tiding them over the most dangerous period of their existence and turning them out in the spring in good shape.

In 1887, under the provisions of the Animal Contagious Diseases Act, inspection and a 90-day quarantine were imposed upon all cattle entering the North West Territories, except those which were settlers' effects or were for breeding purposes. The quarantine ground was an area bounded by the Milk River, which described a shallow arc in southern Alberta, and the international boundary; it was to be kept clear of all animals except those in quarantine. In effect, little use was made of the quarantine ground as such, since few cattle were imported during the period of its operation.

However, developments on the American range focussed special attention on the Canadian range and particularly the designated quarantine ground. The American range was rapidly deteriorating from overgrazing and competition between cattle and sheep; and there was a natural tendency for cattle in northern Montana to drift towards the better range and water of the Milk River area, just across the boundary in Canada. Soon, American cattle were intruding upon the quarantine ground, moving right up to the Milk River.

The task of keeping the quarantine ground clear of these cattle fell to the North-West Mounted Police, but keeping the cattle out proved virtually impossible. The police notified the Montana Stock Growers' Association in 1890 that its members must keep their cattle off the quarantine ground, but as Supt. R. Burton Deane commented in his 1890 annual report, "It goes without saying that cattle cannot be educated to respect an imaginary line—they will go to water—and the water they cannot be prevented from seeking is that of the Milk River. During the past year I have, therefore, adopted the Milk River as the natural boundary to the north." He added that there was no place in the south to which to drive the cattle, anyway; there was no feed farther south, or the cattle would not have moved north.

In effect, then, the northern boundary of the American range became the Milk River. The Mounted Police attempted to keep the American cattle on the south bank of the river, but, of course, many cattle crossed the river to the north bank, and mixed with Canadian herds. In 1896 the police made arrangements with the Floweree Cattle Company and Conrad Kohrs, both of

Montana, by which the two outfits stationed one rider at Coutts and another at Writing-on-Stone to drive the cattle back across the Milk River. The Circle Ranch in Montana later detailed a man to work out of Pendant d'Oreille as well. The Canadian government allowed the police to hire special constables to herd the intruding cattle, thereby relieving the regular police of the job. In 1902 the quarantine ground was reduced in size and the Montana Stock Growers' Association began to fence part of the boundary south of Writing-on-Stone. However, the problem of American cattle continued to plague Canadian ranchers at other points along the boundary.

In 1896 there were an estimated ten thousand American head of cattle south of the Cypress Hills and fifteen thousand in the Milk River Ridge area where the police hired Indians to drive them back. The American stockmen drove thousands of cattle from their southern ranges to within a few miles of the boundary, and allowed the animals to drift across the line to fatten on Canadian grass. Canadian cattle were subject to quarantine in the battle against mange; the American cattle which freely crossed the boundary continued to be a source of the disease. The situation was further exacerbated by American roundups sweeping north into Canada and also by the system of brands. Cattle belonging to the Circle outfit of Montana for example, were all branded with an "O." As the company leased range on both the north and south sides of the border their herds could wander across at will, since it was impossible to tell their American cattle apart from their Canadian counterparts. Other Montana ranchers soon discovered that they could obtain leases in Canada, too, and registered their American brands in the North West Territories.

The Mounted Police asked the government to fence the boundary to stop the American intrusions, but Canadian ranchers strongly opposed such a move. While they complained about the American cattle, they were afraid that their cattle which drifted south in storms would pile up against the fence and die; the ranchers much preferred that the police simply continue to herd the American cattle back to the boundary.

The Dominion Customs Department was aware of the opportunities the unfenced boundary presented for smuggling cattle, and frequently sought Mounted Police assistance in gathering information, charging owners and seizing cattle. But the Canadian ranchers also objected to this manner of dealing with the Americans, claiming it made for bad relations with their southern neighbours. The police were thus caught between the demands of the Customs Department and the ranchers. The establishment of a border patrol and hiring cowboys under the supervision of the police to drive the American cattle back across the boundary helped alleviate the situation for a while, but American cattle continued to pose problems.

Incursions of American cattle were reported to a special Customs Department officer, who was stationed at Lethbridge. In 1903, as the situation continued to worsen, the commissioner of Dominion Customs issued the following bulletin:

> Roundup parties entering Canada for the purpose of taking out cattle or other livestock are required to report at the nearest Customs House after crossing the frontier, and obtain a permit from a Customs Officer in the regular way. This permit will be subject to the conditions that the roundup while in Canada shall be accompanied by a member of the Police Force or by an Officer of the Customs, whose duty it will be especially to see that Canadian cattle are not disturbed on their ranges and that American livestock are taken across the line and properly reported outwards, and also that foreign livestock unentered for duty are not branded on Canadian territory.
>
> The pasturing of foreign livestock is not permitted without duty entry at the Customs House. The owners will be held strictly accountable after June 1, 1903, for keeping foreign live stock out of Canada, under penalty of seizure and forfeiture. Casual estrays will be especially dealt with from time to time, but the onus of proof that the cattle are estrays in any instances will rest with the owners.

In 1904 Superintendent Deane instructed Staff Sergeant Allen of the Ten Mile detachment that the number of American cattle gathered in Canada by the North Side Association, with headquarters in Chinook, Montana, was to be reported to him for reference to Mr. Stunden, the special customs officer at Lethbridge, before the cattle could be taken out of the country. Allen duly made his report and on October 13 Deane advised the cattle owners in Montana that the roundup in question had gathered about one thousand head. Deane asked whether they had any instructions regarding the cattle; the Americans replied by telegram that the Chonkin Pool roundup should return the drift cattle to Montana under police supervision.

Deane dispatched this message by courier from Montana to the Ten Mile detachment, but before it had time to reach its destination the foreman of the roundup took the law into his own hands and drove his herd into Montana. The foreman had previously arranged with Allen to hold the herd on Willow Creek, about three miles north of the boundary, so that the 200 Canadian cattle might be cut out. But several days later, Allen became suspicious when he discovered that the roundup camp was set up in Montana.

Soon after, Allen met the American herd being driven as speedily as it could south towards the boundary. He called upon the herders to stop, but they said they were acting under instructions from the foreman. Allen found the foreman and ordered him to stop the herd, but the American paid no attention. When Allen attempted to arrest him, the American put spurs to his horse and got safely across the boundary. The police officer then turned his attention to a herd of about 450 cattle, which was being driven south by Canadian cowboys. He called upon the Canadians to assist him in driving their cattle back from the boundary. They did so, pushing them 12 miles to the north during the night.

The mange ordinance stated that no cattle could leave a quarantined area without permission from a veterinary inspector, so the remaining American cattle were held until they could be checked. The inspector found that the 450 head in question were infected with mange, and ordered them to be dipped, at the owners' expense. Two ranchers representing the Montana owners travelled north and made the necessary deposit for the release of their cattle. Although the Americans repudiated the actions of their foreman, Deane was convinced that the man had not acted strictly of his own volition. He suspected the Americans were afraid that all their cattle would have to be dipped before leaving Canada, and the expense of doing so would have been substantial.

The problems which arose along the boundary were well illustrated by the activities of the brothers Sam and John Spencer, who first came to the attention of the ranching community and the Mounted Police in 1887, when Superintendent McIllree received orders from the Customs Department to seize a herd belonging to Sam for violating the Customs Act. McIllree, at the Mounted Police's Maple Creek divisional headquarters, hired a party of cowboys and rounded up about 180 head of Spencer cattle, which were sold at auction after the Spencers refused to pay the duty and fines. During the same year, Sam Steele of the Lethbridge detachment seized cattle belonging to the Spencers near Pendant d'Oreille Coulee, on the information of the customs officer at Lethbridge.

The Spencer brothers, who had a small hut near the Milk River, several miles east of Pendant d'Oreille, told police patrols that they intended to apply for a lease in the area as they badly needed range on the Canadian side of the boundary. They purchased some dogies (motherless calves) in Ontario and turned them out along Manyberries Creek after branding them with their American brand, 3CU. With Spencer cattle in the Sweet Grass Hills on the American side of the boundary as well, it was virtually impossible to determine the origin of the animals in Canada—whether they were in fact American or Canadian. In 1899 the two brothers leased five townships along the Milk River, arranging their land in such a manner as to control and deny other leaseholders access to the Milk River, and thereby effectively acquiring additional grazing land at no cost.

There were many complaints from Canadian ranchers about the Spencer cattle—stockmen noted the remarkable increase in the Spencers' herd—and Superintendent Deane investigated the situation. The Customs Department then sent out a special officer with instructions to inform the Spencers that they were charged with having smuggled into Canada about five hundred head of cattle in April 1900, with a duty due value of $15,000. The officer was to demand payment of a deposit of $7,500 on the cattle, subject to the final decision of the minister of Dominion customs.

Deane and the special customs officer, John Bourinot, travelled to the remote Spencer ranch along the Milk River to inform the brothers of the charges, but were unable to locate either of the men. Deane and Bourinot did, however, meet the Spencers' manager, W.A. Taylor. When Taylor insisted that the Spencers had paid duty on all imported stock and "would not put up a dollar," Deane and Bourinot returned to Lethbridge.

Shortly afterwards, Deane met George Lane at a stockmen's meeting and discreetly inquired as to the cost of rounding up a crew of 15 riders and all their gear for 21 days. Lane estimated $1,500 and upon further inquiry quickly guessed the purpose of the proposed roundup.

By mid-May the roundup crew was gathered, and headed east from Lethbridge. It included Billy Henry, a cattle buyer; George Voice, an American cowboy lent by his employer to Deane; John Bourinot, and the captain of the outfit, William Playfair. The roundup gathered 585 head of Spencer cattle, with a value of over $20,000 and Deane, knowing that there were buyers who would quite willingly pay $20,000 for the cattle if the Spencers refused to pay duty and fines, recommended that the Customs Department require from the Spencers a deposit of $10,000 (the maximum allowable).

W.A. Taylor and Bourinot went to Medicine Hat where Taylor deposited $10,000; upon receiving word of this, Deane released the cattle to the Spencers. Much to Deane's disgust, however, the Customs Department returned $4,000 to the Spencers; the superintendent considered that the department allowed itself to be defrauded of about $14,000, since he felt that the department should have demanded a deposit of $20,000 in the first place.

The Spencers then brought suit against the Dominion government for the remaining $6,000, and the case was heard in Medicine Hat in December 1904. The Spencers filed streams of affidavits attesting to the propriety of their operations and importations, but the result was foregone when even the judge commented that the affidavits contradicted evidence given by the same persons in court, and that the amount sued for represented only a small proportion of the value of the cattle seized for nonpayment of duty. The result of the case, as Deane observed, "was not entirely to the satisfaction of the Spencers."

During the early 1900s the pressure of American ranchers along the boundary eased somewhat as many obtained leases in Canada and moved their cattle north. The government also took steps to stop the shuffling of cattle back and forth across the boundary by requiring American ranchers to register different brands in Canada.

The protection of Canadian cattle from diseases was a major interest of Dr. Duncan McEachran. Unfortunately, much of his outstanding work in this regard was too frequently overshadowed by the controversies which swirled about him as a manager of the Walrond Ranche.

When McEachran became concerned about the possible spread of cattle diseases from Europe in the 1870s and pushed the Dominion government on the issue, the Liberal administration of Alexander Mackenzie asked him to set up a system to protect Canadian livestock. McEachran not only put into place an effective quarantine organization, but in 1884 he was appointed Dominion veterinarian.

He was also determined to maintain Canada's access to the expanding British market for live cattle. In 1878 the British government passed legislation which excluded from Britain live cattle coming from countries where certain diseases existed. In addition, Britain listed certain countries from which cattle could be landed live but had to be slaughtered within ten days if healthy, or immediately if found to be diseased. Canada, which was exempted from these regulations, passed the Animal Contagious Diseases Act in 1879, with stiff rules to keep its cattle herds healthy and off the British list. In the North West Territories cattle were allowed to be brought across the boundary only at certain points where they were inspected by veterinary surgeons who refused to permit diseased animals to enter the country. The rules were tightened after 1884 to prevent the entry of cattle with pleuropneumonia, a disease which affected many cattle in the more humid eastern parts of North America, but far less so in the drier western areas.

When the British government listed cattle from the United States, fearing the introduction of pleuropneumonia to British herds, the Wyoming Stock Growers' Association asked Moreton Frewen to persuade the British to admit American western range cattle free of pleuropneumonia through Canada. Although Frewen assured the British Privy Council that his plan had the support of the Canadian authorities, the British government consulted

Ottawa and found the Canadians opposed to the scheme. The Dominion government replied that they were not in favour of any relaxation of the quarantine laws regarding cattle, even though the American ranges were virtually isolated from pleuropneumonia.

Despite all of McEachran's precautions, the British government listed Canadian cattle in 1892 on the grounds that pleuropneumonia had been discovered in a recent shipment. The diagnosis was strongly debated even in Britain, and infuriated McEachran, who insisted that there was simply no evidence of the disease in the North West Territories, though there might be in Ontario. While Canadians continued to export cattle to Britain, their animals had to be slaughtered shortly after landing and before recovering from the stresses of the journey. As a consequence, ranchers suffered a considerable decrease in the market value of their cattle.

Other stock diseases presented challenges to the ranchers and caused frequent losses. In horses, glanders, an incurable and fatal swelling of the glands beneath the lower jaw, was transmissible to other animals and to humans, so ailing horses were killed and their carcasses burned.

Blackleg, an infectious disease of cattle and sheep, also usually resulted in death. Perhaps the most common and serious malady was mange, a skin disease which was spread by tiny parasites. Afflicted animals lost large patches of hair from rubbing against trees and fences to relieve the terrible itch of mange. These animals suffered badly during winter storms and there were sizable losses.

In the early 1880s mange appeared in several parts of the North West ranges, and was an early concern of the South West Stock Association. According to the Macleod *Gazette's* report of the meeting of the association in 1885,

> Letters were ... read from Lieut.-Governor Dewdney, in reply to certain ones sent regarding the mange. The letter regarding the treatment of mange was read by the President amid roars of laughter. The wise manner in which the Association was instructed in the treatment of mange by His Honour, was thoroughly appreciated and enjoyed. It was facetiously moved that Dewdney be thanked for his valuable information which, however, was not asked for.
>
> Moved by Capt. Scobie, seconded by J. Garnett, that the reply of Governor Dewdney, having afforded considerable amusement to the meeting, is of no further use, and be placed on file. Carried.

Dr. McEachran reported in 1886 that the problem of mange had been brought under control, though a further appearance of the disease in 1888 brought accusations that McEachran was confining his inspections to the Walrond lease where the Dominion veterinarian had his own business interests. Small outbreaks of mange cropped up throughout the next decade, but were not taken seriously. Both the government and ranchers believed that the disease would disappear as cattle fattened on grass during the summer. By the spring of 1898, however, a serious outbreak along the Little Bow River and the rapid spread of mange caused alarm. Once again the problem was a major concern of a meeting of the Western Stock Growers' Association at Calgary in April 1898. The stockmen decided that the best method for controlling the disease was dipping the infected cattle in a solution of lime and sulfur, and consequently a number of dipping vats were placed at strategic locations on the range.

The Dominion government also became concerned and placed the whole cattle country from the CPR mainline to the international boundary under quarantine. No cattle could leave the quarantined district without the inspection and permission of a veterinary surgeon; all cattle entering also had to be inspected. Efforts to have every infected animal treated, however, were only half-hearted, as many ranchers still considered the problem an insignificant one. Indeed, by 1901 the cattlemen felt that mange in the country had been pretty well cleaned up and asked the government to lift the quarantine. J.C. Hargreaves, a veterinary surgeon, reported that the ranchers were simply refusing to acknowledge the prevalence of the disease in their herds, and strongly recommended against a lifting of the quarantine.

Dr. J.G. Rutherford, who succeeded McEachran as Dominion veterinarian in 1902, advised the government and the ranchers that he considered the threat of mange to be very serious. He arranged to meet members of the Western Stock Growers' Association to discuss methods for most effectively attacking the problem and eradicating the disease. By this time, too, stockmen were taking the problem of mange rather more seriously. The disease had appeared all over the range, from High River to Gleichen, from the Milk River in the south to the Red Deer River in the north. The ranchers decided to try the dipping method again and make a more thorough search for infected animals. Some smaller ranchers hand-scrubbed their cattle, actually the most effective method, though such a procedure was obviously impractical for the larger operations.

But this new campaign against mange also failed. By 1904 the stockmen realized the disease was still a serious threat. Rutherford once again met with the stockmen and noted that, despite their efforts, their losses from mange were actually increasing. The association then adopted a resolution for the compulsory dipping of all animals twice between September 1 and October 1.

The 1904 quarantine ordinance specified that proper treatment for mange required immersion for not less than two minutes in the solution of lime and sulfur. One successful formula for dipping solution called for ten pounds of lime and twenty pounds of sulfur to every one hundred gallons of water, all to be boiled for about two hours and applied warm to the animals. If the treatment was by hand-scrubbing, the recommended solution was two pounds of sulfur, eight ounces of oil or tar and one gallon of raw linseed oil. Dipping was to be repeated after an interval of ten to fifteen days.

The ordinance also specified charges for the treatment of stray cattle, or of the cattle whose owners neglected, or refused to comply with, the order. These charges were 25 cents per head for each dipping, with an additional one dollar per animal if it became necessary to collect the cattle for a second application.

At Raymond, Ray Knight built a dipping vat 60 feet long, 8 feet deep, and 4 feet wide, with corrals and yards to hold 3,000 cattle. He estimated that he could put through fifteen hundred range cattle in a day, half that number if they were dogies since they would not run the chutes. John Spencer, in association with a couple of other ranchers south of Medicine Hat, built a large vat and set of corrals in southeast Alberta. Many stockmen put their horses as well as their cattle through the vats. In the Fort Macleod district over one hundred and sixty thousand head of cattle were dipped, while in the Calgary district over one hundred thousand were treated. In 1905 over a half million head were treated, and many stockmen were pleased to discover that the treatment also checked other skin diseases and even lice. Within two or three years, the mange situation improved dramatically and the compulsory dipping order and quarantine were rescinded.

During the early days of the cattle industry the ranchers' concerns about theft were directed principally towards the Indians. The attitudes of southern Alberta ranchers towards the native people varied considerably. Some, such as Fred Stimson and Ed Maunsell, got on very well with their Indian neighbours; others disliked them intensely and constantly complained about them to the Mounted Police and the government. The Cochrane Ranche people, whose lease bordered the huge Blood Reserve, grumbled incessantly about the Indians, while H.M. Hatfield, a close neighbour of both the Cochrane Ranche and the Bloods, complained of just about everything else—wolves, gophers, cutworms—but never Indians. (The Cochrane Ranche apparently had less trouble with their Indian neighbours after they paid the Bloods for wintering their cattle on the reserve.) Major-General Strange of the Military Colonization Company Ranche found Indians offensive (Chief Crowfoot possibly excepted); his Blackfoot neighbours reciprocated the feeling by making his life uncomfortable, if only by their presence.

The early ranchers expected that they would lose some stock to the Indians, who were, after all, only recently removed from the days of the great buffalo herds and a nomadic way of life. Considering the strains on Indian society in a period of painful and often degrading transition, the native people showed remarkable restraint towards the cattle ranging freely on the plains. The police checked on ranchers' complaints about cattle killing, but found that actual instances were relatively rare. Early in 1887, during the severe winter of that year, a rancher told Supt. Sam Steele at Lethbridge that he had seen a few lodges of Indians near the mouth of the Bow River, and since the Indians were not likely to receive rations there, they must be killing and living on cattle. Steele dispatched an interpreter and four constables with orders to examine the whole country from Lethbridge as far as the mouth of the Bow and then some distance down both sides of the South Saskatchewan River. They were to question all Indians as to their business in the area, enter their lodges, and note any traces of dead stock. If any evidence of cattle killing was found near or in an Indian lodge, the occupants were to be arrested and taken to Lethbridge. The police party carried out Steele's instructions, but found no evidence of cattle killing. The Indians were living on antelope meat and Steele was convinced that they had not killed any stock.

There were, of course, many dead cattle as a result of severe winter weather. Ranchers often suspected that some of these animals did not die from natural causes. But as one policeman reported, there was no lack of unscrupulous men who would take advantage of nearby Indians to blame for losses which resulted from their own actions—or inactions.

Nevertheless, bands of Indians wandering over the range without any apparent supplies did annoy the ranchers. "They undoubtedly kill cattle, occasionally," reported Commissioner Herchmer, "although it is almost impossible to catch them in the act." By the 1880s, with the buffalo gone, the Dominion government was feeding the Indians, but there was certainly not enough work on the reserves for the Indians to earn their food. As a result, they spent much time off the reserves and, for a while at least, engaged in the traditional pursuit of horse-stealing, particularly from Indians across the boundary. In order to control the movements of the Indians, the ranchers and other settlers pressed for a system of passes under which the Indians would be required to obtain permission to leave their reserves. In arguing for such a system, the *Gazette* acknowledged that:

> We are quite aware that this is not a new suggestion. It has, however, always been contended in reply to it that the right to travel at will from one part of the country to another was granted to these Indians by treaty. While we have, unfortunately, been unable to recently examine a copy of this treaty, we have no hesitation in saying that an examination of it will prove that this clause only held good for ten years, and consequently expired in 1887. That being the case steps can at once be taken to enforce what, by antithesis, must be the law now. There is no excuse or reason for these Indians travelling about the country, demoralizing themselves, and a menace to whatever localities they visit ... The punishment for leaving the reserves without passes and other details could be very easily arranged. The main thing now is to bring the Ottawa authorities to a realization of the grave dangers which are threatened through all parts of the country being infested by marauding Indians, who once loose from their reserves, kill cattle, steal, get drunk, and in various other ways prove that they are not fit to be trusted abroad.

The Department of Indian Affairs instituted such a system in the 1880s and it fell to the Mounted Police to enforce the regulations, even though the policy ran directly counter to the spirit of Treaty No. 7 signed in 1877. Superintendent McIllree at Calgary reported in 1889 that the Indians as a rule "submitted quietly to be sent back to their reserves, but I doubt the legality of such a proceeding, as according to the treaties made with them they can go where they like as long as they behave themselves." Superintendent Deane at Lethbridge, on the other hand, felt that the pass regulations should be tightened:

> Apropos of roving bands of Indians, I would respectfully submit that the issue of passes from the reserve to Indians, enabling them to roam about a cattle country, such as the Little Bow, is much to be deprecated. I recognize the difficulty of an Indian agent in refusing a pass to a plausible Indian; but there are two main points to be remembered: one, that the cattle must be protected; and the other, that Indians will never work on the reserve so long as they are permitted to roam the country.

The pass system placed the Mounted Police in an awkward position.

They were expected to enforce it, but because the regulations had no validity in law, offenders could not be prosecuted. Their task of maintaining peace between Indians and the ranchers was made even more difficult when the Department of Indian Affairs began to operate in 1879, relieving them of much of the responsibility for the welfare of the Indians which they had skillfully exercised under the steady and sympathetic hand of Col. James Macleod. Macleod and other officers had relied upon the co-operation of the chiefs, who not infrequently turned over to the police offenders among their people, but the Department of Indian Affairs sought to diminish the influence of the chiefs. When the government decided to try to make the Indians self-supporting by cutting their rations and forcing them to farm their reserves, the police warned the Department of Indian Affairs of trouble, but were accused of interfering.

During the 1870s and 1880s the Mounted Police tended to be more lenient towards the Indians during their period of transition than to white offenders, a policy which brought numerous complaints from cattlemen whose feelings were reflected in an 1890 editorial in the Macleod *Gazette*:

> Different stockmen have, during the past summer almost caught them [Indians] in the act of killing cattle ... They are beginning to think, however, that, to bring an Indian in is only a waste of time. In the first place it is extremely difficult to secure a conviction, and when fortunate enough to convict, the punishments awarded have not generally been of such a nature as to cause an Indian much uneasiness when in the act of slaughtering a ranchman's animal ... There was a time long ago when leniency was justifiable, but that time is past. The Indians are now thoroughly aware that they are committing a serious crime when they kill cattle; they are well fed and cared for on the reserves, so that there is no excuse in the way of hunger, and when they do kill cattle, it is only through pure cussedness.

In 1886 Commissioner Herchmer established a patrol system which effectively covered the range country with five divisions of the North-West Mounted Police: two at Fort Macleod and one each at Lethbridge, Maple Creek, and Calgary. Under each divisional headquarters there were subsidiary detachments and outposts. Patrols from each outpost or detachment connected with those from other outposts, and in this way the whole cattle country from the Rockies to Wood Mountain could be policed. Police outposts were also established within a few miles of some of the major ranches, such as the

Cochrane Ranche in southern Alberta, the Oxley on Willow Creek, and the Bar U at Pekisko.

Despite their complaints about the Mounted Police, most ranchers realized that their losses would have been much greater without the Mounted Police. Any move by the Dominion government to decrease the police presence in the range country drew vigorous protests from the cattlemen and their stock associations. Resolutions at annual meetings of the associations regularly took note of the Mounted Police's assistance. In May 1885 William Black, secretary of the South West Stock Association, wrote to Supt. Cotton of the Mounted Police at Fort Macleod:

> In accordance with the instructions of the South-Western Stock Association, I have very great pleasure in forwarding herewith a copy of a resolution expressive of their appreciation of the efforts of yourself and your command in the interests of the stockmen, which was unanimously adopted at the annual general meeting held here on the 29th ultimo ...
>
> At the annual general meeting of the South-Western Stock Association of the North-West Territories held at Fort Macleod, 29th April, 1885.
>
> It was moved by Mr. F.C. Inderwick, seconded by Mr. John Garnett, and carried unanimously—
>
> That this Association desires to express their appreciation of the efficient manner in which Major Cotton and his command have performed their duty in helping the cattle ranches, and the prompt steps taken during the present troubles to keep the Indians quiet meet our fullest confidence, and approval, and that the secretary be instructed to forward a copy of the same.

Chapter Eight

RANCHERS AND SETTLERS

Although the Canadian range country did not suffer the sometimes explosive violence between Indians and whites, and later between the ranchers and the sheepmen and farmers, as in the United States, settlement in Canada did not always progress peacefully. Ranchers were hardly established when farmers and other settlers moved in; the struggle between the two groups was long and frequently bitter.

Many settlers entering the district of Alberta moved to the well-watered lands north of Calgary. Others settled in the better known country south of Calgary and sought to establish themselves as small stock farmers or grain growers. In the 1880s, however, the techniques of dryland farming were neither well understood nor widely known, and access to open water, preferably a spring or stream, was considered essential. Water, of course, was equally important to the ranchers, and it quickly became an issue in the conflict. Initially, though, hostility between the settlers and the ranchers focussed on the Dominion government's lease system.

The system had hardly been put in place when opposition to it began to grow. In October 1882 50 settlers met in John Ellis's billiard parlour in Calgary to air their views of the land policy of the Dominion government as it related to the region. The chairman of the meeting called upon Edward A. Baynes (Senator Cochrane's son-in-law), who moved to condemn the Dominion government's lease policy—by which so much good land was reserved for large ranchers, townsites, and Indian and other government reserves, leaving little land for settlers—as not only unfair and unjust, but also as preventing full development of the country.

Baynes's resolution was passed unanimously, though a second resolution, calling for the termination of the existing leases, was vigorously opposed by Baynes, John J. Barter, and a number of others with interests in such leases.

A report in the Toronto *Globe* not only carried details of the meeting, but also listed some of the abuses of the lease system, including the fact that many leases had been granted to people who had neither the ability nor the inclination to do anything more than hold the land for speculative purposes. The *Globe* went on to list companies and individuals holding large tracts of land with little or no stock, among them Baynes, who held two and a half townships of land with only half a dozen horses.

Sir John A. Macdonald, minister of the interior as well as prime minister, was aware of these abuses. In a letter to Minister of Justice Alexander Campbell, on the matter of the minister's brother's application for a lease, Macdonald wrote that he

> ... should like to help Charley [Campbell's brother] as much as possible, but look at this application.
>
> Some 8 or 9 Companies got Ranches on giving the assurance that they were both able and willing to stock them. It turns out that they all lied and merely got their leases for the purpose of selling them—other parties were prevented from getting and stocking these lands. A year or so has been lost and not a hoof or home put on any one Ranche.
>
> These Speculators now club together to make one large Company with a [range] the size of a Province to speculate upon, and propose to hawk this round in England. Neither Charley nor Beatty nor Mills have capital—to work or stock these Ranches—and don't intend to do so.
>
> It is too transparent a job. It cannot be concealed and next session it would be aired in such a manner in the Commons as to work great [disadvantage] to all concerned.

The Macleod *Gazette* carried many complaints by both settlers and small stockmen regarding the lease system. One correspondent, signing himself "Nor-West," wrote:

> Why is this fine country shut up entirely against settlers, and given to a few individuals to the detriment of many? ... As things stand now no man, except the favoured few, can build a cabin or plough a furrow .... There are plenty of men in the country now, and others coming in every day, who would willingly invest money and time to the great improvement of the country, but are debarred from doing so by this most unjust system ... by existing regulation a man cannot even homestead 160 acres, so that literally the country is corralled and the gate shut.

In 1883 settlers in the range country forwarded a petition to Ottawa in which they recalled that pamphlets from the Department of the Interior had encouraged them to settle in the North West; but once they had put up houses, broken land, and made improvements, they were told that the land was under prior lease. Their protests were taken up by the Macleod *Gazette*, which observed that the Dominion government had not made sufficiently well known the fact that it was their intention not to permit settlement on the leases.

The lease-holders certainly knew the government's policy—they had their leases in front of them. The government, though it advertised for set-tlers, failed to inform them where they could or could not locate. Further-more, between the leases, the Hudson's Bay land, the CPR lands, the school lands, townsite lands, and land company lands, many newcomers were in a quandary as to where they might settle. "Why, a Philadelphia lawyer could not ascertain anything if he were to try for a month to unravel the present Government Land regulations … "

In a letter to the *Gazette* editor C.E.D. Wood, A.M. Burgess, secretary to the Department of the Interior, outlined the government's policy. By the provisions of their agreement with the Dominion government, the leasehold-ers were precluded from interfering with any actually resident settler who may have occupied land before the date of the lease. The government was not bound, however, to respect any claim more than the area of a homestead— that is 160 acres—which must be the quarter section covering the settler's most valuable improvements; and in no case would the settler be allowed to obtain more than 320 acres, the area of a homestead and a pre-emption.

Nor would the government permit any person, under the pretence of being a settler for agricultural purposes, to start a stock operation within the boundaries of a grazing leasehold, in opposition to the lessee. In the case of settlers who went upon agricultural land within a leasehold subsequent to the date of the lease, and the lessee proposed to eject them for any reason other than that they had located where he elected to place his buildings and corrals, or that they were engaged to stock-raising, the settlers were invited to com-municate with the minister of the interior, who would consider their claims in a fair and equitable manner.

Burgess also emphasized that it was the policy of the Dominion govern-ment not to permit grazing leases to check or interfere with the advancing tide of agricultural settlers, and with that view, power was reserved in the leases to terminate them on two years' notice. On the other hand, the grazing leaseholders were fulfilling an important function in the development of the North West. Several had introduced cattle selected from the very best herds in the world and had invested large amounts of capital in their enterprises. These facts, concluded Burgess, entitled the leaseholders "to the good will of the people among whom they have cast their lot, and to just consideration from the Government."

Antagonism between the large leaseholders and the smaller stockmen and settlers continued to intensify, however. F.X. Girard, a doctor on the Blood Reserve near Fort Macleod, wrote to Sir Hector Langevin, minister of public works.

> Our population is divided into two well distinct clans; the Stock-Raisers who have the monopoly of the lands in this part of the country, and the *bona fide* farmers including the old squatters and the new Ranchers ...
>
> Everywhere the will of the strongest is the law to which they have to submit. The Stock-Raisers claim this right, though they have no title to it, and proclaim loudly and in every way: "No farmers in this Country we have no need for them. The land is good but for pasture and nothing else; why, then, attempt, uselessly, to establish farms. Farmers coming here to establish themselves, choose the lands on the rivers. It is a nuisance [sic] for us, because our cattle will soon be unable to reach water. Down with farming."
>
> ... Our farmers astonished and surprised at such a state of things proceed to Mcleod [sic], if they have not already been there, to find the land office. They, then and there, get the following plain answer: There is no land office, and if you are determined to settle on a farm, do like this or this other one; build up a house and do not mind the notice.
>
> Full of confidence and ardour, they return to their first choice and begin work.
>
> Some day or other they are sued with order to appear on a certain day ...
>
> After the usual proceeding, they are condemned to pay costs always onerous, and expelled without mercy ...

John Milne Browning, secretary-treasurer of the Cochrane Ranche, put forth the position of the large leaseholder in an interview with the *Montreal Gazette* in May 1884. Leaseholders, he said,

> ... have no desire to exclude *bona fide* settlers from such portions of their leases which may not be necessary for grazing purposes. The trouble heretofore has been in squatters, not settlers, going upon choice hay lands, valuable river fronts, and lands with springs which are absolutely

necessary for cattle during the winter, with no intention of settling, but with the object of being bought off or selling their *pretended* rights to innocent settlers. What the ranchemen think they are entitled to is that parties desiring to settle upon their leases should ask and receive permission to do so before attempting to take possession, and where there is not good reason for refusing their request, they may rely on being allowed to occupy the land.

When Burgess, as the new deputy minister of the interior, toured the North West, he noted that

antagonism between ranchers and settlers is purely theoretical, such antagonism being forced by small, independent speculators forcing themselves upon the leases of the ranchers and entering into competition with them, and then demanding restitution for being forced to move, or refusing to pay Government rent.

Burgess concluded that farms would actually help the big ranches. If there had been a hundred small farmers in the vicinity of the Cochrane Ranche at the time of its disastrous winter, the company would have been able to purchase hay and prevent much of its loss.

Several court cases involving squatters and leaseholders attracted much attention in Fort Macleod during 1884 and large numbers of people packed the courtroom benches. In each case, the key issue appeared to be the date of occupation of the land by squatters. By the terms of the lease regulations, no man on a lease previous to the date that it was granted could be disturbed. However, if squatting was subsequent to the date of the lease, the lessee had power of eviction.

The law was clear, as the *Gazette* observed, though it questioned the justice of the law. It reported on the case of *Gallagher v. John B. Smith*, which came before the stipendiary magistrate Col. James Macleod, in August 1884.

A man was cutting hay in different parts of the country on shares with John B. Smith, and one of the spots selected chanced to be within the boundaries of Gallagher's lease. After about six tons had been cut, Gallagher warned the man to desist, and at the same time replevied the hay. The case came up the same day, and Gallagher producing his lease, the Magistrate gave judgment in his favor, and he consequently took possession of the hay. A very few words will set all parties right before the public. The Government has leased this grass to different parties, and on the written contract being shown, Col. Macleod could not do otherwise than as he did. Gallagher we cannot blame for wishing to retain what is legally his, but at the same time it is pretty hard that old settlers, or even new ones, in the country cannot cut a little hay out on the open, unfenced prairie. None of the parties interested can justly be censured; it is only one more argument which should forcibly remind the Government of the ruinous policy which is weakening their power in the North West by curtailing and tampering with the liberty of the people.

Despite the decisions against squatters in 1884, the problem continued. William Winder, in a letter to the minister of the interior in March 1885 complaining about squatters on his grazing and hay grounds, noted that he had already bought out various squatters and their improvements, including two ex-employees and one man who squatted on the lease twice. There was, Winder wrote,

> plenty of unleased land and any number of leases which are not used by anyone ... not one of these parties are married men or actual settlers. And have only squatted for speculative purpose, hoping I would become disgusted and buy them off as I did the first three. But there appears to be no end to paying out. Any single man out of work can throw up a few logs into a cabin and demand from five hundred dollars upward for the squatters' claim.

It was sometimes difficult for the ranchers to distinguish between the squatters who went on their leases for speculative reasons and those settlers with more legitimate purposes. For the latter group, matters came to a crisis in April 1885. A number of settlers in the Calgary area responded to a summons to meet at the farm of John Glenn on Fish Creek, a few miles south of Calgary. The meeting took place on Sunday, April 5, and Sam Livingstone, a long-time farmer in the area, was asked to chair the meeting. Livingstone told the assembly that he had been in the country for almost 20 years and had improved and cultivated land in the vicinity of Calgary, yet he could not obtain an entry in the land office even though he had been on his place for nine years and was long ago entitled to a patent for his lands.

Livingstone said that between government reserves, leases, school lands, and Hudson's Bay Company lands, a man was unable to find a spot to settle. And if a man did settle, he was sure to be chased by someone—either by the police, land agents, or government officials of some kind. A settler, Livingstone maintained, was worse off than a wild animal, since a wild animal had a closed season in which he could not be hunted, while a settler was chased at all seasons of the year. "For the present I defend my claim as my neighbours do, behind my Winchester," he proclaimed. "Unless the land is all opened up for homestead entry all must either fight for our rights or leave the country and if I am compelled to leave, I will leave marks on the trail behind me." His sentiments were echoed by John Glenn, who said he would hold his claim with a shotgun. The rest of the settlers would do the same.

The 50 unhappy settlers thereupon formed the Alberta Settlers' Rights Association and drew up a resolution calling for the immediate throwing open of all the townships around Calgary for homestead entry and for the granting of immediate patents to all who had complied with the Dominion Lands Act as to residence requirements and improvements. Moreover, they asked that all leases, the terms and conditions of which had not been complied with, be cancelled and the land be thrown open for homestead entry. And, perhaps to further jolt the Dominion government, at that time trying to cope with the troublesome Métis along the Saskatchewan River, the meeting " ... resolved that the half breeds in these Territories are entitled to and should receive the same privileges as regards lands as have already been conceeded [sic] to their brethren in Manitoba."

Macdonald's response to the petition was to launch an investigation by the minister of the interior. He also cancelled a number of speculative leases, and opened up two townships of government land near Calgary. These measures, however, brought only a temporary peace in the struggle between the farmers and squatters and the ranchers.

In 1886 the Canadian Northwest Territories Stock Association petitioned Minister of the Interior Thomas White to meet with association members, and indeed, White did come to Fort Macleod, the first visit to the area by a minister of the Dominion government. He visited with ranchers and settlers around Fort Macleod and was royally and enthusiastically received. At a big reception and luncheon at the town hall, organized and catered by Harry Taylor of the Macleod Hotel, one of the area's prominent ranchers, Lord Boyle, proposed a toast in which he referred to the confidence the people of the area had in White and the esteem in which he was held, a toast which was received and "drunk with wildest enthusiasm, cheer after cheer ringing through the hall."

White told the gathering:

> ... rather difficult problems present themselves for solution. You have a large territory here, which is said to be—and I have the testimony of prominent Americans who visited the Department at Ottawa, that

the statement is correct—the best ranching country on the continent of America [cheers], and that is saying a very great deal for it. How we can develop that great interest and at the same time not interfere with the reasonable settlement of the country is the problem which presents itself for solution by the Department [hear, hear]. It would be a great misfortune, as it seems to me, if we were to do anything to injure either one interest or the other. They are both interests of immense importance to the future prosperity of Canada. [Cheers.]

It would be the most unfortunate if in our efforts to develop our great ranching industry we were to prevent settlers from going in and making homes for themselves. I believe that men are more valuable than bulls, valuable as bulls are [cheers], and that if this country is really suitable for farming operations in the ordinary acceptation of the term, it would be infinitely better ... if every 320 acres or every 160 acres had a settler upon it, making his farm and adding to the prosperity and strength of the country, [cheers] ... I can, however, express the hope that the settlers as well as the ranchmen will realize that by recognizing each other's well-being, the prosperity of both will be most largely promoted [Cheers].

... I do not believe, from what I have been able to hear, that the ranchmen object very seriously to the settlers going in upon their leases, if they go in as *bona fide* settlers, anxious to settle and make homes for themselves. What they may object to is to settlers going in and taking up the river fronts and bottom lands, and fencing in the access which the cattle have to the water, and in that way very seriously injuring the ranching interest. [Hear, hear.]

One important thing is that the ranchmen would be assured of access for their cattle to the rivers and creeks and springs through the Territory. [Hear, hear.] In our latter leases we have recognized the interests of the settlers. Since February of last year every lease issued contains a clause under which settlers may go in and take up homesteads and preemption, and the moment they do so the portion they take is excluded from the operations of the lease, and the lessee no longer has to pay rental for that part.

White referred to new lease regulations by which homesteaders could take up land on any lease, and could settle without first receiving permission of the lessee. As well, there were to be no more 21 year leases, and the old leases were to be cancelled as opportunities arose. The Macleod *Gazette*, however, pointed out that the changes in the leases were not as beneficial to settlers as might first appear—most of the land under lease in southern Alberta was still under the form of lease with many years to run.

The system of stock water reserves mentioned by White was supported by William Pearce, superintendent of mines and the Department of the Interior's chief representative in the territories. The task of arbitrating between the ranchers and settlers during this very difficult period fell principally to him. He was very concerned that a few settlers (or ranchers, for that matter) would indeed make the range country of Alberta useless for everyone else by simply controlling access to water, and felt that the Dominion government should regulate and encourage the cattle industry in the dry southwest portion of the territories, rather than promote settlement by farmers.

In December 1886 an order in-council of the Dominion government provided for the setting aside of water reserves on lands which would not be available for homestead entry. Pearce prepared a list of suitable areas. The government also reduced requirements for stocking leases from 1 head per 10 acres to 1 head per 20 acres, a concession which allowed many stockmen to retain large areas that might otherwise have been subject of cancellation. (A number of leases were cancelled for failure to stock them as required.) The ranchers could look with a certain amount of satisfaction upon these changes, for despite the apparent defeat in the matter of homesteaders on the leases, they now had greater security, in many cases through lighter stocking regulations and control through the reserves of water outside their leases.

The optimism generated among the settlers and ranchers by White's visit and changes were short-lived. At White's urging, Senator Cochrane agreed to open up two townships near Calgary for homesteading, but this concession took a very long time to materialize and necessitated a second trip to the North West by the minister in 1887. The Calgary *Herald*, speaking for Calgary businessmen, who were adamantly against the lease system and claimed that it was inhibiting the growth of the area, said that the Cochrane lands which were opened were already thickly settled by men determined to stay put until their claims were recognized, and that the Cochrane Ranche was merely making a virtue out of necessity by waiving its claim. The lease system was a dreadful annoyance and detriment to Calgary, the *Herald* continued, and added that Senator Cochrane had done more than any other man to discourage development in the district and that when the townships were opened, every acre had been entered for by settlers within two days.

Farther south there were about twenty-five miles of fence along the Belly River between Kipp and Slideout that kept cattle from access to water and shelter in the valley. Pearce tried to persuade the settlers to leave their fences open in the autumn so that the range cattle could get down into the valley, but the settlers refused to countenance such a proposal, fearing that their own cattle would disappear into the big herds from the large ranches.

In March 1889 G.E. Goddard, manager of the Bow River Horse Ranche, which had taken over part of the Cochrane lease, wrote to the secretary of the Department of the Interior in reply to a request from the department for the ranchers' side of the cattlemen-settler conflict:

> That we bought the Lease on the express understanding that the Government would not recognize Squatting as per enclosed notice signed by Mr. Burgess [deputy minister of the interior].
>
> That all Squatters were aware of the terms of our Lease restricting squatting and had the above notice [prohibiting squatting] served upon them *before they had made any improvements* ...
>
> They are doing much fencing and taking up water rights by which our stock, which used to Winter within 5 miles of the home corrals, are now driven for pasture and water 15 and 20 miles away—the open spring being too near the Squatters' homes for them to water there.

Goddard's complaints were supported by Pearce, who wrote that the squatters would soon cut the Bow River Horse Ranche in two, leaving the operation's headquarters isolated from the best pasture. Pearce feared that if the government granted the settlers near the Bow River ranch what they wanted, every section in the lease would soon be squatted upon, and the process would be repeated on other leases. He contended that most squatters knew very well that the lands were not open for homestead entry, but since the two townships of the Cochrane lease were opened because of squatting, other settlers thought the same thing might occur again. Even so, Pearce did acknowledge the benefits which might accrue from combining settlement with stock-raising, though if the settlers were allowed to squat wherever they pleased, they would take all the well-watered land and ruin the rest of the country for the cattle industry. There was, moreover, still good land available near Calgary.

The conflict between ranchers and settlers on the southern ranges moved towards a critical point, particularly around the Walrond lease. There, the settlers were supported by C.E.D. Wood, editor of the Macleod *Gazette* and a vocal and literate opponent of the lease system. Dr. Duncan McEachran, manager of the Walrond and Dominion veterinarian, had drawn fire from Wood on previous occasions, but an interview with McEachran which appeared in the Ottawa *Free Press* allowed Wood to roll out his fearsome battery of colourful invective. McEachran justified his opposition to settlement by farmers by citing a limited local market, distance from major markets and the uncertainty of the growing season for cereal crops. He defended the lease system as the only way to obtain capital for stocking and developing the range in Alberta.

Wood, who described McEachran as a "blustering and egotistical little man who did not confine himself to the facts," fired off a blistering response:

> The bump of misrepresentation, to use a mild word, must be very nearly as strongly developed in the little man as that of self-conceit, for he evidently finds it impossible to open his mouth without rushing into all sorts of extravagant and untrue statements ... We have heard that, as an obscure and modest horse doctor, Mr. McEachran was not at all a bad sort of fellow, but that, like all such people, he cannot stand prosperity and that the consequent swelling of the head has rendered him oblivious to everything except his own self-importance.

Why, Wood demanded, was the lease system the only way to obtain capital when there were Americans ready to bring in 50,000 head of cattle but for the various restrictions put in place by the Dominion government? He pointed out that the American range, where no lease system was in effect, attracted enormous quantities of capital.

Relations between ranchers and settlers continued to deteriorate. Numerous settlers who apparently squatted on leases were given eviction notices and driven off. Wood called upon the government to exercise the two-year cancellation notice clause in the original lease agreements, and in 1891 he called for an inquiry into the conduct of the Walrond management regarding the Dixon family. Two brothers, James and Anthony Dixon, settled on two quarters on the south part of the Walrond lease. They were served with a statement of claim demanding possession of their land and with an injunction prohibiting them from cutting hay on the Walrond's lease or fencing any lands. Wood noted that, as a result of the injunction, the Dixons were unable to put up hay for their stock, and since they could not fence their property, their crops were left open to the depredations of Walrond cattle and they were required to hire a herder.

In reviewing the Dixon case, Wood also pointed out that their land had been occupied since 1880 and that the Dixons had on June 26, 1884, purchased the improvements built by George McKay, and had finished building a house as well as stables, a granary, corrals, and cattle sheds. They had broken and cultivated 26 acres and had put up two miles of fence for 100 head of stock. Nor had the Walrond interfered while the Dixons made these improvements, which were valued at $1,500. In 1890 William Pearce and Dr. McEachran had visited the Dixons and, as no complaint had been made, tacitly acknowledged the Dixons' right to the place.

An even more celebrated case came to light in September 1891, when the Macleod *Gazette* published the story of the Dunbar family. W.T.V. Dunbar had taken up a place in the southern part of the Porcupine Hills in 1882, a good year before the area was surveyed. In December 1883 a lease was granted to John Hollis, and it included within its boundaries Dunbar's place. Hollis, however, did not object to Dunbar's presence and left him unmolested. The Hollis lease was cancelled in 1887 and the land transferred to the Walrond. Although the new lease was signed well after the new regulations came into effect, the Walrond apparently succeeded in getting the property under the terms of the old "closed" leases.

William Pearce visited Dunbar in 1886, took down information about his holding and forwarded it to the land commissioner in Winnipeg. Dunbar eventually received a letter from the commission telling him he could take a homestead and pre-emption entry for his property. In July 1889 Dunbar got his homestead entry—and a visit from Dr. McEachran. The Walrond manager said that he would not interfere with settlers already on the Walrond lease, but he certainly did not want any more of them.

In the spring of 1890 Dunbar received notice that he was not to go on with further improvements or cut hay pending an investigation into claims by the Walrond Ranche. He prepared to defend his claim, but before the case could be heard in court his entry was cancelled, destroying any chance of a successful defence. The Department of the Interior explained its actions in cancelling Dunbar's entry by claiming that the land agent in Lethbridge had made a mistake in granting the entry. The cancellation notice was accompanied by an offer to transfer his entry to any other land open to settlement, even though this meant that he would have to give up his improvements. Dunbar's brother, Samuel, experienced a similar situation.

The controversy engendered by the Dunbar case eventually reached the House of Commons in Ottawa where J. McMullen, Liberal MP for North Wellington, commented, "In all my experience, which is not very extensive, I admit, in all the hardships that I ever read of, and the ejectments that have taken place in unfortunate Ireland, where the landlords rule with a rod of iron, I have read no case of hardship that exceeds the one I have now presented to the House …"

McEachran found himself at the centre of a storm. Among his various worries was the notorious Dave Cochrane (no relation to the Cochrane family) who squatted on the Walrond lease and had a rather unsavoury reputation for accumulating things in suspicious ways. Cochrane offered to move off the lease in return for $5,000 for his improvements, but McEachran refused to pay such an outrageous price for the supposed improvements. One day, while McEachran and Cochrane were arguing over the matter, the squatter lit his pipe, held up his burning match, and asked the manager if it had ever occurred to him that such a tiny flame could burn out his whole range. Shortly afterwards, McEachran agreed to buy out Cochrane, an arbitration board of three local men having decided on $2,700 as fair value for Cochrane's improvements.

In early January 1891 a fire destroyed about three hundred tons of Walrond hay, and McEachran believed that the blaze was caused by arson. McEachran complained to the Mounted Police that he had received threats from the Dunbars, and reminded the police of Dave Cochrane's presence on the lease. One evening several shots were fired at the Walrond ranch house. As a result, the Mounted Police provided McEachran with protection for the next 18 months.

McEachran's story of threats to burn the range was not unique. Ernest Cochrane at Big Hill wrote that one of his men

> was out among some of the settlers the other day, pretending to be looking for land—he asked one man if the B.A.R.C. Coy [British American Ranche Company] would not turn him off if he settled on their lease and the fellow's answer was "Oh, show them a box of matches and they will leave you alone" and then proceeded to tell how he was on one of the Townships lately thrown open, but if he had not got his entry before long he would have done some burning.

By 1891 the Dominion government found itself under constant criticism for its support of the large cattle companies and ranchers and its apparent disregard for its own commitment to agricultural settlement in the North West. To try to resolve the matter of the leases, the minister of the interior requested a meeting with representatives of the ranchers; the two parties met in Ottawa in February in 1892. The leaseholders were represented by Senator Cochrane; Dr. Duncan McEachran; D.W. Davis, MP; three influential Conservative businessmen from Montreal, Hugh Montague Allan, P.S. Ross, and William Ramsay; some of the more prominent ranch managers in the North West; and the cattle companies' parliamentary spokesman, J.A. Gemmell. The meeting agreed that all the old closed leases held by the companies would be terminated after December 31, 1896, but the cattlemen could, during the interval, purchase up to ten per cent of their leaseholds for two dollars per acre and, after

1896, apply for leases under the new system of regulations. The price of two dollars per acre was later reduced to $1.25 per acre, half the amount charged to homesteaders in the Fort Macleod area for pre-empted land.

The ranchers agreed to the changes on the unwritten promise of expanded water reserves. They drew up lists of desired reserves and sent their recommendation to William Pearce, who investigated their suitability and then forwarded them to Ottawa.

Most of the springs, creeks, and rivers were well protected under the new regulations, and the next series of evictions was not from the government leases, but from the reserves. Squatters were given written notice to vacate reserved lands, with eviction by force threatened if they failed to comply. Notices of squatters who refused to vacate were forwarded by Pearce and the Department of the Interior to the comptroller of the Mounted Police, who in turn instructed his force to take possession of the property on behalf of the Queen. Pearce, who co-ordinated the effort to enforce the new regulations, advised one squatter on a water reserve that:

> it is the policy of the Government to prevent squatting on such reservations even if forcible ejection is requisite. It is in the interest of the small stockman as well as the large one that such watering places should be provided and maintained and while no doubt such a one would seem particularly desirable to the squatter, the public interest and not that of the individual has to be consulted.

In a letter to Frederick Burton, who squatted on the north side of Trout Creek and had built a sod-roofed cabin and some corrals beside a spring, the superintendent of mines wrote that "if people were permitted to settle wherever they liked in a broke country like the Porcupine Hills, half a dozen settlers would in very many cases ruin a township for general grazing purposes."

The settlers, for their part, claimed that there were more water reserves than necessary, they were too extensive in area and some had no water at all. Pearce, caught in the struggle between the farmers and the ranchers, defended the policy of water reserves in his report in 1897. He stated that in cases where settlers protested that there was not stock watering on a reserve, the assertion proved to be erroneous 95 percent of the time. Pearce feared that settlers who claimed they would allow stock watering if they could settle on reserves might well be succeeded by others who would not allow it, and that those who agreed to provide access might well change their minds.

Defending the sizes of the reserves, Pearce said that cattle needed large areas in order to provide access to water by all. There were indeed reserves without water, but they were useful for shelter and also gave access to valleys and valley bottoms where pasture and water were abundant.

The cattlemen were grateful to Pearce for his support of their cause, and in 1899 members of the ranching establishment gathered at the St. James Club in Montreal to offer the superintendent of mines a gift for services rendered "in the interests of the cattlemen." Pearce declined the gift.

The settlers on the leases and near the water reserves continued to insist that these lands, particularly those in the Porcupine Hills, were the only good farming lands in the district and that, if they were driven from them, they would have to settle on the dry plains where they could not exist. They forwarded petitions to Ottawa through D. W. Davis, MP for Alberta, and F. W.G. Haultain, but complained that they were never laid before the House of Commons. Frank Oliver, MP for Alberta, also received complaints about the leases and water reserves from both settlers and small stockmen. D. V. Mott of Nanton wrote that Pearce

> wanted to know why all the small ranchers wanted open water, why we could not build Windmills to pump water for our stock or dig ditches, to run the water from the springs, etc. etc. I suppose it really does seem strange to Mr. Pearce that a man with a small capital would want open water in his pasture and for that reason I think he is a very unfit person for the position he holds and should be granted a long leave of absence with a recommendation to go to Holland where he could study the windmill system to his hears [sic] content.

Meanwhile, there were other parties who were complicating land matters for the ranchers. As part of its contract, the CPR received land grants of 25 million acres which its agents were to choose from the odd-numbered sections surveyed. The company's right-of-way passed through the Cochrane Ranche west of Calgary, and the railway chose 37,000 acres of the ranch's lease for its lands. Although the railway showed little inclination to dispose of its property and continued leasing it to the Cochrane Ranche, it had the right to sell it on short notice, a situation which made the Cochrane uneasy.

The Calgary and Edmonton Railway Company, which was granted a Dominion charter in 1889, completed the Calgary-South Edmonton link in 1890 and by 1892 had extended the line to the Oldman River near Fort Macleod. The government's need to pre-empt land held under lease to make up the Calgary and Edmonton Railway land grant had been a major issue taken up in the meeting of the ranchers and the government in Ottawa in early 1892.

The railway took up its lands in 1895. Many ranchers purchased land from the railway which, together with the 10 percent of their former leases they were allowed to buy, gave them secure tenure for a time. The cattlemen were thus in a fairly strong position when the Dominion government changed in 1896, Wilfred Laurier's Liberals replacing the Conservatives.

The old lease system came to an end in 1896, the same year that Clifford Sifton became minister of the interior. Even though Sifton was determined to encourage and increase immigration and to populate the North West with agricultural settlers, he recognized the southwest part of the territories as an important grazing area. There were problems, however, in maintaining the range country for the cattle industry. Immigrants from the United States passed through the country of the ranchers and many with dryland farming experience in Kansas, Dakota, and Nebraska decided to stay in the area and competed with Canadian cattlemen for the range. Even the weather played a role. During this period average precipitation was considerably above normal, which led many settlers to dismiss the rancher's warnings of the dryness of the country as nothing more than anti-settler propaganda.

Frank Oliver of Edmonton succeeded Sifton as minister of the interior in 1905. Oliver had long opposed the ranching community as a reactionary segment of society (not to mention its ties to the Conservative party) and preferred the development of mixed farms on the prairies. These were more numerous in the North Saskatchewan River area than they were in the southern part of the territory near Calgary. He was in office only a short time when he put up for auction many of the water reserves in southern Alberta.

William Pearce, whose extensive travels in southern Alberta made him familiar with the resources of the area, urged the Dominion government and the CPR to look into the possibility of irrigation on the dry plains. Pearce later oversaw the surveying of an irrigation scheme, and in 1904 joined the CPR in an advisory capacity with responsibility for irrigation matters. (A plaque honouring him was erected near the weir on the Bow River at Pearce Estate Park in Calgary.)

The conflict between ranchers and settlers continued into the 1900s, and even smaller stockmen began to consider the necessity of leases closed to homesteaders. Nevertheless, the ranchers were in retreat, particularly along the route running from Calgary to Fort Macleod and south to the boundary. This area was rapidly developing with farms and a number of small towns along the railway, and pressures on the cattlemen intensified. It was, therefore, with a sense of urgency that George Lane wrote to J.W. Greenway, commissioner of Dominion lands, in 1904:

For the past two seasons settlers were crowding into the country, and
what used to be our summer range is practically all gone now and our
cattle are confined to the hills and rough country along the eastern slope
of the Rockies …

You can easily understand a man, who has some hundreds or some
thousands of cattle, and who can neither lease nor purchase land for
grazing, being in a very uneasy state of mind as to what the final outcome of his business will be if settlement still continues to crowd in
upon him.

There may be good reasons for refusing to lease or sell large tracts
of land for grazing purposes where it can reasonably be contended the
land is fit for farming, but the same reasons cannot apply to the high,
rough, broken country known as the foothills, and I would strongly
urge that the Government reserve this latter country as a permanent
grazing district …

In the past cattle owned in the foothills, drifted out on the plains for
the summer and grass in the hills was thus saved for the winter months,
but the large settlement along the Calgary and Edmonton Railway has
cut off the summer range and the cattle are now practically confined to
the hills all year round.

Further, homesteading in the hills, the only range that is now left,
will simply mean the destruction of cattle ranching in that part of the
country …

But the cattlemen continued to retreat. They moved farther east along
the Little Bow and Bow rivers, northwest to the Red Deer River, and southeast to the Cypress Hills-Whitemud ranges. Even these areas were subject to
settlement through the early 1900s, especially after the disastrous winter of
1906–7 and the collapse of many of the large cattle operations. As the cattlemen retreated and the settlers advanced, the range was turned wrong-side up,
never quite to recover. Not until the 1920s and 1930s, when hundreds of settlers fled from vast areas of the broken range, were the cattlemen vindicated
in their assessment of the country's unsuitability for agriculture.

Chapter Nine

ORGANIZING THE RANGE

The earliest formal stockmen's association in southern Alberta was the Pincher Creek Stock Association, organized in 1882 for the spring roundup. However, in April 1883 the cattlemen of the district of Alberta assembled in Fort Macleod to form a more broadly based association as a means of protection for all stockmen alike against "prairie fires, Indians, and other inimical objects." This general association, the South West Stock Association, was divided into a number of district associations which retained control over matters of specifically local interest. Joseph McFarland was elected president of the new association; representing the northern ranchers was first vice-president Fred Stimson; representing the southern ranchers was second vice-president Matt Dunn; and Duncan Campbell, sheriff of Fort Macleod, was appointed secretary-treasurer.

The meeting went on to discuss the deliberate killing of stock by rustlers, a growing and serious problem in the area, and agreed to post $100 rewards for information leading to the conviction of anyone caught killing cattle, setting prairie fires, or stealing horses. (A further suggestion came from one of those present that the reward be increased to $150 if the horse thieves were killed.) The Macleod *Gazette* reported that "some varied discussion then took place, when Jonas Jones [president of the Pincher Creek Association] called the attention of the meeting to the fact that they were rather wandering from one subject to another and required a slight rounding up themselves." He dodged a cigar butt thrown at him and sat down, and the meeting continued.

One member of the association brought up the matter of the lease system, but another member "acted as if some one had let off a strong spring under him and said 'd__m the leases,' which threw a whole tubful of cold water on the much abused system." Two other ranchers got into a discussion over another issue, the *Gazette* reported; and though both resolved not to get hot, "before three minutes some one was talking 200 words to the minute." Finally, when it was suggested that their concerns be placed before the North West Council in Regina, it was noted that "the North West Council never meets, there is no money in it. If we want the Government to make stock laws for us, we must propose them."

A second meeting of the South West Stock Association was held in June 1883. The members petitioned the government not to reduce the number of North-West Mounted Police in the Fort Macleod district and in ranching country generally; in fact, they felt that additional patrols were necessary. The lease question came up again with many ranchers asking that leases held by speculators be cancelled. Others wanted a return to the free range, with rent based on a per head, rather than a per acre basis.

Another meeting in September 1884 tackled the problem of sheep, which were starting to come in from Montana. Members particularly had in mind the herd brought in by the Cochrane Ranche. The stockmen insisted that where sheep and cattle were allowed to graze the same range, the cattle were driven out, because sheep ate the grass down to the roots. They asked the government to prohibit sheep in an area bounded on the north by the Highwood and Bow rivers, on the east by the Alberta boundary and on the west by the Rockies. This request was approved by a territorial order-in-council in October 1884. And just to make their feelings on the matter clear beyond doubt, the association passed a resolution that no sheepmen be admitted to membership.

By 1885 problems began to develop within the association. The annual meeting that year was postponed for several hours in the hope that the High River delegation would show up. When the northern cattlemen failed to appear, association president John R. Craig expressed his regret and hoped that dissatisfaction with the association was not the cause of their nonattendance. The High River stockmen were indeed unhappy with the association. They were also concerned with several specific issues. In particular, they did not like it that the sale of beef was possible without producing the hide, that venting (cancelling of old brands on animals using a special mark) was not required upon sale of an animal, and that the brand recorder's office in Fort Macleod was so far from Calgary. The upshot was that they organized their own association, the North West Stock Association (NWSA).

A meeting to reorganize a general stock association was held in Fort Macleod in early March 1886. The South West Stock Association (SWSA) was criticized as being too cumbersome, ineffectual, and too concerned with purely local problems. The association simply could not cope with such a diversity of interests and try to frame laws for them, particularly in regards to the annual spring roundup.

William Black, the secretary-treasurer of the SWSA, addressed the meeting. He had done a good deal of travelling in order to canvass the views of ranchers in each district and now had several proposals for a more effective association. First, he suggested that each district have its own local roundup, conducting it in the interest of that district, but working with others for their mutual advantage. Second, each district would send two delegates to meetings of a general association as a means of cutting down the time wasted in useless discussion. Third, Black suggested that the old association suffered from the fact that members had nothing to lose by dropping out of it. For the new association, he proposed that some provision be made whereby a man would lose much by either dropping out of the association or by not joining it at all. Lastly, he felt that incorporation would give the association both power and a legal status, and was therefore very necessary. The stockmen often looked to the associations in Wyoming and Montana for ideas and models, though they also recognized that what was suitable in the United States might not be at all practical in Canada.

Many of the southwestern ranchers were anxious to get on with the formation of a new association right away, even though there was no representative from High River at the meeting. The chairman, Jack Garnett of Pincher Creek, told the assembly that he had recently talked with Fred Stimson of the Bar U, the acknowledged "mouth piece of the High River stockmen," and that Stimson and others wanted to form a district similar to the original Pincher Creek district, but to be governed also by a general association. It would therefore be a great mistake, Garnett felt, not to have every district represented, in the formation of a new association. Stanley Pinhorne of the Oxley and F.C. Inderwick of the North Fork Ranche protested that if they waited for the High River people, they would never get organized. Garnett soothed the two men and insisted that they must give all the stockmen sufficient time to discuss the matter thoroughly and that they couldn't take too much trouble to make this new association a lasting one.

The assembly struck a committee of five men—Stanley Pinhorne, William F. Cochrane, W. Bell, F.W. Godsal, and John J. Barter—to draft a new constitution and bylaws. It then tackled the problem of establishing the boundaries of each stock district. The afternoon session concluded with a resolution expressing appreciation of the NWMP's efforts during the recent difficulties caused by the Métis Rebellion of 1885. A short evening session considered the question of hiring a stock detective, but took no further action in this regard.

In April 1886 representatives from all the stock districts, including High River, convened in Fort Macleod to consider the proposed constitution and formation of the new association. First, there was the heated discussion over whether John Craig, former manager of the Oxley Ranche, would chair the meeting. F.C. Inderwick pointed out that a vote was not necessary because Craig was president of the South West Stock Association until its annual meeting in May, and was therefore chairman by right. Pinhorne objected; it was not a meeting of the SWSA, but was an assembly called for the purpose of forming a new association. One of the northern delegates drew attention to the fact that some of those present were not members of the old association, to which Inderwick replied, "Then you should not be here." Pinhorne and a number of other delegates left the session in a body, and Craig took the chair.

Craig compared the condition of the southern Alberta stockmen with that of people abroad; he had interviewed farmers in England during his recent visit and found them in a deplorable state. Beef from North America was so cheap that it made it impossible for the British to profitably produce their own. Adding that he was speaking now to men of experience on the range, he said it did not behoove them to be taught by men who came from abroad with very crude notions of what was wanted, and that Alberta stockmen should be careful not to yield their experience to them. Craig then defended the old association, though he admitted he had not seen the draft of the new constitution.

The evening session started with an election, and J. Garnett took the chair. The assembly then read through the proposed constitution and chose a new name, the Canadian Northwest Territories Stock Association. There was further discussion on the boundaries of the four stock districts—Calgary, High River, Willow Creek, and Pincher Creek; the boundary between the Willow Creek and the Pincher Creek districts was a particularly contentious issue. Mr. Inderwick, reported the *Gazette*, broke the tension when he "arrived with a very big umbrella, which caused considerable excitement and curiosity—not Mr. Inderwick, but the umbrella."

Having settled the matter of districts, the meeting moved to the subject of electing delegates to the general association and decided that there should be three from each district, rather than two. Pinhorne returned to the evening session and proposed that each member of the association vote for district delegates according to a sliding scale based on the number of cattle owned. Inderwick immediately protested—that this was exactly the issue which split up the old association, and Pinhorne wanted to vote the small men down. Doc Frields of the Walrond jumped into the fray—if members were assessed fees according to the number of cattle owned, they should vote according to the same. Inderwick, never afraid to express his views, contended that under the plan proposed by Pinhorne and Frields, the men who represented companies would have more influence than men who had invested in their own ranches; the representatives of the large companies would run the country. Several other ranchers supported Inderwick—the big companies would always be able to elect their own men as delegates, and they could not see small stockmen joining the association if Pinhorne's plan was adopted.

C.C. McCaul, the solicitor for the Oxley Ranche who had a hand in drawing up the new constitution with its controversial system of representation, defended Pinhorne's plan as a compromise, and further suggested that the sliding scale, worked out by both large and small stockmen in the old association, had tied the ranchers together, rather than driven them apart. John Craig said he thought the intention of the meeting was to thoroughly reorganize the association because the usefulness of the old one was gone, but he had yet to hear anything adopted which was different from the old organization. The reason for forming a new association, Pinhorne snapped back, was simply that the old one was unmanageable. The *Gazette* reported that a Mr. Pace

> intimated he was a Conservative to the backbone, but there was no use in getting up Conservative ideas. They must all have the same voice whether they owned ten cattle or 10,000. There was no good in two or three getting together and thinking that they were going to run the world. Why get up a paltry meeting like this you can't do it [cries of order].

The assembly adopted the constitution in the end, including the much debated system for voting. Each stock owner was entitled to vote in proportion to the number of cattle he owned in accordance with the following scale:

One vote	500 head and under
Two votes	500 to 1,000 head
Three votes	1,000 to 2,000 head
Four votes	3,000 to 4,000 head
Five votes	5,000 to 8,000 head
Six votes	8,000 to 12,000 head
Seven votes	12,000 to 17,000 head

In early May a few members of the old South West Stock Association met, appointed president John Craig and secretary William Black a committee to wind up affairs, and passed a resolution that an assessment be levied on the members of the SWSA which, together with other dues, would be sufficient to meet all the remaining liabilities. They also discussed the advisability of holding an annual exhibition of livestock and agricultural products, but Craig felt that, in his experience at least, the most successful exhibitions were the outcome of the enterprise of the towns in which they were held. Therefore, it was decided that the suggestion for an exhibition should come from Fort Macleod, though a committee was formed to work with the town. (The first fall exhibition was held in Fort Macleod that year.) Duncan Campbell moved that a vote of thanks be tendered to John Craig for the manner in which he had conducted the association's affairs; F.C. Inderwick seconded the motion, saying that Mr. Craig had been the right man in the right place.

The first meeting of the Northwest Territories Stock Association took place in mid-May 1886 at Fort Macleod. All the districts in southern Alberta save Calgary were represented. Delegates included Walter Skrine and Tom Lynch from High River, with authority to act for the absent John J. Barter, the third delegate; John Herron, F.C. Inderwick, and Jim Dunlap from Pincher Creek; and Doc Frields, Ed Maunsell, and Stanley Pinhorne from Willow Creek. They elected John Herron as president of the association, Jim Dunlap and John J. Barter vice-presidents, and appointed C.E.D. Wood of the Macleod *Gazette* as secretary. Two observers from Montana also attended, but since their arrival was unexpected and their stay short, the stockmen regretted that they were unable to extend to their visitors their full hospitality. However, the next time the Montanans attended, the stockmen resolved, "it will be seen that Rome everlastingly howls!"

The second meeting of the NWTSA was held on May 31, 1886, with seven delegates attending. Herron explained that the association wished to give anyone the opportunity to join before the spring roundup—scheduled to begin June 1—and ranchers could propose names for acceptance by the delegates. He also expressed pleasure that a large number of smaller owners, who had never belonged to the old organization, had joined the new one, and that both small and large owners seemed to be working in harmony.

A number of motions were made and carried: that members be assessed one-half cent per head to provide the association with funds for its running expenses; that Stanley Pinhorne and the secretary be authorized to pay all bills; that the president take steps to have the association incorporated, and that the association send a communication to the Montana Stock Association requesting that they use their influence with the Montana legislature to have a law passed that would punish anyone taking stock stolen from Alberta into Montana.

The association met again in Fort Macleod in May of the following year. Having just come through the severe winter of 1886–87, the secretary in his remarks noted that the way the cattle came through the winter proved "that our claim that Southern Alberta and Western Assiniboia contain the best ranges in the world, is not confounded," and that "the clerk of the weather will have to rustle harder than he has yet done to scare up a winter that will come anywhere near ruining the range cattle business." He also reported that he had it on good authority that a law had been passed in Montana providing heavy penalties for persons taking stock stolen from Alberta into Montana.

Then the meeting moved to elect new officers: F.W. Godsal was elected president, and Doc Frields and George Emerson, vice-presidents. A motion to change the name of the association to the Alberta Stock Growers' Association (ASGA) carried unanimously. The members in attendance then formed various committees to deal with such issues as assessments, rewards, and Indian depredations. The proposed changes to the association's constitution elicited a heated and prolonged discussion. Everyone agreed that the committee system for disposing of association business should be adopted, but the question arose of whether the stockmen should speak and vote at meetings, or only the delegates. In the end, it was decided that it would be unfair to allow everyone present at meetings to vote, as those members who lived nearest the headquarters of the association could outvote those who lived at a distance. The meetings would be open to all members who wished to attend, while the actual work would be done by committees of members, each committee being selected in accordance with the fitness of its members for the particular job to be done. The committees would hand in their reports, which would then be open to discussion by all association members present. The district delegates, however, would decide whether the reports were to be accepted or rejected, coinciding as much as possible with the will of the general meeting.

By 1889 complaints about the general stock association began to surface once again. Fred Stimson urged the formation of a new association, stating that the ASGA was carried on in the interests of a few stockmen in the Fort Macleod district, and was of no benefit to the interests of Alberta as a whole. He acknowledged that there was still a need for a strong organization to represent all the ranchers, and suggested that the headquarters should be in Calgary, as that was the most central point. However, the meetings could be held at High River, or wherever desired.

John J. Barter of the Quorn further remarked that the brand recording office at Fort Macleod was very inefficient and the difficulty of registering a brand was more than it was worth. G.E. Goddard of the Bow River Horse Ranche west of Calgary agreed with Stimson and Barter that the old association was of no use to anybody and not worth belonging to, but there was plenty of work for a good association which would have all the support it required.

The Alberta Stock Growers' Association dragged along for a few more years, but gradually disintegrated. A committee of stockmen met at the Oxley Ranche in September 1892 to try to organize something, but other than naming A. Ernest Cross as secretary and appointing two stock inspectors at $100 a year, it accomplished little.

In 1894 the Macleod *Gazette* appealed for another attempt at forming a general stock association which would take action to control rustlers, stamp out wolves, press for better inspection and control at shipping points, and make representations to government. A new association, the Southern Alberta Stockers' Association, was formed in November 1894, but lasted little more than a year.

All efforts to incorporate previous associations had failed. An organizational committee met under the guidance of A. Ernest Cross in 1896 to form the Western Stock Growers' Association. It received its incorporation on October 30, 1896 and held its first general meeting at Calgary on December 28. The issues raised at the meeting were familiar but still pressing ones: rancher opposition to the removal of the quarantine on cattle coming into Canada from the United States; homesteading or leasing by settlers of watering places; shelter areas and driving routes for cattle; compulsory recording of brands; the wolf bounty; enlargement of the stockyards at Cochrane and Calgary; and the vesting of ownership of mavericks in the stock association.

The Western Stock Growers' Association did manage to survive; actually, many of its moving spirits were the same men who had been involved in the previous organizations, but whose personal interests had doomed them all to failure. With a growing list of problems which had long troubled stockmen, the new association set to work.

The WSGA grew in membership and prestige and became a strong voice for Alberta stockmen in their relations with the provincial and Dominion governments, and it continues to be active to this day.

During the early days of the range the rancher's property and investment were represented by cattle and not by land; it was necessary, therefore, to mark the cattle in order to establish ownership. As the range was gradually fenced and cattle more confined, the need for branding diminished. Nevertheless, wherever cattle ran in mixed herds, branding remained essential.

Originally, brands were run on stock with a running iron, a simple steel bar with a hook at one end. But laws were passed in some areas of the American range prohibiting the carrying of running irons; it was too easy for rustlers and others to find unbranded cattle and quickly run on any brand they wished. To be caught with a running iron became a hanging offence. Stamp irons then became the custom. These made the complete brand in one piece so that it could be put on an animal in one operation.

The first recorded brand in the Canadian North West was issued in January 1880 under an ordinance of the North West Territories respecting the marketing of stock. This brand, the number "71," was granted to Percy R. Neale and Samuel B. Steele and was to be placed "on the near ribs" of the animal. The second brand, CD, was allotted to Capt. Cecil Denny of Fort Walsh on April 22, 1880. The original brand recorder was William Winder, but he held that position only during 1880 and was succeeded by T. Dowling. Altogether, 95 brands were recorded under this ordinance.

The oldest continuously held brand in Alberta is the a7, which was taken out by the Cross brothers in May 1886. The original application was for the brand a1, to indicate that all stock carrying the brand was of first quality. However, officials pointed out that the figure 1 could be easily reworked, so the Crosses substituted the number 7, as there were seven brothers in the family. In 1900 the brand was transferred to A. Ernest Cross, and the Cross family and the a7 brand have been identified together since then.

The brand ordinance was revised in 1887 and the system of recording was reorganized to allow for expansion and changes in the cattle districts and a sub-recorder of brands was appointed for each district, as well as a recorder of brands for the whole territory. Two suitable persons were also appointed by the territorial council, who, together with the recorder, formed a brand committee for all the districts. The brand committee met at the office of the recorder of brands at least once every month to consider applications for brands which were forwarded through the sub-recorders. This committee designated the particular brand to be used by an applicant and the place and position it should occupy on the animal. It was also required to consult "always the convenience of applicants, so far as may be, without interfering with previously recorded brands."

The ordinance stated that any person using a like brand in the place or position recorded by another, or obliterating, altering, or defacing the recorded brand of any other person, was liable to a fine not exceeding $100 or 40 days in jail. And much to the satisfaction of the stockmen, the presence of a recorded brand on any animal was considered *prima-facie* evidence of ownership of the animal by the owner of the brand.

The Macleod *Gazette* advised cattlemen that it was definitely in their best interests to pay the fee for recording a brand. A man might have a brand unlike anything recorded, and decide to take his chances and not record it. If someone later came along with the same brand and recorded it, the original brand user could be fined for using a brand similar to a recorded one. A brand should never be made, much less put on cattle or horses, until it was ascertained whether or not it had previously been recorded.

As brands on the cattle were permanent, a system was also needed to indicate the legal transfer of an animal. The practice was to have a vent brand—which cancelled the original brand—placed on the animal sold, in a manner which did not alter or destroy the original brand, but was clear evidence to transfer.

The ordinance of 1887 did not specify that stockmen *must* brand their cattle, an omission which caused many ranchers a great deal of distress and led to considerable conflict between cattlemen and settlers in later years.

In order to cut down on theft and loss of stock, cattlemen pressed for a thorough system of brand inspection. During the early years of the range cattle industry there was no attempt to have stock inspected at shipping points. Cattle were gathered together and driven across the open range, and it was natural that strays should get into the herd and be lost to their actual owners. As the cattle industry expanded, the stockmen demanded that inspectors be present at all shipping points, as well as at Indian reserves and other places where slaughtering took place. They did not feel it necessary to have inspectors present at the time of slaughter, but wanted laws requiring hides to be kept for inspection, perhaps at the end of each month. The inspector could then examine the hide to ensure that the animal had not been stolen and had in fact belonged to the seller. The general feeling was that the government should bear the cost of organizing and maintaining an inspection system, since it would be for the benefit of the country and the protection of property. While strays might accidentally get drawn in with another herd, thieves could just as easily gather up cattle, alter brands, and then sell the animals. Thieves were also adept at changing brands or putting brands on calves before roundup. The running iron was still quite useful in this regard, as were such methods as burning brands on cattle with acid. The lack of inspection left the field wide open for such activity.

The Western Stock Growers' Association meeting in Calgary in 1896 recommended the government appoint stock inspectors at all points of shipping, and went so far as to list individuals it considered suitable for the job. Most of the nominees were ranchers who lived near each point. However, most of these folk were understandably reluctant to take on the job, since it required a long ride to the inspection point and the loss of a day's work. Even the suggested remuneration of five cents a head for inspection was not a sufficiently strong incentive.

Nonetheless, a stock inspection law was passed in 1897 and came into effect in 1899. One of the first stock inspectors was Jim Patterson, the capable foreman of the Walrond Ranche. The job demanded an extensive knowledge of brands and cattle and a keen eye, and Patterson possessed both. R.G. Mathews of the WSGA felt that if there was ever an expert in cow business, Patterson certainly was it. One day Mathews and Patterson were looking through a herd of two thousand head of mixed cattle, when Mathews suddenly heard Patterson shout, "Well, I'll be damned if that ain't old Emma," and he pointed to a cow's head sticking up from the middle of the sea of milling animals. Patterson explained that Emma was an old acquaintance from his early days on the Alberta range.

Even with brand inspectors, cattle theft remained a major problem for the stockmen and for the Mounted Police, who were often called upon to track down stolen animals. In 1905 Supt. R. Burton Deane of the NWMP reported the case of a certain cattle dealer who imported a number of calves from Manitoba which he proposed to sell to persons requiring stockers. According to Deane's report:

> The man had rather bad luck with this importation, for some got away from him before they were branded, and a much larger number got away from his herders in a bad storm. There were then upwards of 100 unbranded calves on the range, and the possibilities were too obvious to be neglected. A local stockman ... whom I will call A, conspired with two employees, whom I will call B and C, to acquire some of these motherless and masterless calves. The *modus operandi* was to brand a certain proportion of the calves with A's own recorded brand, and these would constitute his share, while the other proportion were to be branded 7 11 7 which would form the share of the other two conspirators. This 7 11 7 (seven-eleven-seven) brand was invented by C, and was not a recorded brand. He explained that he invented it because a lateral line would at any time connect the two perpendiculars of the figure 11 thus converting it into a letter U, and a slight extension of the top of the first figure 7 would convert it into a T—the converted brand would thus read T U 7; this was also unrecorded.
>
> I was never able to satisfy myself as to the reason of these men breaking up their connection, but this is what happened. B and C had a scheme on foot to take up and brand certain calves on a particular Sunday, and A and B came together and gave information to me.

The result was that two constables watched the Sabbath morning operations and arrested C red-handed—he was handling the branding-irons and apparently directing the operations. He was subsequently convicted to the penitentiary for three years upon very simple and indisputable evidence, but while he was awaiting trial in the guard-room here he gave away the story of the conspiracy between himself and A and B. B got wind of it and left the country, while A was tried and convicted here last March and dispatched to join his confrère at Stony Mountain.

Particulars which came to light in the course of the trial indicated that the "rustling" of calves had not been confined to the principals of this performance, and a feeling of insecurity has since existed in more than one thitherto unsuspected quarter.

A brand expert was called as a witness for the defence in a rather unusual case in 1901. Two men, Wells and Percival, were charged with killing an animal belonging to King and Jones. The prosecution allowed that the accused had killed an animal and that its hide had been found in the pit of Wells' latrine. Half of the carcass was found at Wells' place and half at Percival's. Half of the head was found under a chicken coop and the other half had been buried in a dung hill. The entrails were discovered behind a pig pen. Three pieces of the unsavoury hide, which were presented in court, were purported to represent the left ribs, with a part of the brand on each piece. The owners of the animal had traced their brand on these pieces of hide. But an expert witness testified that one of the pieces did not belong with the other two. In addition, the hair on one piece grew in the opposite direction; therefore, the pieces could not possibly have come from the same animal. The court attempted to obtain an opinion from other experts, but no one could be induced to examine the offensive hide. The accused were acquitted for lack of evidence, but the judge intimated he had made that decision with regret, since it was clear that they had killed an animal which did not belong to them.

Mavericks were another long-standing problem for ranchers. A maverick is an unbranded calf whose ownership cannot be determined. (The name derived from a Texas lawyer named Sam Maverick, who, for a short time, ran cattle which he did not brand.) Each spring, with the new batch of calves, the decision on ownership was made on the basis that a calf will follow its mother, and that no matter how large the herd, a cow will always know her own calf. Thus, calves were given the brand of the cows they were following. Since the law recognized that a brand was evidence of ownership, it was difficult for a rancher who suspected that some of his calves had disappeared into another herd to prove that the calves might originally have been his own.

Stockmen found various ways of creating mavericks which they could claim and brand. Some slit the calf's tongue so that it could no longer suckle and would stop following its mother; others simply separated calves from the herds until they could no longer find and follow their mothers. One reason for holding all outfits to one day for starting the spring roundup was simply to prevent some ranchers from getting an early start and branding any mavericks they found.

The Wyoming Stock Growers' Association dealt most decisively with the maverick question. In 1884 it defined mavericks for its purposes and gave explicit directions for their disposal. The foremen of the association's roundups were to take up the mavericks and offer them for sale at auction on the range every ten days. The money from the sales went into the association treasury for payment of inspectors and other employees. The Wyoming association also ruled that there was to be no branding of stock in the territory between February 15 and the starting date of the spring roundup. As the rules of the association were recognized by the Wyoming legislature, the association became a powerful force in the territory. The Wyoming rules were adopted by the Montana stock association, but they never received the sanction of legislation in that territory. The early Canadian stock associations followed the Montana model, but also failed to achieve the power of the Wyoming association.

There were always mavericks found on roundups, and the stockmen in southern Alberta addressed themselves to the problem through their associations. At the meeting of the South West Stock Association in March 1886 the secretary, William Black, recommended that members adopt a definite policy so that "these strays will become the property of the local or general associations, as you may deem best. If we quarrel about them it is probable that the laws of the territory will interfere, and the chances are that the revenue derived from them will go to the general government."

J. Garnett, however, felt that mavericks belonged to the Queen and this created problems for their disposal. "A maverick may be sold, and then a man who thinks that he has a claim on them can sue for them at law. We want a law to dispose of these mavericks at our own pleasure."

Doc Frields replied to Garnett's interpretation of the situation: "The Queen has got no cattle in this country, and she is a Jo Dandy if she gets ere a maverick from the W.R. [Walrond]."

The legal status of mavericks remained vague, and early roundups customarily killed mavericks for the camp food supply. In later years, if ownership was not claimed and proved, stock associations sold the animals and turned the money over to a general fund. In November 1896 J.P. McHugh was charged with stealing a Circle Ranch steer from the Conrad brothers' herd at Queenstown. McHugh was acquitted by Mr. Justice Charles B. Rouleau, who then justified the decision, saying that it had become customary for the Conrads to take up and brand all unbranded stray cattle in the district during roundup. The stock associations could not make such rules to suit themselves, Rouleau went on, and he would severely punish anyone brought before him on such charges.

In 1901 the situation was further complicated when, at a meeting of the Western Stock Growers' Association, Howell Harris and George Lane moved that all blotched brands found by roundups should be sold by the roundup captains the same as mavericks were, unless ownership could be proven. The revenue from their sale was to be used for the general benefit of all stockmen who belonged to the association.

The practice of selling mavericks as followed by the roundups antagonized many settlers and smaller stockmen who did not belong to the associations. A Pincher Creek settler wrote to Frank Oliver in 1897 on the issue:

> I notice that at the last Annual Meeting of the Western Stock Growers Association that it was resolved to petition the Dominion Gov't asking that "the ownership of mavericks be vested in the Stock Growers Association." Undoubtedly the matter of mavericks needs some regulations but this proposal, if carried out, will cause endless trouble and gross injustice. Settlers with small bunches of cattle and rangers who look after their cattle closely, do not belong to this Ass'n. and consequently, any calf missed by them or temporally [sic] separated from its cow, accidentally or otherwise, will be scooped up by this Association, many members of which are noted for a keen eye for mavericks. In the spring and fall round ups they drive their herd of range cattle thro' a bunch of gentle stock, picking up everything as they go along and if one does not belong to this Association and this proposal becomes law, are hopelessly lost to him.

Even the small ranchers became alarmed and fought with the larger ranchers over representation on roundups. Many objected to the ruling that owners of 500 head or any fraction otherof must have a man on the roundup to protect his stock, a regulation which put small owners to as much expense as the large operations.

The matter of disposing of mavericks was finally settled in 1903 in a case before Chief Justice A.L. Sifton of the Supreme Court of the North West Territories at Medicine Hat. Sifton (later premier of Alberta from 1910 to 1917) had already drawn the attention of cattlemen, as attested to by the Macleod *Gazette*:

> In the old days stock rustlers hardly feared the law and its punishments as meted out from the old dingy court room at Macleod. Perjury was rife, indifferent jury men, and jury men prejudiced, often turned aside the blow that justice would have dealt to the offenders. Court sittings that dragged so weary a length owing to the absence of a court stenographer made business at the sittings something to be dreaded. But a new man donned the ermine. He had been at this bar before, pleading, and had seen the evidences of perjury and prejudice. Backed by the power he knew was behind him, reinforced in his determinations to be just by the memories of these past offences he dealt out his justice liberally to those convicted. At the last court stock thieves received their proper punishment. Perjurers were given full time to reflect on the crime of lying with their lips on the Bible. Besides these reforms, Hon. Mr. Sifton managed to speed along the business of the Court. Lawyers who plead before him and who array their witnesses in his hearing know for a certainty that they have a mighty good chance of getting through before the crack of doom if they use reasonable judgement.

An unusual maverick case was heard in Medicine Hat. A German settler near Josephburg, who spoke no English, lost a 14-month-old steer when it was driven off by a May snowstorm. He eventually heard that the Plume Creek roundup had gathered up his steer, and went to the captain of the roundup to claim it. The settler could not, however, make himself understood, and so his English-speaking son claimed it for him shortly afterwards. The captain made little of the son's claim and admitted that he took no steps to determine whether the claim was well founded or not. The steer was sold by auction as a maverick for $19.

Another German settler in the same area lost an unbranded heifer in much the same way, and it, too, was sold by auction at the end of the roundup, for $16.50. In this instance, the owner of the heifer did not know until much later that his animal had been gathered up in the roundup, and so did not make any claim for it. When the facts of these two cases were brought to the attention of the Mounted Police, they laid a criminal charge of theft in each case against the roundup captain, James Crawford, who was duly committed for trial.

The executive of the Medicine Hat Stock Growers' Association met in

late September 1903 to consider the matter. It decided to undertake Crawford's defence and asked that the Maple Creek association co-operate with it.
The two associations, which were separate from the general Western Stock
Growers' Association, engaged P.J. Nolan of Calgary to defend Crawford, and
the case was heard in November.

Crawford said that he had been appointed captain of the roundup by
the secretary of the Medicine Hat Stock Growers' Association, and that he
had taken no steps to discover to whom the cattle in question belonged. The
proceeds of the auction sale in each case had been handed over to the secretary of the association's eastern branch, and a letter from the secretary to the
purchaser of the heifer read to the effect that if the association should get a
few more "pay" cattle, it would clear its expenses.

The secretary of the Medicine Hat Stock Growers' Association, J.H.G.
Bray, testified that he had been in the country for nearly thirty years (indeed,
he came west as a member of the North-West Mounted Police in 1874), and
that it had always been customary to sell mavericks to pay roundup expenses.
He also said that the stock associations had been trying for years to get the
custom legalized, but had failed to do so. Witnesses who had acted as captains
of roundups in previous years also testified to the custom, and claimed that
they would have acted exactly as the accused had done. One man said that he
would not even have considered it his place to take the trouble to determine
the ownership of the cattle in question; it was the owner's business to make
and prove his claim.

Nolan, for the defence, stressed the fact that there had been no feloni-
ous intent in the captain's actions, and that the money had gone to general
roundup expenses and not to the accused's benefit. He also pointed out that
though Crawford's actions may have been illegal—and he did not intend to
justify them on legal grounds—they were not criminal as applied to the accused, who happened to be captain this year and merely followed the custom
of his predecessors. Nolan contended that the law was imperfect, in that cattle
should not be allowed to go unbranded on the range and so become a temptation to people of weak resolution.

Chief Justice Sifton agreed that punishment by way of imprisonment
was not necessary, and considered that the requirements of the case would be
satisfied by the record of a formal conviction against the accused, who was released on suspended sentence. But Sifton also said that there was no question
that conviction was proper, and that the secretary and members of the stock
association were equally guilty with the accused. They were well aware that
the sale of mavericks was unlawful; they had been making efforts for many
years to have the custom legalized. As to the intent, Sifton noted that a direct

benefit accrued to the stock association by application to their revenue of the amounts realized by the sale of mavericks. Finally, he said in effect that people had a perfect right to allow their cattle to range unbranded if they so wished, but that no roundup had the right to gather cattle which were not the property of members of the association without the consent of their owners.

This decision marked the end of the arbitrary power of the roundup captains, and perhaps more significantly, the end of an era. For as the open range became more settled with homesteaders and enclosed with barbed wire fence, the general roundup, so characteristic of the cattle kingdom, disappeared.

Chapter Ten

THE COWBOYS

The cowboy has long been a captive of his own public image—living a free and exciting life on the open range, chasing rustlers with his trusty, inexhaustible horse, livening up dusty cowtowns with his good-natured high jinks, and defending the honour of his ranch and women. His real life was much different, of course; it was hard work, discomfort, long hours, and short pay. There was, nevertheless, enough of the freedom and excitement of the popular image in the cowboy's life to attract and hold many men; for others, however, cowpunching was simply a more acceptable job than working in a factory or on a dirt farm.

"You didn't see many old cowboys," one oldtimer told Barry Broadfoot. "By old I mean forty or so. Oh, maybe the cook on the chuckwagon or the night wrangler or something like that ... But all the cowboys were young. Young and tough. Young, tough and underpaid." John Clay, who said he did not know where the cowboys disappeared to as they grew old, noted a similar phenomenon in the United States.

It would seem that those cowboys who did not make it on their own as ranchers or small stockmen became hired hands on farms or in the livery and feed barns. But many cowboys worked for large ranches in order to acquire sufficient capital and experience to establish their own operations later on. And many succeeded, frequently with the encouragement and assistance of their employers.

The cowboy was an employee, a fact which defined his position in the economic and social scheme of things pretty quickly. During the late 1800s the ordinary cowboy's monthly wage was about $40, on top of which might be added board. The payroll of the Cochrane Ranche in 1885 showed that the foreman, Jim Dunlap, received $125 per month, the bookkeeper, $67.50, and the cook, $50. At times, wages rose considerably, as they did during the

Saskatchewan uprising of 1885, when cowboys were particularly hard to find. So many had joined the Alberta Field Force that there was a serious shortage of manpower on the range.

Most ranchers felt that good cowboys earned their wages, but that such men were hard to find. John Craig maintained that there were as many grades of cowboys on the range as men in any other field. There was always something to learn in the cattle business, and the best cowboys added to their knowledge every year. Craig saw plenty of cowboys, both the genuine kind and the "imitation which usually had a little more sombrero and cartridge-belt and gun" than the real sort. Particularly during the early 1880s good hands experienced no difficulty finding work.

Many cowboys found it difficult to save their wages, particularly if they spent much time across the boundary in Montana, as they often did in the early days. On the other hand, American cowboys who worked in the North West swore that it was much easier to keep hold of their earnings north of the boundary. For on either side of the line, there were always professional and amateur gamblers eager to separate cowboys from their cash in games of euchre, faro, and poker. Once their money was gone, the cowboys lived on "jawbone," or credit, until they found new employment or received their next month's wages. The personal accounts of W.F. Cochrane were filled with loans to his cowboys, cook, and teamster.

According to John Higinbotham, Tony la Chappelle's poolroom in Fort Macleod contained two round tables covered with green baize at which there were always men—at any time of the day or night—"sitting with their hats on, usually with the front brim pulled down shading their eyes, smoking black cigars and playing stud poker." If a stranger stopped by, he was invited to sit in; and if he inquired as to the limit, he was informed, "floor to ceiling." Whenever a new herd of cattle and cowboys arrived in town, faro banks did a great business.

Although Fort Macleod, Calgary, and Maple Creek developed into cattle towns, the rowdy centres which sprang up across the American cattle country where liquor flowed, gambling flourished, and women were bold never really developed in Canada. The passage of legislation and presence of the North-West Mounted Police ensured that they never got a firm foothold. In the 1870s the lieutenant-governor of the North West Territories imposed prohibition on the territories by order-in-council, primarily to suppress the whisky trade with the Indians. As there were few white settlers in the country at the time, there was little opposition to the order. The North West Territories Act of 1875 also forbade the importation and manufacture of liquor, except for medicinal and sacramental purposes, and then only by special permits in writing from the lieutenant-governor. This system worked fairly well until about 1882, when the new lieutenant-governor, Edgar Dewdney, began to issue permits more freely. As trails and railways penetrated the North West and brought in more settlers, opposition to prohibition grew and the law became increasingly hard to enforce. It seemed the whole North West was plagued with maladies of various kinds, and particularly those which required the medicinal qualities of alcohol.

Liquor smuggling increased both in scope and ingenuity. As settlers moved into the country, so did liquor, hidden in every conceivable disguise— eggs, tins of sardines, books, and even bags of oatmeal for the local minister. In one instance a shipment of liquor was carried in a coffin past the bowed heads of a respectful police patrol. Saloon operators in Calgary, Fort Macleod, and other centres kept sheafs of liquor permits on hand to cover their stock. Some of the permits were old, but a permit was a permit; and it was impossible for the police to prove that the liquor they found was not imported under the permits produced. Many people who had been granted permits left them in saloons or turned them over to the saloon-keepers; liquor legally brought into the country could therefore legally be in anybody's possession.

The ranchers generally discouraged drinking by their cowboys, especially during the crucial time of roundup. However, none went so far as the giant XIT Ranch in Texas, whose employees were "strictly forbidden the use of vinous, malt, spiritous, or intoxicating liquors" during their time of service on the ranch. But, there were also plenty of illicit stills hidden in the hills and coulees of the range country, and liquor inevitably found its way into the cow camps. Fred Ings recalled how on one roundup a keg of home-brewed whisky was discreetly left beside the cook tent one night. The next day there was a wild and hilarious branding session, and that year the calves wore their brands in all sorts of places and at all angles.

Out of his earnings the cowboy had to pay certain essential expenses, one of which was clothing. Clothes were more expensive in the North West than in such Montana towns as Fort Benton and Miles City. The cowboy's clothes were basically those of most working men of the time—wool flannel underwear, a woollen shirt in the winter and perhaps cotton in the summer, and strong, warm pants. Denim pants, of course, were very popular because of their durability and comfort, especially during the summer, when wool pants were hot and uncomfortable. The serge pants worn by the Mounted Police were also considered very good for conditions on the range. Clothes were designed for hard work and freedom of movement and there was no such thing as the distinctive western cut which later became so popular. Clothes tended to be heavy, and they needed to be, particularly for the winter, spring, and fall work. The ever-present wind on the plains had a sharp bite to it and though daytime temperatures in the summer might be very warm, the nights were cool.

Over his standard items of clothing, then, the cowboy wore his special gear. Leather chaps provided protection for his legs against brush and rope burns and scrapes in the corrals. Early chaps were of the shotgun variety—tubelike and very plain—into which the cowboys stepped. Later, batwing chaps became popular, as they could be easily strapped on without having to remove boots or spurs. In the winter the cowboys wore woolies, chaps with angora on the outside for additional warmth. Chaps also shed water well, and woolies acted as a good windbreak without becoming stiff in cold weather as even oiled chaps did. Chaps were held in place with a special belt which buckled at the back and was designed so that it need not be pulled tight. The two halves of the belt on each leg were held together in front by a thin strip of leather or rawhide which would break easily if caught on a saddle horn.

Western boots were originally high-topped, often as high as the knee, again for protection against brush. Later adaptations lowered the height, scalloped the top and added other features. The pointed toe of the boot allowed it to be guided quickly and easily into the stirrup, and the heel, raised and undershot, prevented the boot from sliding right through the stirrup. There was always the danger for a rider that his horse might fall or "pile up"; if he could not get his feet out of the stirrups quickly, they would slide through. If the horse fell and rolled, the rider's legs might be crushed; if the horse recovered but the rider's foot was caught, or "hung up," the cowboy might be dragged and struck by the horse's hoofs.

The early boots, with their heels back of the sideseams, tended to have weak shanks (the narrow part of the sole in front of the heel) which broke down when the wearer walked. Later designs advanced the heels forward somewhat, thus strengthening the shank. As many cowboys became bow-legged from spending so much time on horses, they naturally tended to run the heels of their boots out, that is, bend the boot out over the heel. To overcome this problem, good boot-makers set the heel slightly towards the outside.

Boots were designed for horseback, and cowboys were often reluctant to dismount and walk in them. Stories abounded of cowhands who refused to perform jobs such as digging a well, skinning a carcass, or building a fence because those tasks could not be done from horseback. Jim Minesinger liked to tell about the time some horses got loose and headed off over the plains, chased by cowboys on foot. It wasn't very long before all the men were sitting on the prairie, nursing their feet and ankles, much to the amusement of Minesinger, who usually wore moccasins.

Because of the different climate, Canadian cowboys wore much smaller hats than their southwestern American counterparts. The cowboy's hat was not for show by any means; it provided protection from the sun, rain, and wind. It took a lot of punishment and so had to be made of good material. The Stetson Company made the best hats and there were many distinctive styles, including a Calgary design with a seven-inch crown and four-and-a-half-inch brim. Nor was the bandana around the cowboy's neck an affectation; it was used to cover the nose and mouth as protection against the dust raised by hundreds of cattle on the dry plains. F.W. Godsal of Pincher Creek discovered another use for his bandana. On one roundup the water supply came from shallow pools on the plains, and he and the cowboys sucked the water through their kerchiefs to strain out the "wrigglers" and other aquatic life. Another necessity was a good vest, with pockets for knives, tobacco, matches and other odds and ends. Buckskin shirts and coats, made mostly by the Indians and tanned to remain supple and comfortable, were prized, especially for spring and fall work. And during winter extra socks in the boots and a long coat were crucial.

According to the popular image, no self-respecting cowboy would venture forth without his trusty "gun" (the North West term for six-shooter). Guns were far less common than generally portrayed by later books and films, even in the United States, for they simply got in the way of a busy, working cowboy. If a cowboy did in fact own a six-shooter, he usually left it in his bedroll at the camp wagon or back in the bunkhouse. Nevertheless there were plenty of guns of all sorts, as might be expected on any frontier. While the six-shooter originated with the early Texans in their wars with Indians because it was a weapon which could be discharged from a fast-moving horse, the principal use of the weapon during the ranching period in Canada was killing varmints, not humans. People in the range country also frequently carried rifles.

As early as the 1880s, novelists had shown the public—including cowboys—a particular image of the wild west and there were some cowboys who felt obligated to live up to that image. John Higinbotham remembered a little Englishman named Williams, who had come out to the North West to be a "wild and woolly cowboy." One evening while two Higinbotham brothers were seated at a table reading papers, "Williams sat on the doorstep toying with his beloved six-shooter. A brainstorm entered his almost empty skull and he decided to shoot out the light ... suddenly there was a blinding flash, a crash of broken glass, and a smoke-filled room ... he was immediately disarmed before he could cause further damage, and, seized by two irate men, was used, in lieu of a vacuum cleaner, for dusting the ranch floor."

Other incidents were less amusing. On one occasion Fred Ings and some cowboys were spending the night at the Little Log Hotel in High River. Weary after a long ride, they spread their bedrolls on the floor of a room in which a poker game was underway. Ings was suddenly awakened by loud and angry voices and the noise of a chair crashing over. He opened his eyes to see two men facing each other across the table, with guns drawn. Ings called to them and suggested that they settle the dispute outside. The two men went out protesting and arguing, but there was no shooting.

In 1885 the Macleod *Gazette* reported a fight between two cowboys from the Walrond Ranche, named Thompson and Wright, under this wordy headline; "The Six-Shooter again is called in to settle a dispute and does it most effectually—one man seriously wounded—the victor leaves for the sunny south." The story went on to note that "shooting seems well on the highway to becoming a common pastime in the vicinity of Macleod." That, however, was not the end of the affair. The following week, Thompson, the wounded party in the incident, published a letter in the newspaper disputing the reporter's facts. Only five shots were fired, according to Thompson, not six, and Wright had been the aggressor, trying to strike Thompson over the head with a gun when accused by Thompson of spreading untrue stories about him.

L.V. Kelly recorded an amazing incident in the quiet Mormon town of Cardston. A young woman, angered that a man was impugning her reputation, took a gun in hand, tracked the culprit down, and confronted him on the town's main street. Forcing him to his knees, she extracted a confession and apology from the villain, who promptly repaired to the local detachment of the Mounted Police and insisted that a charge of assault be laid against the young woman.

Guns were easy to obtain and they were used. While the rampant violence of the American west did not spread into Canada, thanks to the presence of the Mounted Police, there were still enough sensational and brutal crimes—murders, robberies, and assaults—to frighten and anger the population. But there were also practical and essential uses for firearms. A six-shooter was particularly valuable for turning cattle during a stampede, killing injured animals, scaring off range studs, and rifles for hunting the wolves that were a constant menace to the herds. The wearing of side-arms in towns, however, was discouraged by the Mounted Police; though the practice continued in the

Cypress Hills country even after the turn of the century, it had disappeared elsewhere by the late 1890s.

Guns may have been useful adjuncts, but horses were the very instrument of the cowboy's work. There was a saying in the west that a man who did not love his mount did not last long on the range. Indeed, the horse was more than just a work animal—it was frequently the critical factor in life-or-death situations, whether during a stampede or in a blinding snowstorm. Many range country tales revolved around a faithful horse that saved its rider from certain death in a raging blizzard by returning home long after the cowboy had lost all sense of direction or slipped into delirium or unconsciousness while still in the saddle.

To be stranded on the plains without a horse, far from water or assistance, could be fatal. Early range cattle were frequently half-wild animals, accustomed to men on horseback, but to whom men on foot were strange and threatening. Horses were absolutely essential for handling these cattle and keeping out of their way. Horse thievery was thus a great crime in the cattle country—particularly in the United States—and in some parts of the cattle country horse thieves often received far more severe penalties than other lawbreakers.

The cowboy was seldom deliberately cruel to his horse and generally treated it in a manner appropriate to its value. Ranch managers, however, were sometimes reluctant to hire cowboys who had their own horses, thinking they would not get enough work from them; most ranches provided their hands with strings of five or six of their own horses for work.

The first horses in the cattle country were descendants of stray Spanish animals in Mexico. Over the centuries these strays, often called ponies, evolved into small but strong and well-adapted horses. The Indians soon learned to use horses as well (their ponies were called cayuses), and this development ushered in the golden age of the plains natives.

Wild range horses were not well suited for long-sustained work, however, and two or three might be needed by a cowboy in the course of his daily work, especially on a roundup or trail drive. Towards the end of the 19th century, efforts were made to breed horses better suited for various tasks to which they were put, giving rise to a whole new aspect of ranching.

One of the first spring activities in the cattle country was breaking horses. A herd of horses which had been running wild and free on the range was brought in and the biggest and best animals were cut out. Then began a period of intense training to halter-break and gentle the animals to make them suitable either as work horses or cowponies. There were men who travelled the country specializing in breaking horses. These were the famed bronc-busters, or bronc-twisters. Most large ranches also had one or two men of their own who had earned reputations for their bronc-busting abilities. The profession was a dangerous one, for while a good man might break many horses without injury to himself, one bad horse could do enough damage to a rider to end his career. Most bronc-busters got pretty churned up from the jolts they absorbed, and many seemed to leave their vocations soon after they married. Bronc-busting was not the sort of duty the ordinary cowboy took upon himself.

One method of catching a horse was frontfooting. This involved roping the horse by the forefeet and then throwing it down on its side. The procedure was preferred by many skilled bronc-busters, as it was less likely to injure the horse. A horse roped around the neck was liable to panic, because it felt it was being choked. Indeed, the method was called "choking down."

The routine for breaking horses varied among ranches and bronc-busters. In the early days on the range many riders simply attempted to get a bridle and saddle on the horse, mount and stick on the animal, and then let time and hard riding do the rest. But the usual procedure began by driving a green horse into a circular corral of poles, in the centre of which was a stout post. The round corral kept the bronc-breaker within a short roping distance of the horse and allowed him to keep the animal moving around more easily. The cowboy threw a loop around the horse's neck and snubbed the rope securely to the post with one or two wraps. As the horse continued to run around the corral, the roper turned with him, always keeping the rope securely snubbed. Once the horse quieted down after fighting and backing off the rope, the cowboy talked gently to it, often rubbing and patting it to show that he meant no harm.

The next step in the breaking process was to make the horse familiar and comfortable with a bridle. The first bridle put on the horse was in most cases a special one called a war bridle; it was simply a rope with a loop large enough to fit in the horse's mouth and usually wrapped with a piece of cloth to prevent injury. Pulling on the bridle, the horse-breaker led the animal around the corral until it followed easily. Then the horse was turned loose in the corral for the rest of the day to give it a chance to recover from its initial handling.

The next day the procedure continued. Sometimes to gentle the animal, the bronc-buster would take a sack and rub the horse all over so that the animal would become accustomed to things touching it. Some cowboys would also do the same with a rain slicker, which a rider might wear in a storm or heavy wind. If the horse responded badly to the slicker, the bronc-buster might swat it all over with the garment until it learned to stand still. After the horse became used to the war bridle, a regular bridle with a metal bit or mouthpiece and leather reins was put on the horse.

During the next stage of breaking, the bronc-buster required steady assistance. While one man held the reins of the bridle, the bronc-buster eased a saddle onto the horse's back. Once the animal got used to the saddle, the bronc-buster prepared to mount. To distract the horse, he twisted one of its ears, then climbed into the saddle.

Naturally, the horse got excited when a rider first swung onto its back, but a good bronc-buster always tried to keep the horse from getting its head down to buck. The rider pulled tightly on the reins, drawing the horse into a spin, then loosened them enough so that the horse could trot around the corral. Of course, some horses exploded into bucking when first mounted, despite all of the bronc-buster's efforts, and it was essential for the rider to maintain his seat and prevent the horse from getting the upper hand. The bronc-buster did not always win this particular battle, either. But he had to encourage a horse to do the right thing and discourage it from doing the wrong. When the animal bucked, the bronc-buster whipped it with a quirt, a short-handled riding whip with a braided leather lash. When the horse quieted down, it was petted and talked to as a reward for its good behaviour.

In the final stage, the corral gate was thrown open and the horse taken out onto the range. Although it might still try to buck or run, eventually it settled down. The bronc-buster always liked to have another cowboy, called the hazer, nearby, to help him keep clear of fences and pick him up in case he found himself unexpectedly on foot.

After a horse was broken its mane and tail might be trimmed. This not only improved the animal's appearance, but helped set it apart from green horses when they were loose together on the range.

Johnny Franklin, a short, heavily muscled Texan, was considered to be one of the best, if not the best, bronc-buster in the North West. Franklin arrived in southern Alberta in 1888 and worked for the usual wages on the Frank Strong ranch for a while. When he heard that the foreman was willing to pay $75 a month for a bronc-buster to get his horses ready for the Mounted Police, the young Texan asked to try his hand at the job, but was turned down. He persisted, however, until the foreman finally gave him a chance. Franklin so impressed his boss with his skillful and graceful riding that he got a bronc-busting job then and there, and stayed on the ranch in that position for nine years.

According to L.V. Kelly, Franklin was such a natural rider—riding on balance and using no more muscle than required—that he was appointed judge of the bucking competition at the first Calgary Stampede. On that occasion a friend asked Franklin how he would make a decision if two men should tie. The venerable Franklin, astonished that a sensible man should even ask such a question, simply replied, "I'll just ride both them horses my-self. That's the only way to find which bucks hardest."

Franklin was never thrown from a horse, a distinction some people also accorded to John Ware. In comparing the styles of these two famous riders, L.V. Kelly wrote that " ... Ware rode awkwardly, though with great efficiency. The great negro would bounce all over his horse's back, holding by clutch of knees alone, bounding, rocking, laughing, but staying. Johnny Franklin rode with an easy grace that made him seem part of the horse, and as he rode he raked the fighting animal from tail to ear with his big spurs."

Bert Sheppard recalled that Herb Millar of the Bar U also rode "some of the worst outlaws in his day and made it look as if it was very easy ... and a lot of people thought he was the best rider in the country ..."

Frank Ricks, another well-known bronc-buster, arrived in Alberta from Oregon in 1883 in charge of a herd of 250 horses. Ricks worked for a while on the Mount Royal Ranche west of Calgary, but then set up his own opera-tion near Cochrane. One day he arrived on foot at the Cochrane Ranche at Big Hill and asked for the loan of a horse. William Kerfoot offered him a dark chestnut known to be a long-standing outlaw with a thousand different twists and an intense hatred of men. But Ricks calmly saddled the animal and rode the brute until it could hardly stand, much to the astonishment of Kerfoot—and the horse.

The cowboy's routine varied with the seasons. Winter was generally a slack time and most large ranches released many of their hands after the fall roundup. Some of these men, now out of work, did odd jobs in nearby towns such as High River, Medicine Hat, or Maple Creek, often working for little more than their board. Others went on the grub line, drifting from ranch to ranch, picking up a few meals before moving on again. Sometimes they did a few chores or small tasks on the ranches in exchange for food. Winter was a time of insecurity, and many cowboys had plenty of time to contemplate the nature of their life. As Supt. R. Burton Deane of the North-West Mounted Police said, "The chances and changes of a cowboy's life must be seen to be appreciated."

For those men fortunate enough to be retained by a ranch throughout the winter, much time might be passed in the bunkhouse, often little more than a well-chinked log shack that kept out the cold wind. (Most of the ranch houses were little better.) If the operation employed many cowboys, there was a cookhouse near the bunkhouse; on smaller ranches, the cowboys ate with the rancher and his family. On still other ranches, the cowboys might eat in the ranch house, but in a separate dining room.

The bunkhouse smelled of sweat, manure, Bull Durham tobacco, and smoke from cigarettes and coal-oil lamps. Sets of bunks leaned against the walls, while in the centre of the room stood a large pot-belly stove which had to be kept fired up continuously during the cold winter days and nights. A shelf or two near the door held pails for water, a basin for washing, and assorted tins for soap, tobacco, tools, and other items. Pegs in the walls held bridles, ropes, and clothes. Although life in the bunkhouse could be boring at times, there were always card games to play, saddles and other gear to repair, and perhaps some books or newspapers to read. The living conditions may have been fairly primitive, but then, except during the winter, ranchers did not expect their hands to spend time in the bunkhouse, anyway.

There was always work to do, even during the freezing winter. Cowboys had to check the cattle from time to time to ensure that they were not starving or freezing. Waterholes had to be chopped in the ice so that the stock could drink, and often cowboys had to venture out in cold weather, searching for lost animals in thickly falling snow and icy winds. During winter storms cattle turned their backs and drifted with the wind; then the cowboys had to go out and herd the animals back onto their ranges before they piled up against fences and in coulees, or fell on ice and injured themselves. In later years they put out feed for the livestock. Although the ranchers might let the cattle rustle grass during the winter, there were always times when the weather got too severe, or the snow too deep, to leave the animals on their own.

Blizzards, snow blindness, and frostbite were constant hazards on the winter range. Jim Dunlap of the Cochrane Ranche was considered one of the finest cowboys in the country. One winter he froze his feet while travelling from Fort Macleod to the ranch. He was taken to the hospital in Fort Macleod and might have recovered, but when he was told that he would lose both feet, he gave up and died within two days. Another tragic death occurred in 1891, when Constable Herron of the Mounted Police suffered snow blindness while on patrol, and wandered aimlessly over the plains. He, too, apparently gave up because with his last strength he shot himself, never knowing he was only a mile from the sanctuary of a warm ranch house.

Everyone looked forward to a chinook blowing in and breaking the icy grip of winter. The anticipation was almost palpable. R.D. Symons, a cowboy and rancher in southern Saskatchewan, remembered the coming of a chinook:

> It might be −30°, and we'd roll in, with extra blankets or buffalo robes tucked around us … At midnight we might wake feeling too warm, and wondering if the old barrel stove had burned too furiously. One of us

would get up to investigate—no, the big logs were only smouldering. We'd try to sleep again, but sleep wouldn't come. We'd puff cigarettes in the dark and talk. Then someone would say—"Must be going to chinook."

The chinook meant that for a few hours, or maybe even days, cowboys could escape the claustrophobic confines of the bunkhouse. The cattle could leave their shelter and wander onto the prairie. The air and the earth smelled fresh and the trials of a prairie winter could temporarily be put out of mind.

Calving season coincided with the unpredictable storms of March and April. Again cowboys rode over the range, checking for cows having difficulty with calving; many cows gave birth with cowboys as midwives. The new calves were sometimes identified by their owners with a mark which cowboys cut on the ears—perhaps an undercrop (a notch on the lower part of the ear), on overcrop (on the upper part), a grub (the tip of the ear cut off), or any number of different combinations on one or both ears. The earmarks were particularly helpful during the roundup, when hundreds of cows and calves were mixed together.

As spring spread over the plains and foothills, melting the last vestiges of snow and ice, the pace of activity quickened. Rivers and creeks rose as melting snow swelled their courses. The runoff collected in sloughs and sinkholes, and the cattle, tramping in the mud at their waterholes, often became mired. In such cases the cowboy would have to throw a rope around the animal's horns, wrap the other end around the horn on his saddle, and pull the critter out, only to be rewarded most times with a fierce charge and outraged bellow from an ungrateful cow.

Early in the spring the men on the range began to think about the annual roundup. Usually there were two roundups during the year, a big general one in the spring for branding the year's calf crop and returning stray cattle to their home ranges, and a smaller one in the fall for gathering the mature steers for shipment to market. The first real roundup on the North West range took place in 1879 around Fort Macleod. It was a small affair compared to the great operations of later days, with only 16 men and one wagon, and they collected about five hundred to six hundred cattle, which was less than they had placed on the range. The men on this roundup had a few provisions in their wagon, and to supplement their rations they collected wild duck eggs from the sloughs they passed. Since they were not too sure what might be inside the eggs, they boiled them for a long time so that anything inside would be well cooked.

As the great leases were taken up in the early 1880s and more cattle were placed on the range, a general roundup was organized, the first one taking place in 1884. (One of the purposes of an organized general roundup was to prevent some ranchers from having first claim to all the new unbranded calves running free. In the United States ranchers who started working their own cattle—and other ranchers' cattle, perhaps—before the official start of the roundup were known as "sooners.") Originally, one general roundup in the North West covered all of the occupied range, but as the cattle industry continued to expand, the roundup was broken into districts: Fort Macleod, Pincher Creek, Willow Creek, and High River. Later, additional districts were added at Medicine Hat and on the lower Red Deer River, Cypress Hills and Whitemud River ranges. Each district sent a representative to neighbouring district roundups to look after any of its members' cattle which might be found there. The largest general roundup on the North West range occurred in 1885. The operation included 100 men, 15 chuckwagons and 500 saddle horses, and gathered about 60,000 cattle.

For the 1884 roundup, each of the major participating ranches sent its own outfit, consisting of a chuckwagon with cook-driver, a bed wagon, and a number of cowboys with their strings of horses. The horses on a roundup were called a cavvy, and they were placed in the charge of one or two cowboys known as wranglers. There might be five or six horses for each hand on a roundup—two or three for circle riding and different mounts for cutting, swimming, and night herding. Each ranch sent men and horses in proportion to the number of cattle which it had on its books. Smaller ranchers combined their resources and sent a "pool" wagon with their cowboys and horses. On the 1884 roundup there were eight outfits, consisting of thirty or forty cowboys and one hundred and fifty to two hundred horses.

Early in the spring the ranchers gathered to choose one of their foremen as roundup captain, or boss, who then fixed the time and place where the various outfits would meet. In 1884 the cowboys and wagons assembled at Fort Macleod where they worked out final plans for covering the country—all ten thousand square miles of it—and gathering the cattle. Half of the outfits were placed under Frank Strong, manager of the I.G. Baker Ranch at Fort Macleod, and half under Jim Dunlap of the Cochrane Ranche. Then all the outfits moved south to the boundary and began to work their way north. Dunlap led his men to the west and north, and Strong, to the east and north. They took two months to cover the range as far up as High River.

The chuckwagons were the focus of the roundup as they moved ahead each day to a new campsite selected by the captain. There were usually several wagons in the roundup, and they camped some distance apart, far enough for their outfits' wranglers to keep their horses separate, but close enough for co-operation during the day for range work.

The cook was a very important man on the roundup. Besides his cooking chores, he had to handle the four-horse team that hauled his chuckwagon safely and punctually from one campsite to the next. The chuckwagon carried all the food, barrels of drinking water in dry country, and the pots and pans for cooking. Many times extra firewood was strapped underneath the wagon, particularly when the roundup moved into open country where wood was scarce. The big endgate at the back let down, and hinged legs on either side of the gate provided support, making a solid work surface. A collection of drawers and shelves inside the rear of the wagon held the cook's staple supplies and utensils.

The cook needed extraordinary culinary skills, for there was usually little variety in the provisions with which he had to work, particularly near the end of roundups and trail drives. He had to prepare meals for 10 to 15 hungry men; and as the cowboys were quick to complain about any real or perceived shortcomings in the food, he also needed a thick skin. Because of the importance of food to hard-working men, and to keep them contented, ranchers were careful to hire only the best cooks. Charlie Lehr was an outstanding, almost legendary cook. He usually handled the Bar U wagon, and there were never any words heard against him or his cooking. Good cooks also tended to be fussy housekeepers on the range, working with a minimum of bother and keeping things well organized and in their places.

The cook had a helper who drove a second wagon containing bedrolls, spare saddles, bridles, clothing, ropes, tents, and other gear. Once everything had been piled into the wagon, the driver stretched canvas over the load and tightly lashed it. There was rough country to cross, with no roads, and no shops nearby to replace items which might drop off or bounce out.

The day started early, well before daylight brightened the sky at five o'clock on a spring morning. There was plenty of activity as the cowboys crawled out of their bedrolls and collected their equipment in the cool prairie dampness. The cook had already prepared a hearty breakfast and summoned the men to eat with calls of "Grub pile!" or "Come and get 'er or I'll throw it in the mud." Pulling out their tin plates and piling them high with hot meat, potatoes, bread and jam, the cowboys sat on the ground or their bedrolls around the chuckwagon or in a tent. They tended to eat quickly, wasting no time in idle conversation or lingering over cups of the cook's strong, black coffee. (According to Faye Ward, one coffee recipe called for two pounds of coffee in two gallons of water. "Boil two hours then throw a horseshoe into the pot and if it sinks, the coffee is not yet done.")

After breakfast the night wrangler drove the cavvy into a corral formed by heavy ropes strung between the chuckwagon and bed wagon and supported all around with forked stocks. Lariats whistled through the air as the cowboys roped their first horses of the day. The roundup captain then detailed the men in twos and threes to sweep and search the country. Out they rode, seldom hurrying but maintaining a good, steady pace. One of the first lessons a good cowboy learned was to slow down so that his horse would be in condition for speed if the necessity arose; besides, cowboys in a hurry could quickly run off the gain on good beef.

The cowboys, or circle riders as they were called for this job, fanned out from the chuckwagon and worked their way back to its new location. Often there appeared to be a few cattle on the open range, but the riders searched along the coulee bottoms, in the brush and behind the hills. Cattle did not graze in compact herds, but gathered in small groups at favourite waterholes, springs, or grazing areas. By mid-morning the circle riders brought the first cattle into the new camp, threw them into the growing main herd nearby and then went back out to continue the search.

By early afternoon the circle rides were largely completed and most of the cowboys were back at the chuckwagon for dinner. After eating their meal they picked out their cutting horses from the cavvy, horses specially trained to separate individual cattle from the large herd into which the cattle that had been gathered in the morning had been placed. Cowboys from each outfit cut out all the cattle with their brands; the unbranded calves usually stuck close to their mothers or were identified by their earmarks. These cattle were moved off to a separate herd and held loosely by circling riders.

Now the hot, dirty work began, and for cowboys it often called for a change of boots. Each outfit built a branding fire near its separate herd. The fire was tended by a man who made sure the irons were neither too hot nor too cold to do the job properly. Too hot an iron often resulted in blotched brands—parts of the brand running together—and serious injury to the animal's flesh. Too cold an iron would not penetrate the hide to leave a lasting brand. Another man rode quietly through the herd, roping unbranded calves by the heels and dragging them towards the fire. There, two more cowboys, called "wrestlers," worked down the taut rope to the calf, grasped the animal firmly and threw it down, usually on its right side. Brands were most commonly applied on the left side of the calf—58 of the 67 brands registered in Fort Macleod in 1888 were on the left. This custom stemmed from the observation that cattle always turned right and milled that way in a corral, making it easier to check brands that were on the left side. One wrestler held down the calf while the other performed the various operations—branding, castrating, and sometimes earmarking. The pain for the animals seemed to be brief, because after everything was done the calves quickly recovered their feet and ran off to join their mothers. The clean, dry air of the plains helped the wounds heal rapidly, so infection was not a major problem. Occasionally, a cow, angered by the pathetic bawling of her calf, stirred up a little excitement by charging into the centre of things, scattering men, irons, and equipment.

Sometimes calves were taken directly out of the main herd and the wrestlers or roper simply called for the appropriate iron from the fire. If a calf had become separated from its mother, the earmark could be referred to for identification. If the wrong brand was placed on one calf, the error could always be corrected by marking the next animal with the missed brand. Some of the roundup organizations of later years also built corrals at strategic places on the range to facilitate branding operations. The fence poles, however, were frequently too tempting for some of the homesteaders on the treeless plains and quickly disappeared.

As the roundup progressed, the herd—actually a group of herds—expanded as more cattle were gathered in. At a certain point, however, the herd began to shrink. As the roundup reached various home ranges, those respective herds dropped out. Additional cattle for that range were certain to be picked up later, but they would be driven back to their home range at the conclusion of the roundup. Whenever the roundup moved onto a new range, the foreman of that range or ranch took temporary control, as he was the person most familiar with the area.

By evening the heavy work was over and the cowboys gathered around their chuckwagons for supper, a meal perhaps of salt pork, canned tomatoes, black beans, bread and more coffee. Milk was practically always of the canned variety. When the captain allowed a steer to be butchered, cowboys were treated to fresh beef. By the end of supper it was late evening. The men might play some cards or otherwise entertain themselves for a while, but they turned in early; they had spent a hard day, and they had another one like it waiting for them.

Cowboys on the roundup never got enough sleep, but they somehow developed the knack for catching rest whenever and wherever they could. Putting their stirrups over their saddles, they covered up their gear with slickers to keep off the dew, laid out their bedrolls in the sleeping tent or by the wagons, and crawled into bed.

Two men, besides the night wrangler, could not yet look forward to the luxury of sleep and rest. The night herders took fresh horses, tied to a wagon wheel by the day wrangler, and rode out to watch the cattle. "Oh, those night shifts!" remembered Fred Ings. Sometimes they passed in rain or snow; they were nearly always at least cold and uncomfortable and lonely. When the cattle were quiet, there was not enough activity to keep the herders warm, and when the herd was restless, or kept on the move by rain or snow, there was plenty of hard riding for already tired men.

The night herders circled the cattle in opposite directions, throwing back any animals that had worked themselves out of the herd. Singing or whistling seemed to settle the cattle, but the guards had to be careful not to light matches or make sudden movements nearby, because even the swish of a slicker might spook the herd. Cattle most frequently stampeded at night, when they could not see what was going on around them. The guards checked the passage of the night hours by watching the stars in the infinite dome of prairie sky, searching out the Big Dipper and Polaris, whose movements were more accurate and reliable than any timepiece. And there were the ever-present sounds of the night—the cud-chewing and soft blowing of hundreds of cattle, the occasional click of horns, the wail of a coyote. After two to four hours the night herders' shift was done and they returned to the wagons one at a time as the men of the second shift took their place.

By the final stage of the roundup, around late June or early July, all the cattle had been gathered up, the new calves branded and the various outfits had driven their separate herds back to their home ranges. By this time the rivers and creeks running out from the foothills and mountains were at their highest, swollen with meltwater from the high country. Getting the herds across these streams was often a problem. If the cattle would not follow a rider across the river, the cowboys had to cut out a small bunch, hold them tightly together, and then charge them across before they had time to turn back. The rest of the cattle were crowded into the river close behind, with only a mass of heads visible above the churning water. Fast streams presented an additional problem, as the cattle tended to drift downstream with the current. Then, one or two cowboys usually rode with the cattle across the river on the downstream side of the animals, trying to keep them from drifting too far. A safe place to land was carefully selected, otherwise there was great danger of the cattle being swept away and drowning. Crossing a river was a noisy affair, the calves bawling loudly when they struck the cold water, and the mothers in turn bellowing for their young. But once the herd was across and took to grazing on the other side, peace of a sort descended on the range once again.

Once they were back on their own ranges, the cattle were left to graze until the autumn, when they were rounded up again, the mature steers cut out for market and the rest placed on their winter range or feeding ground. The fall roundup was not nearly so strenuous. The cattle did not stray as far during the summer, when there were fewer storms to drive them from their range. Also, branding during the fall roundup was confined to a few late-born calves, or those that had been missed in the spring.

Although the spring roundup was a long and hard job, it was the great event on the range, and cowboys invariably look back on it nostalgically. Despite the long and busy days, the cold and damp nights, and the discomforts and strains, there was the opportunity for visiting, since the roundup brought together cowboys from all the ranches as did no other event. It was a time for swapping stories, pitting their horses against others' in races, showing off their skills, and playing practical jokes. The very strain of the daily work made the moments of relaxation and fun all the more intense and precious.

The pace of work slackened after spring roundup. While some cowboys worked around the ranch buildings—repairing corrals, cutting hay, doing odd jobs—others went on line duty, riding the range and keeping a check on the cattle. The large ranches set up cow camps, a tent or cabin at some distant point on their range, where the line rider made his headquarters; it was impossible to look after thousands of acres from the home place alone. Line riding was not an exciting task; indeed, if life in the bunkhouse was dull and lonely, a summer at the cow camp could be almost intolerably so.

Before he rode out on his solitary duty, the line rider gathered together essential supplies—sowbelly (salt pork), flour, baking powder, salt, coffee, a bag of black beans, tobacco and beef jerky (strips of meat dried over a fire until the outside was dry and hard, but the inside tender and juicy)—and loaded his grub and equipment on a packhorse. Then he wrapped some extra clothes in his bedroll and tied this bundle behind his saddle.

As barbed wire fence came into widespread use and the ranges were enclosed, summer work included riding the fence for breaks and keeping it in good repair. Fences stretched endlessly in all directions, broken every mile or so by a range gate where the cattle and riders could pass through. The gate, typically with twenty-foot posts and a crossbar, made it easier for riders to spot an opening in the fence, saving them the frustration of fruitlessly following the fence in the wrong direction, and also discouraging others from cutting their way through the wire when they wanted to pass.

The cowboy's social life was limited by the character of his job. During the spring, summer, and fall he spent most of his time far from the social amenities of towns and cities. And especially in the early days, there was a great shortage of single white women in the North West. The range was men's country, and most of the few women in the area were already married.

The classic cattle towns of the American west developed where a major cattle trail met a railway. At these places the men on the long cattle drives were

released and paid off. After months on the trail they were ready for excitement and able to afford it. In Canada it was not much different. Calgary, Fort
Macleod, Medicine Hat, and Maple Creek all became important points for
shipping cattle and receiving supplies, and, of course, took on many of the
characteristics of cattle towns. Cattle were even driven down Ninth Avenue
in Calgary while citizens lined the street, watching the excitement, giving the
cowboys a hand now and then, and shooing strays out of their gardens and
yards.

After weeks or months of chasing cattle many cowboys headed straight
for the bright lights of the towns to chase good times. With their wages in
their pockets they wanted to let off some steam—to drink, shoot pool, talk,
and visit the "sporting houses." For two, three, or five dollars, a cowboy might
have his choice of women in a house which nurtured an atmosphere of homey
comfort and hospitality, with proper parlour, kitchen, tastefully decorated
bedrooms, and a Chinese cook, who was always called "boy." It was all very
comfortable, not to say luxurious, at least compared with the bunkhouse and
the line camp.

In a country where men so outnumbered women, cowboys and other
settlers visited the brothels without embarrassment. Many considered the
brothels of Lethbridge to be in a class by themselves. The Lethbridge houses
occupied a triangular spit of land called The Point, which jutted out into the
Oldman Coulee on the west side of town. The madames of Lethbridge were
always happy to welcome the men from the range and ensure that they had a
good time. There were more complaints from the townsfolk about the loud,
happy singing and piano playing from The Point than about the trade itself.
The women in the houses liked the cowboys, who had a reputation for being
freer with their money than the local miners and other workers who made up
the rest of their customers.

Every prairie town had its bars. Maple Creek, in Saskatchewan, was the
service centre for an area stretching from the South Saskatchewan River to the
international boundary. Supt. R. Burton Deane may have remembered Maple
Creek as a "funny little Methodist-ridden place," but R.D. Symons recalled
that the Maple Leaf Hotel there had one of the longest and showiest saloons
in the North West, with lots of shiny mirrors and a gleaming mahogany bar.
Polished brass spittoons were placed at intervals for the convenience of the
"chawing" public, and the usual brass footrail ran along the front of the bar.

One evening five riders from the 76 Ranch decided to raid the Maple
Leaf Hotel. One cowboy got on his horse and galloped up the wooden sidewalk, sending splinters flying in every direction, rode into the bar and threw
a loop at the piano player. That adroit fellow ducked and fled for cover just

in time, and the cowboy roped the piano instead. Hunching his horse down, he dragged the instrument to the door where it inconveniently got stuck. Just then a Mounted Police constable appeared and demanded, "What all is this?"

"Well," answered the cheery cowboy, "it's what it looks like, I guess." His friends attempted to defend him and were supported with the sympathetic intervention of the bartender, who assured the Mountie that everyone was just having a good time; the cowboy was allowed to leave town—after he had paid for the sidewalk.

Claresholm was the setting for a celebrated incident in July 1904, in which farce and near-tragedy livened up the quiet little town growing within the old range country and gave the local editors an opportunity to display their finest literary styles. "Cowboy Runs Amuck" ran the headline in the Macleod *Gazette*, which then went on to report the details. (Shortly afterwards, the cowboy's father complained in a letter to the editor that the report was biased "according to the police version.") The *Gazette* described the cowboy, known only as Gallagher, as

> a young man of 23 years, raised on the prairies of southern Alberta and, of course, a typical westerner. Westerners are all supposed to be bold bad men at any time. When sober Gallagher is an industrious, peaceable fellow. When drinking, however, he becomes a veritable raving maniac, and his one great ambition is to rope the whole North-West Mounted Police force.

The Lethbridge *Herald* dubbed Gallagher "a certain knight of the lariat." It went on to report that he

> came into Claresholm and was surprised … to see it looking like a farming town, so much so that he thought he would show the people they were extremely slow and wanted waking up.
>
> Having got well primed, he rode his bronco into the Wilton Hotel and demanded a drink, which, on account of obfuscated condition, the proprietor refused, whereat the cowboy fired a few shots through the ceiling by way of a start. This caused the proprietor to take refuge in the cellar or somewhere else for fear of his life.
>
> After a lope around the town to the accompaniment of guns the wild man retired to a shack on the outskirts of town for a rest. A "forlorn hope" was enrolled to take him dead or alive, which approached the aforesaid shack on tiptoe and one of the party, bolder than the rest, having opened the door peeped in and found the boy asleep. The

"forlorn hope" then made a rush and the cowboy was seized, pinioned and conducted to the barracks.

Here the cowboy was too much for the North-West Mounted Police as, having been permitted to emerge from his cell on some pretext or other he observed a police gun on the wall, possessed himself of it, over-awed the constable and issued forth again thirsting for blood.

As it happened, however, the only blood shed was that of the cowboy himself for the constable got his rifle and on the prisoner refusing the put up his hand put a bullet through his arm.

This was probably the last serious display of cowboy effervescence in Claresholm although there have been some mild outbreaks since—without firearms however.

Chapter Eleven

SOCIETY AND CULTURE ON THE RANGE

For ten years Fort Macleod was the capital of the cattle kingdom in southern Alberta. As the local headquarters of the North-West Mounted Police, the settlement was not only an important administrative centre, but also an important livestock market. Its connections with Fort Benton, Montana, and the Missouri River made it a transportation, communications, and distribution hub. During the 1870s all mail from southern Alberta passed through Forts Macleod and Benton, and required not Canadian but U.S. postage. Fort Macleod was close to the Pincher Creek area with its numerous and early ranches, and most herds being driven to ranges farther north passed within shouting distance of the town.

The varied backgrounds of the inhabitants of this plains outpost gave Fort Macleod a flavour unique in the southwest. There were probably more characters per capita in that little settlement than in any other centre on the Canadian prairies. Ex-whisky traders, such as Fred Kanouse and Harry Taylor, went legitimate and rubbed shoulders with the Mounted Police, many of whom were just as adventurous as the old traders. Indians from the nearby Blood and Peigan reserves mingled with local ranchers, cowboys, and assorted adventurers.

Not all the citizens in the area, however, found Fort Macleod all that pleasing. Mary Inderwick of the North Fork Ranch on the Oldman River described the settlement as "one of the last places to live in all the world. It is on a bare flat spot high above the [Oldman] River, covered with small stones which the never-ceasing wind drives hither and thither with little clouds of dust ... the effect is disheartening in the extreme. How the people live here happily I do not know." Evelyn Galt Springett, wife of Arthur R. Springett, manager of the Oxley, was hardly more enthusiastic: "There were, of course, a number of ... delightful people in Macleod, but the place itself had little to recommend it, for it consisted of only a few wooden buildings scattered over a bald and stormy waste, with a fierce wind always blowing a gale." Nor was Alexander Staveley Hill especially impressed by the town: "We reached Fort Macleod, and I made my first acquaintance with that somewhat grandly named town, the big type of whose name on the map had inspired me with a certain respect for its importance, and I was not a little surprised to find the town represented by a wide, muddy lane, with a row of dirty, half-finished wooden shanties flanking each side." Although doing business with shop-keepers was certainly not Hill's style, he did acknowledge, perhaps somewhat grudgingly, that the businessmen of Fort Macleod did such business as "would gladden the heart of many a shopkeeper in a country town in England, aye, if he could put his net profit at even one-fourteenth of that which rolled into the pockets of the possessor of one of these shanties."

For many years the most prominent trading firm in Fort Macleod was the I.G. Baker Company, one of the great business houses of Fort Benton. The company was already operating in southern Alberta even before the ar-rival of the Mounted Police in 1874. It took its merchandise to the Indians and shifted its trading posts from one part of the country to another. Alfred B. Hamilton, who built Fort Whoop-Up with Johnny Healy, was a nephew of Baker, and the company possibly underwrote some of the costs of that venture. Hamilton was later elected to the Montana legislature.

After the Mounted Police arrived in 1874 and largely put a stop to the miserable whisky trade, the I.G. Baker Company opened stores in Fort Macleod and at Fort Walsh in the Cypress Hills, and later in Calgary. The company's interests encompassed a wide field: merchandising, transportation, banking, and provisioning the Mounted Police and the Indians. The com-pany also owned a ranch near Fort Macleod, managed by Frank Strong.

In 1882 the I.G. Baker Company partners formed the Benton and St. Louis Cattle Company, with a starting capital of $50,000. Within a few years, the company ran the largest herd in Montana, and in 1886 moved part of its herd to Canada where it secured a lease of about 150,000 acres between the Oldman and Little Bow rivers. It shipped in 82 Hereford bulls from the east, and set up headquarters in Lethbridge. The company was popularly known as the Circle outfit, because of its brand, a large circle.

When the I.G. Baker Company sold its mercantile business to the Hudson's Bay Company in 1891, the news brought forth this tribute from the Macleod *Gazette*:

> To the struggling ranchman, just starting in business, they [I.G. Baker Company] have never refused to extend a helping hand; many a busi-

nessman in the country has been enabled to tide over his difficulties through timely assistance from I.G. Baker and Co ... words fail us in attempting to voice the general feeling of gratitude of I.G. Baker & Co. which exists in this country.

And F.W. Godsal, an early rancher in the Pincher Creek district, wrote,

> I.G. Baker and Co. had the true western spirit and were liberal minded. Their store at Fort Macleod was our hotel. They loaned us the blankets off the shelves and would say, "It is your fault if you sleep cold; we only ask you to fold them up in the morning and put them back on the shelf."

One early resident of Fort Macleod who brought together some of the settlement's diverse elements was D.W. Davis. A tall, striking man with clear-cut features and a thick black beard, Davis was a native of Vermont. He moved west in 1867 at the age of 22 and served as Quartermaster Sergeant in the United States Army. At Fort Benton he became associated with Johnny Healy and Alfred Hamilton, undertaking many trading excursions for them into Canada, and they later placed him in charge of their posts at Fort Whoop-Up and on the lower Elbow River.

During the spring of 1873 a young Indian, Not Real Good, arrived at the Elbow River post, with his thumb and wrist slashed by a knife and a bullet wound in his shoulder. A brother of Red Crow, chief of the Bloods, Not Real Good had been shot and stabbed by another of his brothers during a family feud exacerbated by heavy drinking. Davis dressed the wound, made a bed for the man, and tended him for several weeks, until he was well enough to travel again. Not Real Good presented Davis with a fine horse in gratitude for his care. Later, Davis courted and married Not Real Good's sister, Revenge Walker.

In 1874 Davis was in charge of Fort Whoop-Up when the North-West Mounted Police arrived, but was absent from the fort at the time. The police moved up the Oldman River, then returned to the fort, at which time they were greeted and entertained by Davis. Like many of the early traders, Davis took on a new role after the Mounted Police arrived, and he became the representative of the I.G. Baker Company of Fort Benton. He helped the police build their fort at Fort Macleod and also put up and stocked a store nearby for his company. In 1875 he followed the police to the confluence of the Elbow and Bow rivers and contracted to construct the police fort at Fort Calgary. Just south of the fort, he built another store for I.G. Baker, and remained general manager of the Alberta operations of the company until it sold out to the Hudson's Bay Company in 1891.

Davis and Revenge Walker had four children, three boys and a girl. Two of the boys attended Trinity College School in Port Hope, Ontario, and served with the Mounted Police Rifles in South Africa during the Boer War before returning to Alberta to farm. The third boy became a chief on the Blood Reserve, and the girl moved to Seattle after her marriage. With the pressures of a growing white society in southern Alberta that disapproved of mixed-race marriages, Davis and Revenge Walker separated, and she returned to her people on the Blood Reserve.

Davis then married, in 1887, Lillie Elizabeth Grier, a pioneer in her own right and the teacher at the Fort Macleod school in 1886. Insp. Sam Steele of the NWMP recalled in his memoirs an adventure in which five people were riding in the country when the team ran away, leaving all the passengers thinking that they stood a fair chance of being on their last journey. "D.W. and Mrs. Davis sat as if a runaway on the highest and worst hill in the district was an ordinary recreation. Mrs. C., in very natural terror, clung to Mrs. Davis, whose calm demeanour and soothing manner toward her companion in trouble was one of the finest things in the way of genuine pluck that I have seen."

During the 1880s Davis formed a ranching partnership with Frank Strong east of Fort Macleod. Strong died in 1889, but Davis continued operating the ranch as well as the Baker interests. He also became involved with various ventures in Fort Macleod, offering capital for the community's first newspaper and becoming the first president of the Board of Trade. He was naturalized a Canadian citizen in 1886.

In 1887 the District of Alberta of the North West Territories elected its first member of Parliament to the House of Commons in Ottawa. The employees of the Dominion government, officers of the Mounted Police, and Hudson's Bay Company officials nominated Richard Hardisty, the chief factor of the Hudson's Bay Company at Edmonton, as the Conservative candidate. When the Conservative convention met, however, it did not endorse Hardisty, but rather chose Davis. Hardisty ran as an Independent, and a Dr. Lafferty as a Liberal. Davis was elected by a handy margin and re-elected again in 1890. (Hardisty was later appointed senator.) It was an open ballot in 1887, and Mrs. Davis later recalled that it was hard to see a whole detachment of police march up and vote against her husband.

In 1896 D.W. Davis was appointed collector of customs for the Yukon Territory. He died there in 1906. Shortly after his death, Mrs. Davis and her four sons returned to southern Alberta.

Another character who added colour and legend to early Fort Macleod, and whose hotel became one of southern Alberta's most celebrated businesses, was Harry "Kamoose" Taylor. Taylor was born in England in 1842, and travelled to British Columbia in the 1860s as a missionary to the Indians. Finding little profit in that field of work, he joined the Montana hunters and traders operating in southern Alberta. Taylor and some of his companions were trading whisky in Pine Coulee in the Porcupine Hills in 1874, when they were surprised by a detachment of the newly arrived Mounted Police riding up to their camp. The Mounties not only seized their wagons and goods—rifles, liquor, and buffalo robes—but arrested them and hauled them all back to Fort Macleod for trial. Taylor pleaded not guilty to various charges of breaking the law, stoutly maintaining that he could not have broken it since there was none in the country. Col. James Macleod, in his capacity as stipendiary magistrate, however, found the traders guilty as charged and fined Taylor and another man $200, and three helpers $50 each. Taylor never forgave the police for arresting him, and according to John Higinbotham, never said anything about Colonel Macleod that was printable. Whenever Taylor saw a policeman wearing a buffalo coat, he would comment, "Look at that damned ... wearing one of the buffalo robes he stole from me."

Like other traders put out of business by the police, Harry Taylor had to find a different vocation. He eventually settled upon the hotel business and in 1881 he put up a small hotel on Fort Macleod's single street. Even as frontier hotels went, Taylor's hostelry was not impressive, being little more than a common wooden shanty. There was a kitchen with an adjoining dining room containing three or four tables and benches in rows. Next to the dining room was a large, low-ceilinged sleeping room which accommodated about thirty people—forty in a squeeze. Everybody slept on the dirt floor, wrapped in buffalo robes or blankets. The quarters were dirty and smelly, bad enough, declared Stavely Hill, "to frighten any person from sleeping there unless they were to the manner born."

By 1883 the island location of Fort Macleod was becoming a liability as floods washed away the banks and began to threaten the buildings; the fort and town were both moved to the mainland a short distance upstream. At the new site Taylor put up a more substantial hotel, a two-storey frame building with gabled windows and wooden siding. The upstairs bedrooms were initially partitioned by walls of factory cotton, a common device at the time, but not one to ensure privacy.

One of Taylor's characteristics was a lively sense of humour, and it was for his hotel that he drew up a famous list of house rules, "adopted unanimously by the Proprietor, 1 September 1882 A.D.

Two or more persons must sleep in one bed when requested by the proprietor.

No kicking regarding the quality or quantity of meals will be allowed; those who do not like the provender will get out, or be put out.

Assaults on the cook are strictly prohibited.

Quarrelsome or boisterous persons ... and all boarders who get killed, will not be allowed to remain in the House.

Meals served in own rooms will not be guaranteed in any way. Our waiters are hungry and not above temptation.

All guests are requested to rise at 6 A.M. This is imperative as the sheets are needed for tablecloth.

The Macleod Hotel was frequently the gathering place for the cattlemen in the district, and many early residents had their own favourite stories to tell about the hotel and its proprietor. John R. Craig recalled a visitor complaining about smells in the hotel and remarking to Taylor that the drains must be defective. "That cannot be," replied Harry. "There isn't a drain in the place." On another occasion, when a man protested the condition of the towel hanging above the graniteware wash basin, Taylor's reply was that 20 men had dried themselves on the towel already and he was the first to complain. And when Lord Lathom, a shareholder in the Oxley Ranche, inquired what kind of soup would be served for dinner, he was told, "Damned good soup."

But Harry's dining room had a rival, Fred Pace's restaurant, right across the street. According to Norrie Macleod, the rivalry centred principally over the merits of Fred's hop beer as against Harry's raisin cider. One day Pace and Taylor were standing in front of their respective establishments enjoying the bright sunshine, when Pace called over to Harry, "Mr. Taylor, come over and enjoy a glass of my beautiful beer." Harry turned around, displayed a faded blue patch on the seat of his overalls and retorted, "Your beautiful beer—look what your damned beer did to me the last time I drank it!"

The men of the North-West Mounted Police added another distinct element to the character of Fort Macleod, first as members of the force, and later, after discharge, as part of the ranching community. One of the early inducements for recruits to the Mounted Police was a land grant of 160 acres upon completion of service, and a number of policemen took advantage of the provision to start ranching enterprises on the plains. John Herron, the Maunsell brothers, James Walker, William Winder, J.H.G. Bray, and A.H. Lynch-Staunton were some of the policemen who remained in southern Alberta after receiving their discharges. Then, too, the early years of the Mounted Police coincided with the great expansion of the ranching industry on the American plains and north into Canada, and so it was natural that some of the police, being aware of opportunities, took up ranching. Indeed, William Winder and Insp. Albert Shurtliff, while they were still in the force, purchased stock and left the animals in the charge of others for the time being.

Former Mounted Police contributed to and reinforced certain distinct attitudes within the ranching community, perhaps most notably the attitude towards law and order. At one time, rustlers flourished in the Pincher Creek district, and a group of ranchers met to discuss the problem. The ranchers suspected who was involved, and, feelings running high, some even suggested lynching. However, one of the ranchers, F.W. Godsal, reminded everyone, "Gentlemen, the British just don't settle matters in this way." Thus the meeting ended and the cattlemen went home.

Many of the officers of the NWMP were drawn from prominent and wealthy families in eastern Canada, as were many of the ranch managers. While the Canadian ranchers drew upon the expertise and practices of American cowboys, Canadians and British dominated upper management, which made for a society quite different from the American ranching community. The officers of the Mounted Police and the members of the Canadian ranching establishment identified and shared common interests and views of the world. Both saw the Canadian West as having an upper class, and themselves as part of that class. There were many intimate ties between the two groups. James Walker was Senator Cochrane's first manager, and William Winder was a brother-in-law of Fred Stimson of the Bar U. The Mounted Police were frequent guests at ranch social gatherings, and the commanding officer of E Division in Calgary was always an honorary member of the Ranchmen's Club, the most exclusive club in the city.

There were also former Mounted Police who were persistent thorns in the side of the ranch establishment. C.E.D. Wood, editor of the Macleod *Gazette*, was an advocate of increased settlement and persistent critic of the privileges of the large leaseholders. He was a former member of the police, and prior to joining the force, had been a master at Trinity College School in Port Hope, Ontario. The famous Dave Cochrane, who had caused Dr. McEachran and the Walrond so much grief, was a much smaller thorn. Cochrane was discharged from the Mounted Police at the same time as Ed Maunsell, though the two men served in different troops and their subsequent ranching ventures were very different in scale and style. But Cochrane's feats of survival on the plains were legendary, if not exactly instructive, and he developed a reputation as a "collector" of almost anything and everything he could lay his hands on. Nothing was too useless for him to pick up for himself or someone else.

When the Maunsell brothers began setting up their ranch, they decided
to buy a light vehicle and look over the land. Although rigs were uncommon in the country, J.B. Smith, a rancher in the district, offered to sell his
old buckboard. Ed Maunsell, in checking over the wagon, found one of the
nuts holding a wheel axle was missing. Smith, not wanting to lose the sale,
suggested that Maunsell visit Dave Cochrane to see if he might have a suitable nut in his pile of junk. Smith himself would not go, as he was not on
speaking terms with Cochrane. Maunsell checked with Cochrane, but despite
a thorough search through the latter's collection, could not find a nut to fit.
Cochrane counselled Maunsell to be patient, and that same night brought
a nut to Maunsell that fitted the rig perfectly. Delighted with this turn of
events, Maunsell set out the next morning to look for Smith and conclude
the deal. On the way he met A.C. Farwell, who carried the mail between Fort
Macleod and Fort Benton. Farwell was in a rage: "Of all the doggoned luck.
If I ain't been and lost one of the nuts off my democrat. Ain't that a helluva
note. I crossed the slough and on the other side, off came the wheel. I spent
about three hours wading around in the water looking for it, and I guess it's
floated down the stream." Maunsell felt uneasy, and suspected the nut in his
pocket might have something to do with Farwell's predicament. He made a
few sympathetic remarks to Farwell, and then returned the nut to Cochrane,
saying that it would not do after all. Then he went to see Farwell again, and
suggested that the mail-carrier see Cochrane. Farwell rushed to Cochrane,
who cheerfully searched through all he had, and, sure enough, one nut fitted
Farwell's rig perfectly. Smith, however, lost the sale of his buckboard.

By the 1880s the English element had become part of the ranching community. English investment in southern Alberta was accompanied by a strong
English social presence, particularly in the foothills region between Calgary
and Pincher Creek. Farther east, the short-grass range country was developed
at a later period and was subject more to American than English influence.
The Canadian ranching establishment looked to England as a model for its
life style and regarded itself as the vanguard of a British imperial civilization.
Prints of English hunting scenes were very popular in southern Alberta ranch
homes. Much of the early writing about the foothills ranches was saturated
with this feeling of imperial destiny, a sentiment which seemed justified with
the purchase in 1919 of a ranch at Pekisko by the Prince of Wales. By that
time, however the golden age of foothills ranching had passed its zenith.

John Craig could write unblushingly of being a colonial in association
with the British aristocracy, and Maj.-Gen. T. Bland Strange, in describing
Christmas celebrations at the MCC Ranch, used the analogy of a mediaeval
castle with its lord and peasants. F.W. Godsal, a well-travelled Englishman at

Pincher Creek, was persuaded to become an Alberta rancher by Lord Lorne while he was staying with the Governor-General at Rideau Hall. F.C. Inderwick of the North Fork Ranch originally came to Canada as aide-de-camp to Governor General Lansdowne. Other prominent English or Anglo-Irish ranchers in the south included Lord Boyle, later the Earl of Shannon; his brother, the Honourable Henry Boyle, and the Honourable Lionel Brooke. Walter Skrine, of the Bar S Ranch near Mosquito Creek, was the youngest son of a landed family in Somersetshire. He married the Irish poet Moira O'Neill, who joined him in southern Alberta. The couple returned to Ireland in 1902. In addition to such huge English-owned ranching operations as the Quorn and the Oxley, there were many small ranches established by English immigrants with British financing.

Mary Inderwick, who left her home in Perth, Ontario, in 1883 to visit her brother west of Pincher Creek, and who married Charles Inderwick in 1884, wrote,

> There are so many Englishmen here and a couple of English women. The latter are of very different types, but the men are almost all nice, though they nearly all have no tact in the way they talk of Canada and Canadians. The crowning insult to me is the cool way in which they say "but we do not look on you as a Canadian" and they mistake this for a compliment.

Mrs. Inderwick apparently found the companionship of newly arrived Englishmen very trying at times, and on one occasion burst out with, "Oh, don't England me any more! I am so sick of it!" But she excused her outburst by saying, "The weather is bad and I could not get out; my domestic arrangements were not going very smoothly and this never ending laudation of England got on my nerves."

The Garnett brothers were one of the English ranching families in the Pincher Creek district, and their ranch, called The Grange, stood at the entrance to Crow's Nest Pass. In 1882, the Garnetts built a fine ranch house, the construction of which was supervised by William Gladstone, whose previous credits included Fort Whoop-Up, the whisky post. The Garnetts—Jack, Arthur, Lewis, and Lewis's wife—all tried to maintain the old-country customs. John Higinbotham and Lionel Brooke had once dined at The Grange, for which occasion the Garnett family appeared in evening dress. The eldest brother apologized and explained that it was not "a display of swank or side, but a custom to which they had rigidly adhered since their arrival in the West and designed to keep them from reverting to savagery." While the custom was accepted by many with tolerant amusement, another incident drew an entirely different reaction. On one occasion Mrs. Clarkson of the nearby Roodee Ranch sent a cowboy to the Garnett ranch with a message. The cowboy went to the front door, knocked, and Mrs. Garnett opened it. When the cowboy inquired whether Jack was in, Mrs. Garnett coolly looked him over and told him to go to the back door to deliver his message. The cowboy promptly returned to the Roodee and reported the incident to Mrs. Clarkson, who just as promptly saddled her horse, rode over to The Grange, and gave Mrs. Garnett a piece of her mind.

Within the English population of southern Alberta was a small but colourful group of remittance men. The remittance man of legend was generally one of the younger sons of an aristocratic family who was, according to Bob Edwards of the Calgary *Eye Opener*, "deported for some small lapse from grace, which in the North-West would not afford gossip for ten minutes." One such offence might have been "the unpardonable sin of preferring a pretty barmaid's society to that of a bespectacled aunt coupled with a tendency to staying out all night ... " These young men lived on cheques, or remittances, sent from home, hence the term.

Remittance men were to be found both in southern Alberta (and elsewhere in western Canada) and in the United States. Opportunities in Europe for the sons of the upper and middle classes being limited, the love of adventure, the lure of distant places, combined with assured financial security, drew them to many parts of the Empire and elsewhere.

The traditional view of the remittance man was that his money kept the local bars in business. However, many remittances were used in more productive ways and provided firm financial foundations for some of the early ranches, even though some of these operations could better be described as landed estates than as profitable businesses. In 1908 a reporter for the *Liverpool Post* wrote:

> The speech and tone of Calgary is thoroughly English, but, sad to say, Englishmen in many cases have not proved the best settlers. Too many have imagined that they had only to spend their money in placing cattle upon a ranche and employing a manager to look after them. Having done this, they turned their own attention to the pleasant expenditure of remittances from their relatives at home, until the remittance ceased and they were left to sink or swim ... There is plenty of room for the successful employment of capital in ranching in the Calgary district and along the eastern slope of the Rocky Mountains ... only businesslike

and capable management is required to ensure success. This is impossible without local knowledge and close attention to the details of the ranche's business, which does not consist of leading a life of a cowboy and galloping over the prairie.

The lack of purpose and dissipated actions of some of the remittance men tended to label them, and Englishmen generally, as a unique class. L.V. Kelly wrote in 1913:

> ... to the ordinary Western mind, a remittance man was a rich Englishman who had proven a failure in his home land and had been shipped into the raw land to kill himself in quiet or to work out his own regeneration, if possible ... A remittance man in any particular district was a local pride and his doings were magnified and improved upon for the edification of the inhabitants of other districts, who, if they too owned such a person, listened in superior silence and then came back with more outrageous doings of their own man.

What is probably the classic remittance man story came from High River, where a young Englishman had frittered away not only all the money he had brought with him, but all the subsequent remittances from England as well. Instead of the fine house and herd of prize stock which he assured his family he had, all he could show for his money was a small shack and a collection of empty bottles. One day, he received a telegram from his parents, telling him they were in Calgary en route to California, and though they had only a day to stop over, they wished to visit him and see how he was doing. The young Englishman at once rode over to confer with the manager of a well-known ranch to ask whether he might borrow the place for a day. The manager was immediately sympathetic. He not only agreed to the plan, he even offered to drive to the train station and meet the Englishman's parents for him. The ruse succeeded splendidly. The parents were duly impressed with their son's achievements, gave him another £500, and tipped the coachman handsomely for his services. This was one of Fred Stimson's favourite stories, and some even suggested that he may have had a hand in the business himself.

The era of the remittance men ended in 1914, with the outbreak of war in Europe. When many of them returned to England to enlist, Bob Edwards was prompted to remark that the remittance men may have been green, but they certainly were not yellow.

During the early days of the ranching community the white population was overwhelmingly male and widely scattered. John Higinbotham, soon after he arrived in the country in 1884, was unable to count more than four unmarried white women between High River and the boundary.

> Every arriving stage was eagerly scanned, [he wrote] sometimes from the housetops, with field glasses, for the sight of parasols, the brighter the better; then the news went quickly round, and a goodly line-up of the male sex watched with consuming interest, the passengers leaving the coach. Of course, many of the possessors of the sunshades were brides, and while anything with dresses on was welcome, those who were unattached were doubly so.

The absence of women and families, and the presence of so many young, vigorous, unattached (but not necessarily unmarried) men—cowboys, policemen, ranchers, clerks, railway construction workers and miners—supported a great deal of prostitution in the settlements, a business which involved Indian as well as white women.

For the women who lived on the ranches, life could be very lonely indeed. Loneliness was bad enough in the summer, when everyone was busy, but even worse in the winter, when the country lay stretched and frozen around them for limitless miles with nary a tree or fence or friendly chimney in sight. Evelyn Galt Springett lived with her husband at the Oxley Ranche headquarters on Willow Creek for ten years, and though she was contented and happy most of the time, she acknowledged that it was a lonely life, lacking in human companionship. "For weeks at a time we saw no one outside our own circle; but there was always plenty to do about the house and garden … the nearest shop or settlement of any sort was at Macleod, forty miles away, a long drive behind horses. We went there only when my husband had business to attend to, which was about once a month at the most."

Mary Inderwick at the North Fork Ranch wrote to her sister in 1884: "I sometimes and very often long for a woman to come and live near me … I am at the present the only white woman on this river or the next for that matter, as the next ranche is owned by a bachelor. I am 22 miles from a woman and though I like all the men and enjoy having them, I simply long to talk to a woman." Naturally, the women looked forward to trips to town for shopping, and while Calgary could supply almost anything in the way of luxuries as well as necessities, the smaller centres offered limited choice. Evelyn Springett recalled, "The Hudson's Bay Company had the monopoly of trade all through the North-West Territories. They used to say that the letters

"HBC" with which everything was stamped meant 'Here Before Christ!' and certainly some of their stuff was pretty ancient." Supplies for the ranch were usually bought by the carload. Despite the presence of thousands of head of cattle, many ranchers bought canned milk, preferring that to keeping dairy cows, or using the milk of range cows.

The isolated and lonely conditions under which many ranch families lived made everyone look forward to the various social gatherings held during the year. Chief among these were the dances and balls. In Fort Macleod dances were held frequently, nearly every fortnight, sometimes at the police barracks and sometimes in a town hall. Everyone came to the dances—cowboys, policemen, Indians, Métis, settlers, clerks, babies. Dress was informal and refreshments often consisted of tea and crackers. For lunch, the men and women sat on opposite sides of the hall, pulled mugs from washtubs carried around by the serving committee, and filled up with coffee, sandwiches, and cake.

At Priddis, southwest of Calgary, Monica Hopkins, the English wife of a rancher, noted that the elite did not attend the dances there, but she decided that "they can stay away if they want to but they miss a good deal of fun by doing so … It's simply impossible to be dignified. After our decorous Lancers these dances were simply marvellous and jolly good fun too."

Balls were formal and dignified, and accounts of these events are carefully preserved in the literature of the range. Everyone wore evening dress, the women in gowns with flowers in their hair, and the men in tails or dress uniforms. Elaborate suppers of beef, jellies, and cakes were served at carefully laid tables. There was a master of ceremonies and chaperones for the young people, who generally did not go to the balls until they were 18 or 19 years old. These affairs usually started with a grand march, followed by waltzes which were performed with grace and dignity, and sometimes, as the evening wore on and the atmosphere mellowed, old-time square dances. No smoking or drinking was allowed on the premises, and all proprieties were strictly observed. On one occasion a cowboy rode from Pincher Creek to Fort Macleod, his evening clothes carefully rolled up behind his saddle, to attend a ball. When he arrived in town, he borrowed a white shirt, but was unable to find any evening shoes. He went to the Hudson's Bay store, but the best the manager could find was a pair of low heeled black velvet slippers with red roses on the toes. The cowboy wore them for the evening.

The Mounted Police Ball in Fort Macleod was always a major social event. Attendance was by invitation only, and many guests travelled long distances, often thirty or forty miles by wagon, to attend. The barracks' billiard and reception rooms were thrown open to the guests, and for nondancing men a "smoking concert" was held in the recreation room where cigars and soft drinks were served.

Harder drinks could always be obtained at a ball or any other occasion, despite regulations and proprieties. Mary Inderwick wryly commented: "It is a prohibition country [but] ... I sometimes wonder that I do not develop a fierce thirst for whisky for 9 men out of every 10 seem to suffer from it."

Another important social event in many districts was the annual Bachelors' Ball. In March 1891 the Macleod *Gazette* advised its readers that "a meeting of bachelors will be held at Mr. Haultain's office on Friday next at 2 o'clock to arrange about an Easter dance." Most married women on the range considered it their duty to help the numerous single men in the country and invited them to dinner and generally looked after them as best they could. It was to repay these families for their kindnesses that the bachelors organized their annual ball.

There were, of course, many other dances in the range country, and these were often less decorous occasions than the balls. In February 1886 the Calgary *Herald* reported on a recent dance in that town:

> The old restaurant near I.G. Baker's store, owned by J. Ellis, has been the scene of innumerable dances—stag and breed. Such a night was last night, when one of the old-time half-breed dances took place at the above mentioned academy. As usual the half-breed fair sex were in a large minority, and when the Black Kid, instead of taking his share of the dances—say every third dance—stood up for ten consecutive sets, to the manifest exclusion of ten other—and perhaps better—men, Mr. Hank Forbes, late detective in the employ of the S.W. Stock Association at Macleod, felt it to be an outrage and said so.
>
> It is well understood all over the world, at dances, that when one gentleman insults another by saying that the other "ain't no good anyhow," the insult has to be wiped out in blood. The Black Kid proceeded to wipe it out in the customary style, and with such fair average success that Mr. Forbes felt it incumbent to return to town over the midnight plain to fetch his shooting iron and proceed in a more scientific manner.
>
> This is how at exactly five minutes after one this morning, a small but enthusiastic poker party on Atlantic Ave. was startled by a double report. The reports followed each other in quick succession and may be explained by saying that on Mr. Forbes reappearance at the soiree with his little gun, the Black Kid, who had smelt powder before at Loon Lake and other celebrated fields, jumped for the gentleman's legs in an effort

to upset him. The trigger was pulled three times, first time no report followed; second time, the bullet went through the Kid's hat into the floor; third time, grazed his arm and ribs and entered the floor, when the Kid bolted for fields and pastures new.

This is how the dance broke up last night. The Black Kid, alias John Bertrand, is well and hearty. As for Mr. Forbes, he must be having a particularly cold ride for the boundary line, with the wind at fourteen miles an hour behind him and the thermometer fast approaching the zero point. But when a man misses three such shots as he did, he deserves to be congealed a little.

The ranch wives' concern for the many single men was one expression of the range country's famous hospitality. This characteristic is well expressed by the old saying, "The latch-string is always out." Doors were seldom locked, and travellers passing by a ranch were expected to go in whether or not anyone was home. People who had been away from their homes often returned to find that someone had been in their house and made a meal or stayed the night. But the dishes were always washed and everything put away, though the cups might be turned upside-down on the saucers to indicate that someone had been there. And the owners, of course, may very well have taken advantage of similar hospitality on their own journey. When strangers arrived at a ranch, they were usually simply told to put their horses in the stable and come in for the dinner—no questions asked. The conditions of travel and the distances between settlements and houses made hospitality a necessity for survival.

Living conditions on the range were usually rough and primitive, as might be expected on any frontier. While some ranches operated with sufficient capital to provide the residents with many comforts and adequate protection from the elements, most ranchers and their families had to make do with few conveniences. But the women who came to the west were usually proud of their ability to cope with isolation and hardships, and there was little tolerance or respect on the range for whiners and the faint-hearted.

For many families, the first summer and fall on the land were spent in a tent or other makeshift shelter while the men hurried to build a cabin before winter set in. The first houses were built of logs cut from the bluffs of cottonwoods which grew along the rivers, or, more frequently, trees were cut in the foothills and either floated down the rivers or freighted out. Ernest Windham, near Carseland, decided that floating logs down the Bow River from Calgary would be faster than hauling them with a team of horses. He estimated the time the logs would arrive at his ranch, tied the logs together in a raft and rode the raft downstream. Unfortunately, he had miscalculated the speed of the Bow River's current, and arrived at his ranch in the middle of the night, hours before he was expected. But his shouts eventually roused enough help to pull the raft off the river and up onto the bank near the ranch.

When Ed Maunsell set out to build his first cabin, he thought that the other cabins in the district looked rather sombre. To get around this, he decided to peel his logs so as to have a white, clean-looking house. His neighbours warned him against doing this, but he went ahead, anyway. When it came time to chink the logs with moss and mud, Maunsell discovered that the smooth logs would not hold the chinking. The mud around the door frame gave him particular problems: he had to learn to be careful to control his temper and not slam the door, or the mud would fall from the walls.

Once the log walls were up, poles were laid across to make a frame for the roof. On top of this went layers of slough grass, mud and, finally, sod to hold everything down. Although a well-chinked cabin with a good sod roof could be quite comfortably warm in winter and cool in summer, there were certain drawbacks. After a good rain, for example, the water-soaked roof would drip long after the rain outside had stopped. John Higinbotham remarked "It might be truthfully stated that there was running water in every room." The residents might be seen carrying umbrellas inside the house as they worked at the stove, read by the lamp, or moved about the cabin dodging the assorted pails, cans and other containers positioned to catch the water and mud. Higinbotham's brothers found that the oilcloth-covered kitchen table provided excellent cover for their bed when it was tilted over the bed in a slant position. The Inderwicks on the North Fork Ranch had a different problem with their roof. One memorable winter a roaring chinook carried off one whole end of it.

Ranch women tried to make their homes as comfortable as conditions allowed. One common practice was to cover the walls with cheap factory cotton, material which was also stretched across the beams to form a ceiling. The walls, however, quickly became streaked and stained with leaking mud and water. Some women pulled apart magazines and pasted the pages on the walls, and as these pages yellowed with age and smoke, they were replaced with new pages, providing the residents with an ever-changing picture gallery and stories to read.

There were exceptions to these conditions, of course. In later years the establishment of sawmills in the Crow's Nest Pass and then the importation of lumber from British Columbia on the CPR certainly made building easier. But even in the early days there were notable houses, such as the Garnett brothers' near Pincher Creek and the mansion on the MCC Ranch. A correspondent from the Calgary *Herald* visited F.W. Godsal's ranch near Pincher Creek in

October 1902 and described the ranch and its buildings for his readers:

> Mr. Godsal's new house is well worth a paragraph by itself. It was just receiving the finishing touches during our visit, and it is safe to say there is no house in Calgary that excels it in point of convenience and up-to-dateness. It has a complete system of waterworks and sewerage, and also an independent gas system, electric bells, speaking tubes, furnace, and other twentieth century conveniences. The house is particularly well built. All the rooms are beautifully finished in cedar, the walls being so deadened with linings of prepared seaweed that ordinary sounds cannot be heard from one room to another. The main hall and drawing room are splendid apartments, the latter having a wide and homelike fire place. Mr. Godsal, being a bachelor, has devoted his energies to travelling a great deal, and during his travels he has picked up such a great number of curiosities that his house is a veritable museum.

The early residents of the range country moved about on a surprisingly regular basis, considering the distances and conditions of travel. John R. Craig was not unique in his frequent trips between southern Alberta and Montana. Travelling alone may have been risky, but it was also necessary and it continued the year round. Many early pioneers, in fact, judged the severity of winters not by the temperatures, but by the ability to travel during them. The winter of 1886-87 made even the shortest journey difficult, because of both prolonged low temperatures and heavy snowfall.

The principal route in southern Alberta was the trail from Calgary to Fort Macleod; there it divided into two branches, one leading southwest to the Pincher Creek district and the Crow's Nest Pass, and the other east towards Lethbridge and then south along the old Whoop-Up Trail to Montana and Fort Benton. This latter trail was well marked by the deep ruts of the bull trains which in the 1870s and 1880s carried cargo from Fort Benton into southern Alberta. Frederick Haultain wrote in the Macleod *Gazette* in 1888 that there was a general feeling in the country that it was time for the trails to be permanently marked and located, and that they should be based on the length of time they were in existence and the shortest distances between settlements.

The communities along the Calgary-Fort Macleod trail were served during the mid-1880s by the Royal Mail Stage Line, organized by Capt. John Stewart, who was awarded the contract to provide a weekly mail, express, and passenger service between the two centres. One of the first passengers on the stagecoach was Mrs. Duthie, the wife of the manager of the Alberta Ranche.

She came west as a young girl in 1884 to visit her sister at Pincher Creek, and after alighting from the CPR train at Calgary boarded the stagecoach for the south. The coach was a Concord, a carriage suspended on straps made from ox hides. The floor of the coach was a foot lower than the door, so passengers literally stepped down into the carriage. For this trip, Mrs. Duthie's fellow passengers were an old prospector and a woman with three small children.

When the coach and its passengers arrived at Sheep Creek, they found the water unusually high because of melting snow and rain. The driver was reluctant to cross the river, as the coach was top-heavy and he feared that it might topple over if anything struck it. But the passengers were not inclined to wait for the next week's trip, and urged the driver on. Mrs. Duthie, considering the possibility of the coach upsetting, decided to ride outside with one of the children. However, she could not share the driver's seat, as he needed all the space to handle the horses, so she climbed on top of the coach and hung onto the baggage railing with one and the the child with the other. The crossing was difficult. The horses plunged and swam, icy water washed into the coach up to the level of the seats, and the passengers inside were drenched. When they finally got across the river, they had to struggle up a steep bank, but the horses managed to pull the coach up without damage. Then the driver opened the door and fished out the shivering passengers, who all headed for the nearest settler's house where they dried their clothes. Meanwhile, the driver bored a hole in the floor of the coach to drain the water before continuing the journey. Crossing rivers, especially during spring break-up and high water, was one of the greatest hazards of travelling, and drownings were common occurrences.

The most famous stagecoach driver in the range country was Frank Pollinger, better known as Polly. Described by one oldtimer as a "magnificent driver when sober, but when drunk, sublime," Polly once boasted to Higinbotham that he could drive his coach and four where Higinbotham "couldn't trail a whip." The Lethbridge *News* called him

> one of the best drivers in the West, Montana included, and we think he thoroughly deserves it. There was probably never a more difficult performance in the driving line than that of Polly, when he drove four horses and a concord coach both down and up the terrible hill across the river, without accident, except that one wheel fell down, which made it all the more difficult. The hill must be seen, covered with ice and snow, with deep gullies on either side, and very sideling [*sic*], to appreciate what kind of driving is required to make it. But "Polly" won't take it again, and what he won't tackle should not be attempted by anyone else.

And the *Gazette* recognized his abilities during the terrible winter of 1886–87. "In all directions," it reported, "travelling is bad, the roads being heavy and drifted badly in many places … Polly continues to pull through with only an hour or two added, but then Polly can make his team do almost anything."

There were a number of stopping places along the Calgary-Fort Macleod trail where travellers could rest and get a bite to eat and the stagecoach drivers could change horses. The stopping place at Mosquito Creek was operated by Joe Trollinger, an early arrival in the district, and his wife Lucy, a Blood Indian renowned for her excellent cooking. Trollinger later sold his land to the 76 Ranch, and the property eventually passed into the hands of Fred Ings, who named it the Midway Ranch, for it was almost exactly midway between Fort Macleod and Calgary. Ings also preserved the portion of the old rutted Macleod Trail that crossed his property. This piece of trail has been maintained by his family to the present time.

One of the most popular sports on the range was horse-racing, both on a formal and informal basis. Cowboys naturally enjoyed matching their horses against each other, and there was also plenty of competition to be had among the Indians, for whom racing was one of life's great pleasures. A particularly famous race took place in Fort Macleod during the 1870s. Although time and embellishments have clouded the details, whatever has been detracted from the facts has been compensated for with legend.

The central figure in this race was Fred Kanouse, the old whisky trader, sometime rancher, blacksmith, hotelier, raconteur, and "sport." Kanouse had a great fondness for gambling. A cowboy named Fischer drifted into Fort Macleod from Montana, accompanied by a woman called August, who had eloped with him. Kanouse had a big sorrel horse which had won many races, and he took on Fischer in a match, not only winning the race, but August as well. Fischer promptly retaliated by stealing Kanouse's horse and disappearing. This was a terrible loss for Kanouse, as he had scheduled a race with some Indians and had bet heavily on the outcome, and here he was without his dependable horse. He then learned of a rancher near Pincher Creek who had several horses imported from eastern Canada, one of which was a big bay named Village Boy. Village Boy's price was steep, but the rancher agreed to lower it on the condition that since he was an ex-jockey he ride the horse in the race. Kanouse demurred, but finally agreed.

The day of the race, Village Boy's rider appeared in full racing outfit, while the Indian boy riding the competition wore little more than a confident grin. Spectators crowded the roofs of the buildings and the walls of the fort as the two horses raced past Fort Macleod, across the river and out onto the prairie. The Indian cayuse kept well in the lead, and returned to cross the finish line some time ahead of Village Boy. Kanouse was mortified at the result—and the $500 he had just dropped. In disgust, he turned Village Boy out to pasture for the winter and went hunting.

When Kanouse brought Village Boy off the range in the spring, he found the horse had developed a bad case of mange. He rubbed down the animal with a liberal application of coal oil and sulfur to kill the mange parasites, and then led Village Boy to the blacksmith shop on the edge of town to brand him, because he had been warned that horse thieves were active in the district. Kanouse took up a red-hot branding iron and pressed it on the flank of the horse. Poor Village Boy, still wet with coal oil, burst into flames and rolled over and over in the dry prairie grass, setting the range ablaze. While Kanouse shot the burning horse to put it out of its agony, townspeople struggled to stamp out the prairie fire. Kanouse, feeling rather uncomfortable in the settlement after the fire, left for the western hills.

As the range grew more settled, race tracks were laid out in such centres as Fort Macleod, Calgary, High River, Cochrane, and Medicine Hat, as well as many of the smaller communities. The races at some of these tracks were major social occasions; special trains from Calgary carried spectators to the racing meets at High River and Cochrane. Many of the ranchers had fine-blooded horses and were eager to show them off, jockeys had their colours, and excitement always ran high. There was usually plenty of betting—and drinking—on the side.

The races at Millarville, a community in the foothills southwest of Calgary, with the Rockies as a dramatic backdrop, were conducted by the Millarville Race Club, organized by a number of local ranchers in 1905. A track was laid out along the north fork of Sheep Creek on the property of two ranchers, who offered free use of the land as long as they were its proprietors. The first race in the 1908 meet was run at 10:30 AM. and the last at 5:30 PM. Horses of almost any type were given the opportunity to compete. As usual, there were many side bets, but in 1911 the club started a pari-mutuel book for five per cent. The club operated its informal and illegal pari-mutuel for many years under the very noses of the law, the judiciary, and even the church, whose members were among the faithful race-goers. (The federal government finally caught up with Millarville's races in 1951. That year, the club followed prescribed regulations, with the result that Millarville's day of races was listed in the roster of Canada's leading race centres.) The Millarville races became such an important event in the district that missing them was considered a major social gaffe. In addition to the races, there were athletic competitions for the children, and most families packed a picnic lunch to eat under the poplar trees on the grounds.

Other horse sports were popular, too—gymkhanas, polo, and hunting. The English ranchers introduced hunting to the foothills, complete with hounds, with the lowly coyote substituting for the traditional fox. Moira O'Neill wrote that "in some ways it [winter] is quite as pleasant as the summer; and when one can get coyote-hunting, summer is not to be named in the same breath with it. The fun we had coyote-hunting with our friends last Christmas-time passed all." George Ross of the Little Bow Ranch near High River organized a polo team in the late 1880s, but E. W. Wilmot of the Alberta Ranche is generally credited with bringing polo to the southern country in the early 1890s. A number of teams were formed among the ranchers and the Mounted Police in the Fort Macleod, Pincher Creek, Standoff, and Calgary districts, and they competed very successfully as far afield as Montana, British Columbia, and eastern Canada.

Among the cowboys, less aristocratic sports were also popular. The country provided excellent bird and big game hunting and the rivers and streams of the foothills afforded exceptional fishing.

Members of the ranching establishment of the foothills were predominantly Anglican, but in the early days of settlement, there were few clergymen in the district and only occasional religious services. One of the more interesting ranchers' churches was Christ Church, Millarville, built in 1896. This church was noted for its upright log construction, unlike most log buildings in which the logs are laid horizontally. The church also had a distinctive way of raising money. It financed the cost of buying about thirty calves, which were distributed among the parishioners. When the fattened calves were later sold, the profit went to the church coffers. The church even had its own brand—M96.

Monica Hopkins described a service which she attended at St. James Church in Priddis in November 1909.

> There was a good turn out of people and dogs. The latter predominated in numbers, every breed imaginable and most of them of many breeds judging from their looks … As the members of the congregation drove or rode up, our hounds would rush out and challenge their dogs to mortal combat … It was a cold day and the man who looked after the stove (a tin one which stood in the middle of the aisle) evidently was determined that we should be warm … Soon the stove was red hot and all those who had seats near it were practically cooked on one side and

a trifle under done on the other ... It was so stifling that the clergyman asked for the door to be opened and when that was done a small
procession of dogs ambled in searching for their masters ... Billie [her
husband] shooed the crowd out, much to their indignation and a couple
of fights took place before he could get the door shut. After the decorous
services at home this made a pleasant change and I think I'm going to
enjoy attending church here.

Initially, many clergymen in the range country were missionaries to the
Indians, and attended to the needs of the ranching community as circumstances permitted or demanded. The dispersive nature of the ranching community made organized church activities difficult; the church as an important
element in southern Alberta society developed principally with the expansion
of towns and farming settlement, and it was the railways that speeded this
development.

When the CPR rails reached Calgary in September 1883, there was a major
change in the orientation of the ranching community, as its centre shifted
from Fort Macleod to Calgary. The old north-south axis between Fort Benton
in Montana and Fort Macleod was replaced by the new east-west axis of the
railway. Calgary became the entry point for the ranching districts, and the
area's principal banking, communications, and provisioning centre. Fort
Macleod's role in the ranching industry and its economic aspirations were
dealt a second severe blow with the completion of a narrow-gauge railway
between the CPR mainline at Dunmore, near Medicine Hat, and the small
mining village at Lethbridge. Lethbridge then entered a period of vigorous
expansion based on the local coal mines, and as it developed, took over much
of the police work and distribution functions previously centred in Fort
Macleod.

The role of Calgary as the centre of the cattle industry was further
strengthened with the founding of the Ranchmen's Club in 1891. The club,
modelled on the St. James Club in Montreal, soon became the social headquarters for cattlemen visiting Calgary (though some might give that honour
to the Alberta Hotel, with its long, splendid bar). At first, the Ranchmen's
Club leased rooms over a restaurant on Eighth Avenue. The proprietor served
meals by dumbwaiter from the kitchen below, and was requested to put in a
good stock of beer and claret. The club later moved to its own property on
Seventh Avenue and then in 1913 to Thirteenth Avenue, where it remains in a
brick-faced building decorated with terra cotta monkeys, beavers and bucking horses.

Although the Ranchmen's experienced various financial crises, it was, from the beginning, the bastion of the economic and social elite of both the town of Calgary and the surrounding ranching community. Among its 45 original members were Fred Stimson of the Bar U; Stanley Pinhorne of the Oxley; William F. and Ernest Cochrane; W.R. Newbolt, Arthur H. Goldfinch and W.C. Alexander, all of whom ranched along the Bow River below Calgary; A. Ernest Cross of the a7 Ranche at Mosquito Creek; George and Harry B. Alexander, Irish brothers who established the Two Dot Ranche near Mosquito Creek; and T.B.H. Cochrane and C.W. Podger, ranchers along the Little Bow River. Other founding members of the Ranchmen's Club included lawyers C.C. McCaul of Fort Macleod and James Lougheed of Calgary; Mr. Justice Charles B. Rouleau; William Pearce of the Department of the Interior; and Col. A.G. Irvine of the North-West Mounted Police. Despite the name, cattlemen did not dominate the Ranchmen's, since most of them remained on their ranches, even though many also had business interests and perhaps a home in the city.

Calgary, of course, developed a reputation as a cattle town, although its style was never that of American cattle towns or even Fort Macleod. But with the Calgary Stampede, first organized in 1912, the presence of cowboys and ranchers on the streets, and finally the adoption of the white hat as the symbol of Calgary, the cowtown, or western, image stuck. And yet that image was probably drawn as much from Hollywood and American "western novels" as the experience on the ranges lying just outside the city's boundaries.

One oldtime cowboy, W.J. Wilde, expressed his feelings about the misrepresentation of the heritage of the range:

The Big White Hat

Today we try to live the past
The West's romantic days
The dress, the habits of the ranch
In many different ways.

The Stampede breathes the spirit
That was out upon the range,
The cowboys and their outfits
All show the greatest change.

The boots are a good deal splashier now,
We all go along with these,

The shirts are gaudier than we knew,
As they blow out in the breeze.

The one thing that a cowboy didn't do
In the days of long ago,
Was to wear a big ten-gallon hat,
The colour of the snow.

It is good to see the town's folk,
Dressed up in ranch attire,
With shirts of blue—and overalls,
And handkerchiefs red as fire.

But let's get back to cowboy hats,
Small, and the colour of dobie dirt,
We can string along with the shiny boots
And the multi-coloured shirt.

But to the big white hat,
Every cowboy should say "no,"
It's too much like a gopher-hole mound,
That's all covered over with snow.

Chapter Twelve

THE PASSING OF THE OLD RANGE

"Is the range passing?" the Macleod *Gazette* asked rhetorically in a 1902 review of ranching business. One the one hand, the newspaper pointed out, the range was attracting plenty of "small men," the types whom the old-time ranchers often saw as a menace; but on the other hand, some of the largest ranchers in the United States were driving in herds of cattle running into the thousands, particularly to the shortgrass ranges around Medicine Hat and the Cypress Hills, and along the Red Deer and South Saskatchewan rivers.

There were also new settlers moving into the range country who combined ranching on a small scale with farming, and who would undoubtedly make a go of it. It would be a peculiar year indeed when both branches of these settlers' businesses failed. Even many of the "real" ranches were breaking up some of the range and putting in crops of oats as they recognized the wisdom of making some provision for winter feeding, given the limit to the natural hay crop. The ranchers no longer despised the lowly dogie, the term applied to stocker cattle brought in from some district outside the range country, often Manitoba and Ontario. Whereas dogies previously were considered to have not much life in them and to be too mulish and stubborn, the ranchers now conceded that once the animals got through their first winter, they were all right.

"It is true that there are old-timers who do not look with favour upon the many new range ventures," the *Gazette* report continued. "To them the country wants what is called an 'evener'—a hard winter to even down the dogie man, and a dry summer to even up the farmers. Both prospects are bugbears in the range country."

By the late 1800s most of the range in the favoured corridor along the foothills between Calgary and the international boundary was fully occupied and stocked. Conflicts developed as farmers began to look at the land for its good soil and capacity for crops. As more settlers moved into the corridor, ranchers began to look farther afield for range, particularly to the east where the shortgrass plains, which were unattractive to farmers still not skilled in dryland farming techniques, lay largely vacant.

In June 1900 John Ware moved from his Sheep Creek location in the foothills to the Red Deer River, north of Brooks. He decided that the easiest way of getting his herd across the high spring waters of the Bow River to his new place was to use the bridge in east Calgary. He planned his drive directly through the city. Calgary, however, believed it possessed a certain sophistication and had bylaws prohibiting such use of its streets and bridges. But neither wild horses nor city bylaws could throw Ware. He simply held his peace until the middle of one night and then proceeded to push his cattle across the bridge. By the time the citizens of Calgary were up the next morning, Ware's cattle were well past the city and none of them had a drop of Bow River water on their hides.

Ware built a cabin in the Red Deer River valley, close to the river. The family was forced to move to higher ground when the river flooded one spring; Ware hauled the cabin to a new site about two miles from the river. When his wife Mildred died of typhoid and pneumonia early in 1905, he sent their five children to live with their grandmother at Blairmore. A son, Robert, later returned to work with his father on the ranch. While Robert and Ware were herding cattle one September, Ware's horse stepped in a badger hole and stumbled, rolled over on him, and crushed him. Friends brought Ware's body to Calgary where, after a large and moving funeral, he was buried in Union Cemetery.

A Calgary lawyer, R.B. Bennett, later prime minister of Canada, settled Ware's estate and amused the local folk by selling all the horses first, and then had to hire saddle horses to round up the cattle. Ware's brand and cattle were sold to Roderick Macleay and the horses went to J.T. Bell and Sons, who drove them to Medicine Hat.

The first ranch in the Cypress Hills area was that of Michael Oxarat, a short, dark-skinned Basque from the French Pyrenees, who arrived in Canada via Texas, Oregon, and Sun River, Montana. Oxarat put up a couple of crude log buildings on his chosen site in 1883, thereby establishing his squatter's rights. Sensing an opportunity to make some money from the growing demand for horses by homesteaders in Manitoba and eastern Saskatchewan, he returned to the United States and passed the winter in Oregon assembling a herd of horses. The next spring, 1884, he and his partner Charlie Thebo started north with about one hundred horses which they intended to drive to Manitoba for sale.

At the end of June Oxarat and his outfit arrived in Fort Macleod where the local customs official counted the horses, accepted Oxarat's valuation of the animals at $35 a head and collected the duty. While sojourning in the district, Oxarat met D.W. Davis of the I.G. Baker Company. Davis asked Oxarat if he were interested in taking along 100 head of the Baker Company's stock for sale in Manitoba. Oxarat agreed to do so, and concluded a deal with Davis for a number of horses which the Baker Company had imported from the United States and presumably paid duty on.

With about two hundred head of horses now, Oxarat and Thebo struck north to Calgary where trouble began to dog them and sorely tried the Basque's renowned patience and courtesy. Mr. Bannerman, the Calgary customs official, noted that Oxarat's herd contained many more head than Oxarat was known to have paid duty on, and assumed that the Basque had smuggled some of the horses into the country. Consequently, he ordered the whole herd seized. Oxarat protested loudly and bitterly, but Bannerman held firm and released the horses only when Davis and the Fort Macleod customs official had travelled to Calgary to identify the extra horses.

Unfortunately, Oxarat tarried in Calgary, giving Bannerman time to mull over the situation; for the customs official, convinced that there was something peculiar about the herd, ordered it seized again on the grounds that it was undervalued. Oxarat protested this new outrage until Bannerman reluctantly acknowledged his possible error and once again released the herd. However, there were now 45 horses missing from the herd which the customs department had been holding; most people merely assumed that they had been stolen and run out of the country. Oxarat, furious at the carelessness of the customs people, held the department responsible for his losses and threatened to take the case to the American authorities if he did not receive the satisfaction from the Canadians.

By now, however, it was late summer, and Oxarat decided that it really was time to be on his way. But first, he had to deliver 60 head to the Mount Royal Ranche west of Calgary under the terms of a deal that he had made while the horses were still under seizure. That done, he started east with about ninety head and arrived in Brandon in September.

Oxarat may have been out of Calgary, but he was certainly not out of the minds of Bannerman and the police. One day they drove out to the Mount Royal Ranche to look at the 60 horses that Oxarat had so recently delivered. To their surprise, they found 105 head with Oxarat's brand, the fleur-de-lis, and concluded that the Basque had stolen his own horses while they were being held and then sold them in addition to the other 60. The customs department ordered all 105 horses seized and the police issued a warrant for Oxarat's and Thebo's arrests.

Oxarat was arrested in Manitoba almost immediately upon his arrival at Brandon and sent back to Calgary, where he appeared before Inspector Dowling as magistrate on September 19, 1884, and was charged with larceny. The evidence was insufficient, however, and both he and Thebo were acquitted. They returned to Brandon, sold their horses, and then headed back to Montana for the winter.

The following spring, 1885, Oxarat brought in stock for his Cypress Hills ranch and started up operations. He was particularly well known for his fine Morgan horses and thoroughbreds, as well as for his generous hospitality. Despite the unpromising beginnings in Canada, he lived and worked on his ranch until 1896, when, his health failing, he decided to return to France. He died while travelling east on the train.

The matter of the stolen horses remained something of a mystery, though a letter from Maj.-Gen. T. Bland Strange of the MCC Ranch to a friend, written in February 1885, provides an interesting perspective on the case and the sale of the Mount Royal Ranche in 1886.

> As regards the Mount Royal Ranche. I better explain this ranch. Gunn wrote last year suggesting there might be some sort of amalgamation of ranches. I objected, told him Baynes was a rascal. As he & Benson chose to trust Baynes with their money and give him the support of their names, that was their affair. Baynes wrote me demanding an apology. I refused. He then threatened an action for libel. I took no notice. Now it turns out Baynes paid his private debts with the money he got for the sale of Ranche horses and gave a receipt for 20 horses he did not receive as to account for the money misappropriated—the Sec. & Treasurer Mount Royal Ranch [sic] went down & reported to Gunn & Benson who did not prosecute Baynes, but let things slide, hearing which other creditors have put the Ranch & stock in the hands of the sherriff. In addition the horses bought by Baynes had not paid duty and therefore should not have been sold. Thirdly some horses were brought in by a man named Oxhart [sic] on which full duty was not paid—They were seized by Customs officer, stolen from him, and found on Mount Royal Ranche branded with the brand of one of the shareholders Mount Royal Ranche. The police seized them. It was a mixed up swindle ...

The Spencer brothers of Teton, Montana, extended their operations into Canada during the 1890s, causing other ranchers, the North-West Mounted Police, and the customs department no end of grief. When a nephew, William Taylor, bought into the operation, it became known as the Spencer-Taylor ranch.

In 1885 William Inkerman Ross, a native of Quebec and a contractor for the CPR, joined up with Tom and Matt Brown and two other men to form the Brown Ranching Company. The outfit purchased 400 Shorthorn heifers in Ontario and shipped them by boat to Fort William, then by rail to Medicine Hat, and the following spring trailed them to range near Cardston. Twenty years later, Ross drove the Brown herd, now about three thousand head, to a new location on Rosebud Creek, north of Gleichen. By 1906 Ross was sole owner of the Brown Ranch. He sold his interests along the Rosebud and threw in with J.H. Wallace, originally of Oregon, to form the J.H. Wallace and Company outfit. Ross and Wallace bought herds of cattle from ranchers prostrated by bad winters and ran them on the huge CPR holdings east of Lethbridge, as well as on a lease along the Milk River. In 1912 the company obtained a 300,000-acre lease in southwestern Saskatchewan and southeastern Alberta, moved its cattle there, and continued to buy up leases along the Milk River, including Tony Day's and the Spencer brothers' spreads. Eventually, they controlled 500,000 acres in the area. The Ross Family were not only very successful as ranchers, but were distinguished as conservationists as well.

The English had a talent for unusual ranching ventures, as the Quorn on Sheep Creek and the MCC near Gleichen can attest. The shortgrass range was able to claim its own exotic Englishman in the person of Sir John Lister-Kaye. This young aristocrat might be called the Moreton Frewen of the Canadian range because of the breadth and brashness of his plans—and his persistent lack of success. In fact, by a strange twist of fate, Lister-Kaye became heir to one of Frewen's ventures, the Powder River Cattle Company herd known as the "76."

In 1884 Frewen and the Powder River outfit leased seven townships along Mosquito Creek in the name of E.W. Murphy, the company's foreman. The directors of the company, however, vetoed Frewen's plans to move some of their cattle to the lease. Frewen subsequently resigned from the company, but the directors later adopted his plan. On August 6, 1886, the Calgary *Herald* reported that 10,000 head of cattle were on their way north from the Powder River range, in four bunches of about 2,500 head, and each herd about two or three days apart. Each bunch was accompanied by a wagon and crew. The cattle arrived in Alberta in fine condition and half the crews then returned to Wyoming.

The "76" outfit purchased Joe Trollinger's squatter's rights at Mosquito Creek crossing and built a log house and barn there in 1887. The company suffered considerable losses in the severe winter of 1886–87, but far less than most of the other Alberta ranches. Many stockmen attributed this phenomenon to the fact that most of the cattle brought north were dry stuff (no calves) and thereby better able to withstand the ravages of the weather. The Powder River Cattle Company took a terrible battering in the United States, however, and in 1889 it sold its Canadian cattle and the 76 brand to the Canadian Agricultural Coal and Colonization Company (CACC Co.) of Sir John Lister-Kaye.

Lister-Kaye, described in the Medicine Hat *Times* as "a tall, blond blue-eyed young Englishman with a deliberate, easy manner, a fine sandy moustache, and a shapely head filled full of schemes," arrived in the Canadian North West in 1884, fresh from successfully promoting a land settlement scheme in California. The Yorkshire baronet purchased 7,000 acres near Balgonie, east of Regina, and started raising livestock. Since this Canadian venture was profitable, Lister-Kaye decided to go on to bigger things.

He rented a private railway car from the CPR and, accompanied by his wife Natica, inspected the land along the CPR mainline. In January 1887 he purchased 100,000 acres of land more or less equally distributed at sites along the railway between Calgary and Moose Jaw—Rush Lake, Swift Current, Gull Lake, Crane Lake, Kincorth, Cypress Lake, Pichie's Lake, Langdon, Namara—from the Dominion government and the CPR. He also bought the entire Canadian holdings of the Powder River Cattle Company, including 5,800 cattle. His objectives were to cultivate the land, raise horses, cattle, sheep, and pigs, and bring in English farmers and workers as colonists. Lister-Kaye first organized his massive venture as a syndicate called the Alberta Land, Stock, and Coal Company, but failed to win financial support in England. He subsequently reorganized the syndicate as the CACC Co. in 1888 and this time, with the help of D.J. Wylie, an early settler in the Maple Creek district, succeeded in bringing some of his wealthy friends and acquaintances into the venture. (Wylie took over Oxarat's ranch in 1897, managed Lister-Kaye's Kincorth operations, and later sat in the Saskatchewan legislature.)

Lister-Kaye imported good quality sheep, horses, boars, and sows and distributed his resources among his ten farms and ranches. He brought in labourers from England, and had butcher shops and abbatoirs built at Dunmore and Medicine Hat, as well as a packing plant at Calgary. At first, the venture seemed to prosper, but then its good luck began to peter out. In 1890 January and February blizzards made grazing impossible, and stocks of stored feed were quickly used up. Lister-Kaye was in eastern Canada at the time, en route to London. He knew that beef could be carried by refrigerated ships from eastern ports to Liverpool, and since it was winter across Canada, decided that beef could surely be moved across the country in railway cars. He directed his western managers to slaughter 800 head of cattle and allow the carcasses to freeze in the winter air. He then arranged with the CPR for 30 regular cars and shipped the carcasses east. Unfortunately, a thaw set in before the train reached Montreal, and practically the entire shipment of dressed meat was spoiled. It was a staggering blow to the enterprise.

After several years of losses, the directors of the CACC Co. replaced Lister-Kaye as manager and, in 1895, reorganized the syndicate as the Canada Land and Ranche Company Ltd. Almost all the shareholders of the new company held stock in the old syndicate, but they managed to freeze out Lister-Kaye. The directors hired a new manager, D.H. Andrew, and under his administration the Canada Land and Ranche Company consistently produced profits and dividends.

In 1903 the company began to divest itself of its land holdings, although it retained land at Gull Lake and Crane Lake. There was much pressure on the company from homesteaders moving into the country, but even with various troubles with settlers, government, and the weather, the shareholders continued to receive dividends and bonuses on invested capital, thanks primarily to D.H. Andrew's careful management.

Andrew's death in May 1905 was a considerable blow to the company. The directors, in their search for a replacement, chose Arthur R. Springett, formerly of the Oxley Ranche, and appointed him general manager. But the company suffered a second blow the following year when almost two-thirds of its cattle died during the terrible winter of 1906–7. Springett's major task became the winding-up of the company. In 1909 the directors disposed of the remainder of their lands to the meat-packing firm of Gordon, Ironsides, and Fares. This firm operated the "76" until the 1920s, when it sold the ranch to Canada Packers and the old "76" finally disappeared.

Ranching in the shortgrass country of southeastern Alberta and southwestern Saskatchewan (until 1905 the district of Assiniboia) developed relatively slowly during the 1890s, and then boomed between 1900 and 1905. Increased rainfall made for good pasture, and rising prices for cattle and horses made ranching in the area an attractive proposition. Maple Creek, Swift Current, and Medicine Hat became important cattle-producing areas. According to the Mounted Police report for 1899 from the Swift Current-Maple Creek area, "the district is in a most prosperous condition, and the livestock industry, in which almost the entire population may be said to be engaged, to a greater or a lesser extent, is bringing large sums of money into the country. I doubt very much whether there is in the whole of Canada a district where all the residents are in such easy circumstances as they are here."

The police report certainly exaggerated the district's prosperity, but the area was indeed growing rapidly. Between 1900 and 1905 there were 25 new ranches started by individuals, partnerships, and companies in the Swift Current district alone. A significant number of these ventures were American, for unlike the foothills ranges farther west, the shortgrass districts experienced a great influx of American money and management, and developed a somewhat different style and culture. Some American ranchers moved their operations into Canada, as they felt the pressures of the advancing tide of agricultural settlement in Texas, Oklahoma, Montana, and other states. Probably the most famous of these American outfits in Canada was the Turkey Track and its colourful manager and part-owner, "Uncle" Tony Day.

Born in southern Texas in 1849, Tony Day started his career in the cattle business by rounding up some of the wild Texas cattle and marking them with his brand. In 1875 he formed a partnership with his brother, and together they drove their cattle north to new range in Nebraska. The two brothers also took on another ranch in the Indian Territory (Oklahoma) where they ran about fifteen thousand head.

The Days were cleaned out by the disastrous winter of 1886–87, and Tony went back to Texas where he joined up with a new partner, Frank Cresswell, an English-born rancher running cattle in the Texas Panhandle. Crosswell and Day moved their cattle north in about 1895 and established a new base of operations in South Dakota. There Day trailed in about four thousand head and, within a couple of years, was running about twenty thousand in South Dakota with another ten thousand in the Panhandle. The Texas cattle were purchased from Charlie Goodnight, one of America's most colourful and successful cattlemen.

Cresswell did the steer-buying and marketing, while Day ran the ranches with strict economy and good results. Day was a well-seasoned raconteur and one of his favourite anecdotes was about the time he stayed on the ranch trailing and shipping, while Cresswell in Chicago watched the cattle market, advising him when to come on and when to hold back cattle. Only once did Day go against Cresswell's advice, figuring that other ranchers, similarly informed of a glutted market, would hold back their cattle. Day had a huge shipment ready; the cowboys were holding the cattle on a creek near the railway depot. He asked the operator to check on cancellations of stock trains at all the big shipping centres. When he was satisfied that others were holding back, Day wired Cresswell, "Cattle runnin. Can't hold em." It was just as he expected—a light run and a big market. What a celebration he and his partner put on for the boys that time!

Homesteaders moving into South Dakota prompted Cresswell and Day to move again, and in 1902 they shipped their northern cattle by rail to Billings, Montana, and then trailed them north. The Turkey Track moved across the boundary into Canada with about thirty thousand cattle and one thousand horses; it was rumoured that Day paid more than $40,000 in duty to bring his herd into the country. The Turkey Track spread its operations over a number of leases along various watercourses south of Medicine Hat, the Cypress Hills, and Maple Creek.

In 1904 the Matador Ranch extended its operations into Canada. The Matador, one of the greatest and most successful of the American ranches, was organized in 1879 by a group of Texas and New York investors. In 1882 a Scottish group based in Dundee purchased the Matador for 1.25 million dollars and within a year had about sixty thousand head of cattle, 300,000 acres of land, and range privileges on an additional 2 million acres. Much of the ranch's prosperity was attributable to the very capable management of the Scotsman Murdo Mackenzie.

In November 1904 Mackenzie secured a 21-year lease of 130,000 acres north of Rush Lake, along the South Saskatchewan River. The Matador, which had land in Texas, Colorado, Montana, and elsewhere, used northern ranges for finishing cattle. The lease along the South Saskatchewan was used just for range feeding and finishing the company's Hereford cattle, which were shipped in from the Matador's American ranches and then returned after fattening to the American market. The Matador raised no cattle in Canada. In fact, it had an unusual arrangement by which the company shipped in two-year-old cattle "in bond" to avoid paying duty, fattened them for two years, and then shipped them out again to market at Chicago.

Lord Delaval Beresford, a member of the Anglo-Irish aristocracy whose ranching interests were centered in Mexico, also expanded his operations into Canada. Beresford's distinction in the development of the Canadian range probably stemmed more from his personal life and association with a black woman than from his achievements as a rancher. At least, his personal affairs attracted more attention.

Beresford was born in 1862 into a distinguished family which traced its pedigree back many centuries and owned a large estate in Waterford county, Ireland. His four brothers were all outstanding in their own ways.

One, Lord Charles Beresford, rose to the rank of admiral in the Royal Navy and commanded at various times the Mediterranean and the Channel fleets. Lord Charles also nearly came to blows with the Prince of Wales—later King Edward VII—over the latter's *inamorata*, who was considered "the prettiest married woman in London."

Delaval Beresford landed in Mexico in the early 1880s during the cattle boom, searching for adventure and investment opportunities. Near Chihuahua he bought two ranches, considered some of the best cattle property in Mexico. Later, he also acquired land in New Mexico and property in El Paso. Although he spent much of his time on his Mexican ranches, Beresford periodically visited El Paso where he gained a reputation for heavy drinking.

In Chihuahua Beresford met Florida J. Wolfe, an attractive black woman from Illinois, who was working as a nurse in the home of the American consul. She and Beresford fell in love, and he persuaded her to give up her position and live with him. While there was little trouble in Mexico over this liaison, people in Texas did not look on it with favour. When Beresford and Wolfe travelled to El Paso, he would enter the town in one carriage while she followed in another. Once he was arrested and fined for appearing on the street with her.

Beresford, like other ranchers, felt the encroaching settlement and looked north to the Canadian ranges for relief. He leased land along the Red Deer River, shipped in 2,000 Texas steers and 900 horses, and called his operation the Mexico Ranch. The livestock ran free on the open range along the river, and Beresford's foreman hired men only for spring and fall roundups. In 1903 Hansel Gordon Jackson, just arrived in Alberta with a trainload of cattle for a ranch south of Calgary, joined the Mexico Ranch as a rider and shortly afterwards as foreman.

Much to the consternation of many ranchers and the federal government, Beresford constructed an illegal fence, enclosing nearly four townships of land and about thirty-six miles of river front. One year, during a stormy February and March, hundreds of cattle from the north and east drifted before the wind and snow and struck the fence. Being unable to reach the shelter of the river bottom, they piled up against the fence and perished.

Beresford and Wolfe visited the Canadian ranch two or three times each year. There was a widely circulated rumour that he had a wife in Ireland (he did not). It was said he tried to induce her to join him on the Canadian prairie by building on the ranch a replica of Curraghmore, the Beresford's stately home in Ireland. (Wolfe did not figure in this story; in fact, her association with Beresford was scarcely acknowledged in the United States until after his death.) Actually, the ranch house was a very simple affair of logs and driftwood salvaged from the river, roofed with split pine poles and sod, and chinked with badlands clay. There were only three rooms—the "bull room" where the ranch hands slept, a combination kitchen and living quarters for the foreman, and the "blue room" where Beresford and Wolfe slept on their visits.

In Texas Wolfe was ignored by the same newspapers that reported Beresford's whereabouts and activities and she was segregated by law. In Canada conditions were less constrained for her. Sometimes she drove from the ranch 20 miles to the railway station to meet Beresford. If he wasn't on the train, she went on to Medicine Hat and searched the bars until she found him and took him home.

In December 1906 Beresford visited the Mexico Ranch for the last time. After spending three weeks on the ranch and in Calgary and Medicine Hat, he left for the United States. The train on which he was a passenger was running late and at high speed through the foggy night. As it rounded a curve near Enderlin, North Dakota, it plowed into the rear of a switch engine on the right-of-way. Beresford and ten other persons were killed when their light wooden smoker-car was completely crushed between the heavy steel-framed cars preceding and following it.

Lord Charles Beresford, executor for Delaval's will, ordered the body shipped back to Ireland for burial and began the lengthy process of carrying out his brother's will, a task which entailed travel to Mexico, the United States, and Canada. In his will, Delaval bequeathed Wolfe approximately $10,000 from an estate that was valued in 1906 at $200,000; the rest was to be divided among the surviving brothers. Wolfe appealed to Lord Charles for a larger share, but to no avail. She considered contesting the will as Beresford's common-law wife, but found that she had no legal basis for such an action; Mexico recognized only state marriages, and Texas law, which did recognize common-law marriage, prohibited inter-racial marriage, common-law or otherwise. In the end, Wolfe received the $10,000 and an additional $5,000 on condition that she waive any further claims. Lady Flo, as Wolfe styled herself, moved from Mexico to El Paso and lived there quietly until her death in 1913.

Lord Charles Beresford decided to wind up the Mexico Ranch operations in Canada. The livestock were sold to the Circle outfit and the buildings and headquarters passed to Hansel Gordon Jackson. Jackson filed a homestead patent on the land and discovered, much to his chagrin, that he had to pay $125 for the improvements, which he had put up in the first place.

Jackson never ran a large operation—about three sections of land—but was self-sufficient and independent. He liked to shock his good, upright neighbours, though, and his gruff manner and stern outward appearance earned him the sobriquet "Happy Jack" Jackson. Much of his early life remained a mystery to his neighbours on the Red Deer River range, for he chose not to disclose it and there was an accepted rule that people did not pry into a man's history.

Certain things were known about "Happy Jack," however. He was born in North Carolina, later moved to Georgia with his family, and then to Arkansas and New Mexico where he spent his first years in the saddle keeping out sheep herders. "They warr mostly a mean lot, them greasers," Jackson once told a writer for the Calgary *Herald*, "specially when they made up their minds to keep a waterhole, but we never had to shoot many of 'em. We just got 'em on the run and larruped 'em with a doubled rope where it done them most good. They didn't come back."

Jackson watched with skepticism as homesteaders rushed into the shortgrass range country in the decade before World War I. "This is the fifth open ranch country I've seen homesteaded. Kansas had three waves of settlers before the last ones finally made it stick. I've seen aplenty of 'em put out the fire, lock the door, call the dog and hit the trail." But then, he did not like neighbours to be too close; one long-time neighbour observed that Jackson never lit a lamp without first covering the window with a cardboard. "To keep the nesters from shooting us ... seen more'n one man shot through a window in my time," Jackson explained. He always slept with a six-shooter under his pillow.

During the 1890s and early 1900s ranchers saw their ranges increasingly sliced up by homesteaders' fences. As competition for land and water forced the ranchers to make more efficient use of their grazing lands, stockmen also fenced and cross-fenced their property and leases, so that in many areas the open range virtually disappeared.

In the late 1890s a small number of cattlemen experimented with importing Mexican yearlings and two-year olds, thinking these cattle might provide good profits if they could be purchased cheaply in Mexico and then finished for market on the northern grass. H.C. McMullen, livestock agent for the CPR, reported that the Mexican cattle "made remarkable gains, as might be expected when young cattle are turned from a scant and wiry pasture that requires constant hustling on the part of the youngster to subsist into one where the matter of finding a big fill of fattening grass is but a question of loitering about awhile in almost any spot."

McMullen warned, however, that while grass was abundant during the preceding years, conditions were unusually favourable and stockmen could not always count on such good conditions to carry large numbers of animals. He further advised cattlemen to drive only well-bred Mexican cattle north, because the market for cattle from the northern ranges was chiefly for a class of animal that could be finished in condition for export directly from the range, something that could not be expected of the many scrubs being imported simply because "a ten acre lot of them could only be bought for little money."

Nevertheless, a number of cattlemen brought in large bunches of Mexican stock. George Emerson and George Lane both shipped in many Mexican cattle. Emerson declared that he had no fear of the Mexicans' wintering well, as they were naturally born rustlers and would fight a storm and take care of themselves even better than the northern cattle. Frank Cresswell and Tony Day brought several thousand Mexican head into the Medicine Hat district in spring, 1903. Gordon, Ironsides, and Fares thought so well of the Mexican cattle that they bought a 200,000-acre breeding ranch in Mexico where they planned to maintain a herd of about twenty thousand to provide well-bred stock for their operations on the Canadian range. J.H. Wallace imported about five hundred Mexican longhorns which he bought from the governor of the state of Chihuahua in 1910. He shipped them north and trailed them from Coutts to his range in southeastern Alberta. But Wallace had difficulty with his Mexican stock: "Enroute the long horns tore out many barbed wire fences. A homesteaders' dog would bark as we drove them along the road allowance and the Mexicans would gallop into the opposite fence and tear it out (along with considerable crop damage) for hundreds of yards."

Despite the many pressures on them, cattlemen generally felt optimistic about their future in the early 1900s. They had faced many challenges, but had met them, adapted, and survived. Then came the winter of 1906–7. After 20 years the disastrous winter of 1886–87 had largely receded from memory, although there were other hard winters which people remembered. An April blizzard in 1892 caused very heavy losses. Spring in 1903 was also hard: March in that year was a cold month, April brought more snow, and a May blizzard caused tremendous losses, burying cattle and horses in coulees and enormous drifts, and killing hundreds of dogies on the range, in the stockyards, and in railway cars. These winters, however, paled beside that of 1906–7. "Speaking of the killer winter of 1906–7, what you read and hear, if it is bad, believe it," wrote Chris Christianson of the Red Deer River range near Brooks.

A few cattlemen took note of nature's warnings in the fall—the beavers' extra-large caches, the horses' heavier-than-usual coats, the hares' early winter coats. The winter started early; a light snowfall in early November was followed a week later by a powerful three-day blizzard that left 15 inches of snow on the range south of Maple Creek. The temperature plunged to minus 20 degrees Fahrenheit, and there were few breaks in the freezing until late February. December brought more snow and storms. The Calgary *Herald* commented in early January that:

> Although the cold weather is seasonable it is a little too seasonable. Alberta is not in the habit of having regular spells of seasonable weather. Real Alberta weather is a month or so of warm spring-like weather and then a week or so of about 20 below. Although the weather is what might be looked for as seasonable weather, the preparations made by the ranchers go to show that seasonable weather is not looked for in Alberta.

Smaller ranchers who held their stock close by and had put up hay were able to feed their cattle, though they worried when it became necessary to start feeding stock in late November and early December instead of January as in other years. The greatest danger, though, faced strictly range cattle on ranches which had not bothered to put up hay. As the snow piled up in hard, coarse drifts, the cattle were unable to rustle feed, and when the cold northern winds blasted the range, the stock began to drift, moving before the storms and seeking shelter in coulees, behind buildings, or wherever else there was refuge from the wind. Cowboys tried to force stock up out of the river breaks and coulees in order to drive them to feed on open range which was sometimes blown clear. But the cattle seemed to sense that worse was yet to come and were difficult to handle. The cowboys also tried to keep cattle on their home ranges, but after riding day after day in the freezing, biting wind, their faces browned and continually peeling from frostbite, they gave up. The cattle would be better off drifting and finding shelter and range by themselves.

Livestock wandered into coulees where they huddled, starved, and were buried under the drifting snow. Other cattle died on top of them until the frozen corpses were piled in layers. By mid-January reports from various parts of the range country indicated that many cattle were so gaunt and hungry that they were a pitiable sight, stringing aimlessly across the prairie. So many cattle were starving that it was a question of whether a chinook or death would come first. At the CY Ranch on Belly River, north of Taber, Archie McLean reported that a vast herd of strange cattle wandered onto the ranch in search of food and shelter. In Claresholm numerous animals wandered into the town and huddled up in the lanes and alleys. Scores of dazed cattle were killed by trains, and many farmers had difficulty protecting their stacks of hay from the ravenous wanderers. Ironically, for the Shaddock family of east of Calgary, a store of hay resulted in disaster; they had put up several big stacks in the summer and fenced them, but the drifted snow allowed hungry cattle to walk right into the enclosure and on top of the stored hay. Starving cattle plunged and piled on top of each other to get at the hay, and they died in droves in the process. In other areas cattle piled up against fences and died by the hundreds.

In late January a chinook blew across the southern Alberta ranges, but it was of short duration. While it lasted, the prairie was covered with water and sloppy snow, but ten minutes after the warm wind changed direction and the temperature dropped, the prairie became one vast sheet of ice. Outside work virtually stopped as people stayed indoors. The Medicine Hat *News* reported that "it is next to impossible to secure accurate information from the outlying sections, as the low temperature has put a stop to all communication for the present."

The terrible weather took its toll of people as well. On the Red River range Lee Brainard, his young son, and another hand got so far away from their camp while trying to herd their cattle that they became lost when night fell. They struggled through a furious storm until they saw the light of a homesteader's shack. Brainard's son, however, was so exhausted that he could go no farther. Brainard picked him up in his arms and headed for the light. The other man stumbled into the shack, but Brainard did not follow. A search was made, and they found Brainard hung up and unconscious on the lower wire of a two-wire fence. Brainard survived, but the boy died. On the Maple Creek range a man became lost as he went from his house to the barn; his frozen body was discovered some distance from the buildings several days later.

The weather moderated somewhat in February and March, but it was late April before spring really began to clear away the snow and bring some relief to the battered range. The ranchers' sense of relief was quickly tempered by the devastation which appeared as the snow melted away. Thousands of dead cattle lay heaped in coulees, against fences and buildings, and scattered across the prairie. Their corpses clogged the rushing streams and even hung from the branches of trees as the snow disappeared beneath them. In his book *Wolf Willow*, Wallace Stegner called that season of 1907 "carrion spring."

The range cattle which survived were so mixed up and scattered that it took months to gather them together and sort them out. Stock from the Canadian range were found as far south as the Missouri River and, according to one report, Wyoming. East of Calgary, twelve thousand head were brought together at Deadhorse Lake, where dozens of reps from various outfits spent four days trying to sort out the different brands.

Spring saw a rash of ranch sales as many stockmen, staggered by their losses, sold out and left the business. Losses were strangely distributed. Some ranches reported losses of 70 percent, while others escaped virtually unscathed. The old Cochrane range west of Calgary came through the winter in fine condition, as did the Pincher Creek district. The shortgrass ranches, dependent as they were upon the open range, were particularly ravaged, and for some the winter was the fatal blow.

Tony Day looked around at the ruins of his herd and cried out in despair to a group of farmers at Medicine Hat, "You fellows can't possibly know, but the men of your profession have chased me from the lands of Old Mexico north, across the Canadian border, and now you can have it all." Day sold his remaining cattle, though he continued to raise horses for a few years before retiring. Some of the ranchers in the foothills belt, seeing the wreckage of the industry on the shortgrass plains, decided to stay where they were. The rancher's despair was indeed often the farmer's hope. As cattlemen withdrew, homesteaders and the Dominion government pressed forward with settlement. Elements of the old range remained, but the winter 1906–7 effectively marked the end of the open range.

The passing of the old range was evident even in the ownership of the ranches. By 1907 the first "big four" ranches—the Cochrane, Walrond, Oxley, and Bar U—had all changed hands. A new generation of cattlemen was making its mark on the industry. In 1898 Roderick Macleay of Danville, Quebec, came to High River to visit George Emerson and family friends. He was impressed with the country and its prospects, decided to stay, and determined to be a rancher. A brother, Alex, and a cousin, Douglas Riddle, joined him in 1900, and together the three men homesteaded and built up a herd of cattle that ranged from the foothills to the Red Deer River north of Brooks.

When the winter of 1906–7 discouraged his partners, Roderick Macleay persuaded George Emerson to buy out their interests, and for a number of years Emerson and Macleay imported Manitoba steers to fatten and mature on Alberta grass. As the country became more settled and fenced, Macleay bought out homesteaders and neighbouring ranches to provide for his cattle.

Emerson, however, accustomed to the old way of leasing range, objected to the land purchases. Macleay then bought out Emerson in 1914 and continued his policy of securing and buying grazing land for the future. Emerson passed his last years in High River where he died in September 1920.

The 1890s and 1900s also witnessed the development of Pat Burns' huge meat-packing and cattle empire. Born in Oshawa, Ontario, in 1846, Burns moved to Kirkfield, Ontario, with his parents when he was nine years old.

There, one of his friends was the young William Mackenzie, later Sir William Mackenzie of the railway-building firm Mackenzie and Mann.

In 1878 Pat Burns and his brother left Ontario for Manitoba, filed on homesteads near Minnedosa, and then returned to Winnipeg for the winter to earn some money with which to prove up their homesteads in spring. The only work available for Burns was blasting rock on the CPR right-of-way east of Winnipeg. He worked at this job for six months. Then, taking his savings, he bought a yoke of oxen, wagon, plow, and other supplies, and returned to his homestead. It wasn't long, however, before he started trading in meat animals. In 1886 his old friend, William Mackenzie, working on a railway in Maine, contracted him to supply meat to the construction camps. After completing this job, Mackenzie and Mann and Pat Burns started work on the Qu'Appelle, Long Lake, and Saskatchewan Railway in 1888. Mackenzie and Mann obtained the contract to construct the Calgary and Edmonton Railway in the early 1890s, and Burns followed, once again contracting to supply meat to the railway camps.

Burns bought cattle in the Calgary district for his meat camps north along the railway and also established a small slaughterhouse on the east side of the Elbow River in Calgary in 1890. The next year, encouraged by George Lane, he successfully bid for the contract to furnish beef for the Blood Indian Reserve. (His predecessor for the contract was the Cochrane Ranche.) At the same time, Burns processed about seven or eight fat cattle per day, as well as some other meat animals at Calgary, and provided wholesale meats for the city's markets. In 1897 he leased from the Canada Land and Ranche Company the buildings and land comprising an abbatoir originally built by the North West Trading Company, a subsidiary of Lister-Kaye's sprawling enterprise. In 1899 Burns bought the property for $8,000.

While still supplying beef to the railway construction camps, Burns began to look farther afield for markets. In 1891 he began shipping cattle to Vancouver and the British Columbia Interior. The mining areas of the West Kootenay proved to be a particularly good market, though transportation of beef to towns in that district was a problem. Burns shipped cattle by rail to Revelstoke, then moved them south by barge and trail. In 1897 the Macleod *Gazette* reported that Burns was "killing 800 animals a month which is practically at the rate of 10,000 a year. Even at the rate of 10,000 per annum, it will take pretty nearly all the beef cattle Southern Alberta has for export. Not the least pleasing feature of the present position is the price at which cattle are being contracted for by Mr. Burns ... $40 for all four-year-old steers without picking them."

Mackenzie and Mann contracted for the Crow's Nest Railway in the mid-1890s, and again Burns received the meat contract; not only was the contract profitable for him, but the railway provided easier access to one of his principal markets, the Kootenay district. Burns also supplied meat to Dawson City during the great gold rush. The Calgary *Herald*, in December 1897, reported that Burns had taken 85 head of prime Alberta beef cattle, shipped them from Calgary by rail to Vancouver and by boat to Skagway, and then trailed them into the Yukon Interior. The cattle packed the outfit's gear on their backs and reached Dawson City in November 1897. They dressed out at eight hundred pounds and sold at one dollar per pound. The next year Burns shipped another herd north, this time under the management of Billy Henry of High River.

By 1899 his business outstripped the capacity of his abbatoir at Calgary, and so he enlarged his facilities, adding a power plant and large cold storage rooms so that he could extend his slaughtering season, hold surplus meats for longer periods and remove some of the seasonal fluctuations in beef prices. Rather than open his new facilities with the traditional ribbon-cutting ceremony, Burns invited George Lane to swing the knocking hammer to drop the first steer before the invited guests, who were duly impressed with the efficiency of the operation and capacity of the facilities.

The year 1901 brought a further dramatic expansion of the Burns enterprise. Pat Burns travelled to London to marry Eileen Ellis, the eldest daughter of one of British Columbia's cattle barons. William Roper Hull, who was in London at the time, attended the wedding, and at the same time worked out an agreement by which Burns purchased Hull's string of meat shops, a small abbatoir, and the Bow Valley Ranch south of Calgary.

As befitting their status as two of the North West's most successful entrepreneurs, both Burns and Hull built large mansions in Calgary. Burns' 18-room house, the interior finished with eastern hardwoods and the exterior with western sandstone, cost $40,000 and became a favourite stopping place for VIPs visiting Calgary. W.R. Hull's imposing three-storey residence, Langmore, stood nearby. The house and grounds covered 22 lots. Hull shifted his activities from cattle to real estate developments in Calgary, among them the six-storey, sandstone Grain Exchange Building on Ninth Avenue.

For many years Burns' silent partner in business was William Mackenzie. Mackenzie was the means of Burns getting his first and subsequent meat contracts and he also advanced significant sums of money for Burns' livestock and meat trade. Burns assumed the money was simply a loan, repayable with principal and interest. Mackenzie thought otherwise, and considered that the money made him a partner in Burns' enterprises and entitled him to a share of the profits. There was no documentation concerning the conditions of the advances, but, as a result of his differences with Mackenzie, Burns reorganized his enterprises in 1909 and transferred them to a new company, P. Burns and Company Limited, with 3 million dollars in paid-up stock, of which Burns held 2 million and Mackenzie 1 million.

Burns' meat trade continued to expand as he moved into hogs, sheep, and then dairying, poultry, and eggs. He also put up abbatoirs at Calgary, Vancouver, Edmonton, and Prince Albert. At the same time, he was also slowly moving into ranching, though of a somewhat different style from that of the old-time ranchers. To guard against shortages in his supplies for the railway camps, he held a number of herds of steers along the railway, and cut and stacked hay to feed them during the winter. He kept no breeding stock, just steers. When the Calgary and Edmonton Railway contract was completed, Burns had a substantial band of cattle left over which he put on good grazing land east of Olds. Burns joined up with Cornelius J. Duggan and bought additional stocker cattle from nearby farmers and purchased land nine miles east of Olds. Duggan largely managed the operation of the Olds Ranch where young cattle were shipped in and fat cattle shipped out. This traffic on the Olds Ranch peaked around 1897.

Burns and Duggan also developed an extensive system of feeding camps throughout the range country, and in 1901 Fred Stimson estimated that Burns was running about ten thousand head of cattle at various places. The feeding system helped Burns further stabilize his beef supplies and prices and move away from the old system of heavy marketing of cattle with low prices in the fall. His system of cutting hay and feeding cattle was not taken up by other ranchers, who retained their custom of leaving cattle to graze on the range, knowing that the stock would lose weight but regain it in the spring. By 1904 Burns was feeding about thirty thousand three-, four-, and five-year-old steers for spring marketing, and had about 45,000 tons of stacked wild hay.

The Bow Valley Ranch was expanded as Burns purchased 17,000 acres, so that his holdings were almost continuous from the ranch to the feedlot near his Calgary packing plant. Cattle from southern Alberta could be driven north and released inside the Bow Valley Ranch fence, then rested and slowly driven on the ranch's good grass to the abbatoir.

In the early 1900s Burns embarked on a vigorous program of land acquisition. He purchased the CK Ranch, about seven miles northwest of Calgary, in 1905. The CK raised mostly sheep which could be driven conveniently to the Calgary packing plant. Shortly afterwards, Burns purchased the Ricardo Ranch, also on the north side of the Bow River near Shepard, about 15 miles east of Calgary. The Ricardo's 4,000 acres of deeded land had a five-mile frontage on the east side of the Bow River just downstream from the Bow Valley Ranch. This acquisition was followed by the purchase and amalgamation of properties southwest of the Milk River in southeastern Alberta, comprising 150,000 acres, known as the Mackie lease. Although the grass in this dry area was nutritious, carrying capacity was light—about seven thousand head.

Closer to Calgary, Burns secured a group of properties called the Kelly and Palmer Ranch, stretching in an irregular fashion from near Milo east to the Bow River. He ran about 2,500 to 4,000 head of cattle and 400 to 500 horses on the 70,000 acres of this property; the cattle were shipped to market out of Milo and Bassano. In 1910 Burns secured a grazing lease, known as the Imperial Ranch, about 30 miles north of Drumheller, fenced the property, and built up a herd of about 7,000 head. One summer he contracted local farmers around the Imperial Ranch to put up 22,000 tons of hay which he fed to the cattle the following winter in feeding camps stretching in a radius of 40 miles around the ranch. On the south side of the Red Deer River, he took over the buildings and property of the Circle outfit in 1910. Its headquarters and 110,000 acres of deeded and leased land were located near the confluence of One Tree Creek and the Red Deer River, northwest of Patricia.

Several well-known ranches in the foothills also passed into Burns' hands. He purchased the Q Ranch of John Quirk in 1910, the Walrond in 1911, and 2,500 acres south of Priddis (on which the owner, H. Ford, had run an operation known as Bradfield College, an institution for training English boys in the ways of ranching). At various times Burns also owned the Glengarry, Flying E, Bar U, "76," Rio Alto, Two Dot, and Bar S and other ranches. His landholdings at one time comprised about 240,000 acres, and it was said that he could ride from the international boundary to Calgary without ever leaving his land.

Although Canadian cattlemen long suspected that powerful middlemen were fixing prices for their stock, it was not until late in 1906 that a commission to investigate their complaints was appointed by the governments of Alberta and Manitoba. The Beef Commission began its hearings in June 1907, and held meetings at a number of centres in the two provinces. One very common complaint was that the two large firms of Pat Burns and Gordon, Ironsides, and Fares not only fixed prices, but had an arrangement whereby the former company took all the lightweight and less desirable cattle and retained the British Columbia, Yukon, and local markets, while the latter company retained the overseas trade and took all the high quality heavy cattle for export. Buyers from the two firms never bid against each other, according to cattlemen who appeared before the commission, and though the big ranchers had some leverage, the small operators where wholly at the mercy of the buyers.

At the Beef Commission's hearing at Medicine Hat it was reported that:

> Walter Huckvale, rancher for 23 years in this district, President of the Western Stock Growers' Association, stated that he always made arrangements to ship his own cattle to Liverpool. Sometimes he sold before the cattle left the country. He did this as the local buyers did not offer a sufficient price. He knew of no case where one buyer would compete against another. He made more money by shipping his own cattle.

Both Burns and Gordon, in their testimony before the commission, vehemently denied any collusion or the existence of a monopoly, even though Burns proudly asserted that were he to close down, the country would be starving in ten days. The commission tacitly acknowledged that Burns possessed a virtual monopoly of the retail meat trade, but also said that the evidence of price-fixing was circumstantial and that "for some reason there is a lack of healthy competition in the buying of cattle in this province."

The CPR was also accused of neglect in its handling of livestock. There were long delays in obtaining stock cars, sometimes the railway shipped cattle in regular closed cars instead of cattle cars, the trains took up to 80 hours running time between Medicine Hat and Winnipeg, rather than the usual 40 hours, and the railway failed to provide feed and water en route for livestock. In one case the Beef Commission heard that John Day of the Medicine Hat district:

> brought in his cattle for the 13th of November, having ordered cars a month before. There were no cars for three weeks and he held his cattle for that length of time. He had almost a trainload. It had cost him about $150 to hold the cattle and the market dropped so that he lost $1,500 to $2,000 because the cars were not furnished him for seven weeks after ordered.

One solution to their marketing problems which the cattlemen wanted to explore was changing the export meat business from one of live cattle to dressed meat. Most stockmen knew that the system of sending live cattle to Great Britain, paying heavy freight charges on trains and ships, and then having the animals slaughtered within ten days of arrival in Britain was a wasteful one. It was a bad enough system with the stall-fed, grain-finished steers of the eastern provinces, and the cattle from that area were shipped at points from which the journey to market was comparatively short and easy.

With the relatively wild, grass-fattened cattle from the western ranges, losses were much greater. A.B. Macdonald estimated that the average dressed weight of three-year-old steers on the Blood Reserve in Alberta was 843 pounds, while experienced buyers and shippers of range cattle asserted that the dressed weight of these same cattle in Great Britain would not average higher than 650 pounds. Furthermore, the shrinkage in weight was accompanied by a decline in the quality of the meat. The export of live cattle also forced the cattlemen to crowd their finished cattle upon the market within the space of a few weeks each year, pushing down prices and making extraordinary demands upon the railway. A trade in dressed and refrigerated meat would help steady both prices and market fluctuations. The cattlemen pointed to the examples of the United States and Argentina which had already established a very profitable trade in dressed meat.

The Beef Commission made a number of recommendations regarding the transportation of stock that benefitted the producers; it also recommended the appointment of a livestock commissioner to be paid by the province to assist the marketing of Alberta export cattle. The provincial Department of Agriculture named W.F. Stevens to that position and he was also able to assist the stockmen by organizing trainload shipments for small producers, pressuring the CPR to deliver cars promptly, and preparing detailed marketing reports.

As Calgary and the surrounding district developed, its residents felt the need for a fall fair exhibition, which would display their produce and achievements in the new land, not just for the local folk, but also for the many skeptics in central Canada. The Calgary Agricultural Society was organized in 1884, but limited its early activity to the shipment of agricultural products for display in Toronto. The deputy minister of the interior, A.M. Burgess, was visiting the Government farm at Fish Creek in 1884 when he was thrown from his horse and broke his collarbone. James Walker drove from Calgary to rescue him. Walker took him home and, with the deputy minister a captive listener, outlined the Agricultural Society's need for land. Walker pointed out that the Dominion land beside the Elbow River was quite distant from the centre of Calgary and would be eminently suitable for fair purposes. Burgess and Walker inspected the land together, and Burgess agreed to try to arrange for the society to acquire it at reasonable cost. In 1889 the Agricultural Society purchased 94 acres in what is now Victoria Park at $2.50 per acre and the society had a permanent home for its exhibition. (The Calgary *Herald* proposed that Burgess's horse, having performed such a fine service for the community, should be nominated for a seat in the Territorial Assembly in Regina.)

The first exhibition was actually held in 1886 for two days in October. As the new grounds were not yet available, the fair was held in a rink and an adjoining field. The fair survived its first shaky years and developed into an annual occasion. The Calgary Agricultural Society reorganized as the Inter-Western Pacific Exposition Company Limited in 1900 and changed its name again in 1911 to the Calgary Industrial Exhibition Company Limited.

One of the outstanding early exhibitions in Calgary was the Dominion Exhibition, held in 1908 under the auspices of the federal government. Twenty-six thousand people, more than the population of Calgary, attended opening day and thirty thousand passed through the gates on "American Day." The exhibition's program featured performances by the Iowa State band, horse races, a polo match, Indian races, vaudeville acts, and fireworks. A hydrogen-filled airship thrilled the crowd as it made five spectacular flights over the city before its equally spectacular explosion. (It was on the ground at the time and there were no fatalities.) Another great attraction was the Miller Brothers' Wild West Show from the United States, bringing the excitement and colour of the Old West to the heart of the Canadian range.

The Wild West Show was the family enterprise of "Colonel" George W. Miller of Oklahoma and his three flamboyant sons. George Miller died in 1903, but his sons carried on the family business and drew upon the traditions of the Rotary Club, southern planters (their mother's background), and western ranchers for their show. The Millers thrived on publicity and once invited the American National Editorial Association to hold its annual meeting at their 101 Ranch in Oklahoma, with its enormous white-pillared mansion called the White House. Naturally, the Millers received plenty of copy for their achievements and hospitality.

The family put the money from its Oklahoma ranch and oil wells into the Wild West Show and first staged rodeos and entertainments for gatherings at their ranch. In 1908, however, the brothers took their show on the road, with the eldest son, Col. Joe Miller, as the star attraction. Miller rode his favourite horse equipped with saddle and gear costing thousands of dollars. The show not only toured North America, but also Europe, where the audiences were fascinated by Miller's "cowgirls," a species unknown on the range (although many ranch women and girls rode well and helped with the cattle when necessary.) Before the Miller Brothers' show closed as a result of bankruptcy in the 1930s, it included Russian Cossacks, exotic animals such as elephants and camels, and even an opening number, called Arabia, featuring dancing girls. American historian Lewis Atherton observed that the Millers managed to "encompass stereotypes from all corners of the earth," and "in doing so, they reduced the code of the West to an absurdity never before achieved."

Among the performers in the Miller Brothers' show was a young vaude-ville cowboy, Guy Weadick, a native of New York state. Weadick learned his craft well, and was possessed of big ideas and a persuasive, talkative manner. In 1908, when the show played in Calgary, Weadick met H.C. McMullen, the CPR's livestock agent. The two agreed that Calgary was the natural location for a world-scale rodeo. After Weadick left with the Miller Brothers, he kept in touch with McMullen. Four years later he returned to press his ideas for a wild west show and rodeo in Calgary.

The city was in the midst of a feverish real estate boom and though almost anything seemed possible, Weadick could not get any firm commit-ments for his idea. McMullen suggested that he and Weadick ask George Lane for his support. The two men found Lane relaxing in the rotunda of the Alberta Hotel. He listened patiently and quietly to the enthusiastic Weadick, and then told him to come back in a few days to give Lane time to talk over the matter with a few friends. Lane put Weadick's proposal before Pat Burns, who was receptive to the idea, and he also brought in A. Ernest Cross and Ar-chie J. Mclean of Taber. Together the four men (the "Big Four" of Stampede fame) comprised a committee with Lane as chairman and agreed to back the project to the extent of $100,000.

Of the four men, Archie McLean was probably the least known. Born in Ontario in 1860, he settled in Virden, Manitoba, in his early 20s. He built up a good trade in horses in Manitoba, but in 1886 moved to southern Alberta where he became manager and a partner in the Cypress Cattle Company (CY) northwest of Taber. As well, he organized a cattle-exporting firm, Bater and Mclean.

By the early 1900s the CY was feeling the pressure of farmers moving into the district; and McLean quietly liquidated the CY operations and tem-porarily left ranching. At the urging of friends and neighbours, he ran for the legislature to represent the Lethbridge district and in 1909 was elected to the Alberta legislature as an Independent Liberal. He was re-elected in 1910 by ac-clamation, and after the fall of the scandal-battered Rutherford government, he entered the Liberal cabinet of Premier A.L. Sifton as provincial secretary and then as minister of municipal affairs. He returned to ranching after retir-ing from politics in 1921.

Ernest Cross's interests had also expanded beyond his cattle operations. An injury in 1888 caused him to return to Montreal for treatment, and his doctors advised him to stay a little closer to civilization. While in Montreal, Cross developed plans for a new venture, and upon his return in 1892 orga-nized the Calgary Brewing and Malt Company. Although Cross subsequently became very involved in the business and social life of Calgary, he never lost his interest in the cattle industry, and his a7 ranch is now one of the largest family-owned ranches in the country.

Guy Weadick was an expert at promotion and scored a major triumph when he was able to announce that the Governor General, the Duke of Connaught, and his daughter, Princess Patricia, would attend the stampede as special guests. He arranged special excursion fares to Calgary on the railways and advertised the stampede throughout the Canadian and American cattle country in order to attract the continent's best rodeo competitors. Even Pancho Villa in Mexico sent one of his best riders. The old whisky trader, Fred Kanouse, was coaxed from his retirement in Chehalis, Washington, to supervise a reconstruction of Fort Whoop-Up for the event. And just to keep things in balance, Weadick also invited every member of the original North-West Mounted Police he could locate.

Gordon, Ironsides, and Fares brought in 200 Mexican longhorn cattle pastured on the Blood Indian Reserve for the rodeo events, and 300 horses were purchased from Ad Day of Medicine Hat. The unheard-of sum of $20,000 was set aside for prizes. The stampede was obviously to be a world-class event. Weadick also made it clear that the stampede was not part of the Calgary Exhibition, even though he was using its grounds at Victoria Park.

On September 2, 1912, Labour Day, the first stampede opened with an enormous street parade assembled at the west end of Sixth Avenue. The parade marshalls and Calgary Citizens Band led off to be followed by the veteran missionary John McDougall, his trader brother, David, and 1,500 brilliantly decked Indians from the tribes of southern Alberta. The procession of Indians led one writer to comment in the Calgary *Herald*:

> One could moralize for a mile on the superiority of the red men for the purpose of pictorial procession. By the side of the iridescent Piegans, even the Big Four looked prosaic. We may have better houses, more loose change, better sanitation than they have, but when it comes to romantic toggery they leave us decidedly in the lurch. They appear to have come out of the sunset whilst in comparison we look like tourists from Bruce County.

As the parade progressed along Sixth Avenue, other units of the procession fell in behind the Indians as the different streets where they were assembled were reached. At Eighth Street the parade was joined by the Hudson's Bay men, miners, fur traders, and other old-timers; at Seventh Street by the Mounted Police and the men of 1874, led by James Walker and Major Page; at Sixth Street by the roundup outfits of cowboys; and at Fifth Street West by the labour section. It turned south on Second Street West, then proceeded along Eighth Avenue, turned south again on Second Street East, and finally dispersed near the exhibition grounds at Seventeenth Avenue. The parade contained upwards of three thousand people, stretched for over two miles, and took an hour to pass Centre Street.

The rodeo performance in the afternoon also started with a parade—this time of the competitors, judges, other officials, and the Big Four. Calgarians and visitors enthusiastically cheered on the contestants in the arena during the various events, but there was also considerable criticism of the apparent cruelty to the animals. There were many American contestants, and it was naturally expected that most of the prizes would go to them, as indeed they did.

The highlight of the stampede was the bucking bronc event which came near the end of the four-day program. This event had generated tremendous anticipation, for one of the horses in it was the great black bucker, Cyclone. During the preceding winter, Cyclone had thrown every rider who mounted him, and had already unseated 12 riders during the week of the stampede. The contestants drew their mounts and the unlucky winner of Cyclone was Tom Three Persons, a Blood Indian from southern Alberta. Well, the crowd decided, that was the end of Tom Three Persons.

Three Persons had not even expected to be present. He had been spending time in the police cells at Fort Macleod for a misdemeanour and was not due for discharge until after the stampede. Edward H. Maunsell, however, was determined that Tom Three Persons should attend the stampede and prevailed upon the inspector of Indian agencies, Glen Campbell, to secure Three Person's early release so that he could compete. Campbell intervened and the Indian entered the bucking bronc event.

The suspense was palpable as Three Person's turn drew near—he was the last contestant to ride in the finals for the world championship. This is how the *Herald* described his ride for its readers:

> The horse thrown to the ground, Tom jumped across him, placed his feet in the stirrups and with a wild whoop the black demon was up and away with the Indian rider. Bucking, twisting, swapping ends. And restoring to every artifice of the outlaw, Cyclone swept across the field. The Indian was jarred from one side of his saddle to the other, but as the crowds cheered themselves hoarse, he settled himself each time in the saddle and waited for the next lurch or twist. His bucking unable to unseat the Redskin, "Cyclone" stood at rest and reared straight up. Once it looked as though Tom was to follow the fate of his predecessors. He recovered rapidly and from that time forward "Cyclone" bucked till

he was tired. The Indian had mastered him. Thousands of spectators created a pandemonium of applause that was not equalled all week. The Princess Patricia and the Duchess of Connaught, the Stampede's Royal Guests of honour, leaned far out over the railing applauding vigorously, along with the native Canadians who had witnessed the ride in the enclosure to the north. It was a thrilling moment. Tom Three Persons had captured the championship of the world, the most coveted rodeo event for himself, for Calgary, and for Canada.

The stampede was a success by most accounts, and even earned a profit. Ironically, however, this celebration of the Old North West was not repeated in Calgary the next year, but was held in Winnipeg. Not until 1919 did Guy Weadick return to Calgary, this time to organize a Victory Stampede in celebration of the end of the Great War. It was only later that the stampede became an annual event and joined with the Calgary Exhibition. By then, however, the old days of the range were becoming a cloudy memory, overtaken by wars, revolutions, strikes, depression, and technology. Somehow, that great ride by Tom Three Persons in 1912, a marvellous demonstration of the cowboy's skill by a native of the range, appropriately marked the end of an era.

Sources

Books

Atherton, Lewis. *The Cattle Kings*. Lincoln: University of Nebraska Press, 1972.

Bennett, John W. *Northern Plainsmen: Adaptive Strategy and Agrarian Life*. Chicago: Aldine Publishing, 1970.

Braithwaite, Max. *The Western Plains*. Toronto: Natural Science of Canada Ltd., 1970.

Breen, David H. *The Canadian Prairie West and the Ranching Frontier, 1874–1924*. Toronto: University of Toronto Press, 1983.

Broadfoot, Barry. *The Pioneer Years, 1895–1914: Memories of Settlers Who Opened the West*. Toronto: Doubleday, 1976.

Canada, Sessional Papers. 1874–1905. "Annual Reports of the Northwest Mounted Police."

Careless, J.M.S. *Brown of the Globe*. Toronto: Macmillan, 1972.

Christianson, C. J. *My Life on the Range*. Lethbridge: Southern Publishing, 1968.

_____. *Early Rangemen*. Lethbridge: Southern Publishing, 1973.

Craig, John R. *Ranching with Lords and Commons*. Toronto: William Briggs, 1912.

Deane, R. Burton. *Mounted Police Life in Canada: A Record of Thirty-One Years Service*. London: Cassell, 1916.

Dobie, J. Frank. *The Longhorns*. New York: Grossett & Dunlap, 1957.

Drago, Harry. *The Great Range Wars: Violence on the Grasslands*. New York: Dodd Mead, 1970.

Dunae, Patrick A. *Gentlemen Emigrants: From the British Public Schools to the Canadian Frontier*. Vancouver: Douglas & McIntyre, 1981.

Farb, Peter. *Face of North America: The Natural History of a Continent*. New York: Harper & Row, 1964.

Foran, Max. *Calgary: An Illustrated History*. Toronto: James Lorimer, 1978.

Forbis, William H. *The Cowboys*. Alexandria, Va.: Time-Life Books, 1973.

Gould, Ed. *Ranching: Ranching in Western Canada*. Saanichton: Hancock House, 1978.

Gray, James. *Red Lights on the Prairies*. Toronto: Macmillan, 1971.

Hagell, E.F. *When the Grass Was Free*. Toronto: Ryerson Press, 1954.

Hardy, W. G. *Alberta: A Natural History*. Edmonton: Hurtig, 1967.

Higinbotham, John D. *When the West Was Young: Historical Reminiscences of the Early Canadian West*. Toronto: Ryerson Press, 1933.

Hill, Alexander Staveley. *From Home to Home: Autumn Wanderings in the North-West in the Years 1881, 1882, 1883, 1884*. (Reprint) New York: Argonaut Press, 1966.

Hopkins, Monica. *Letters from a Lady Rancher*. Calgary: Glenbow Museum, 1981.

Ings, Frederick William. *Before the Fences: Tales from the Midway Ranch*. Calgary: McAra Printing, 1980.

Johnston, Alex. *Cowboy Politics: The Western Stock Growers' Association and Its Predecessors*. Calgary: Western Stock Growers' Association, 1971.

Kelly, L.V. *The Range Men: The Story of the Ranchers and Indians of Alberta*. Toronto: William Briggs, 1913.

Long, Philip Sheridan. *The Great Canadian Range*. Calgary: Bonanza Books, 1970.

_____. *Seventy Years a Cowboy*. Saskatoon: Freeman Publishing, 1965.

Loveridge, D.M., and Potyondi, Barry. *From Wood Mountain to the Whitemud: A Historical Survey of the Grasslands National Park Area*. Ottawa: Environment Canada, 1983.

MacEwan, J.W. Grant. *Between the Red and the Rockies*. Saskatoon: Western Producer Prairie Books, 1979.

_____. *Blazing the Old Cattle Trail*. Saskatoon: Western Producer Prairie Books, 1975.

_____. *Calgary Cavalcade: From Fort to Fortune*. Edmonton: Institute of Applied Art, 1958.

_____. *John Ware's Cow Country*. Saskatoon: Western Producer Prairie Books, 1974.

_____. *Pat Burns: Cattle King*. Saskatoon: Western Producer Prairie Books, 1979.

MacInnes, C.M. *In the Shadow of the Rockies*. London: Rivingtons, 1930.

Macleod, R.C. *The NWMP and Law Enforcement, 1873–1905*. Toronto: University of Toronto Press, 1976.

Macoun, John. *Manitoba and the Great North-West*. Guelph: World Publishing, 1882.

Marshall, Duncan. *Shorthorn Cattle in Canada*. Toronto: Dominion Shorthorn Breeders Association, 1932.

McGowan, Don C. *Grassland Settlers: The Swift Current Region During the Era of the Ranching Frontier*. Regina: Canadian Plains Research Centre, 1975.

Morton, Desmond. *The Last War Drum*. (Canadian War Museum Historical Publications) Toronto: Samuel-Stevens, 1972.

Ormsby, Margaret A. *British Columbia: A History*. Toronto: Macmillan, 1971.

Osgood, Ernest Staples. *The Day of the Cattleman*. Chicago: University of Chicago Press, 1929.

The Ranchmen's Club: A Slight Historical Sketch, 1891–1952. Calgary: The Ranchmen's Club, 1953.

Rodney, William. *Kootenai Brown: His Life and Times*. 2nd ed. Sidney, B.C.: Gray's Publishing, 1973.

Sandoz, Mari. *The Cattlemen: From the Rio Grande Across the Far Marias*. New York: Hastings House, 1958.

Sheppard, Bert. *Just About Nothing*. Calgary: McAra Printing, 1977.

Skelton, Robin. *They Call It the Cariboo*. Victoria: Sono Nis Press, 1980.

Springett, Evelyn Galt. *For My Children's Children*. Montreal: Unity Press, 1937.

Steele, Samuel B. *Forty Years in Canada*. (Reprint) Scarborough: McGraw-Hill Ryerson, 1973.

Stegner, Wallace. *Wolf Willow: A History, a Story and a Memory of the Last Plains Frontier*. New York: Viking, 1962.

Strange, Thomas Bland. *Gunner Jingo's Jubilee*. London: Remington, 1893.

Symons, R.D. *Where the Wagon Led: One Man's Memories of the Cowboy's Life in the Old West*. Toronto: Doubleday, 1973.

Ward, Fay E. *The Cowboy at Work: All About His Job and How He Does It*. New York: Hastings House, 1958.

Ward, Tom. *Cowtown: An Album of Early Calgary*. Calgary: McClelland and Stewart, 1975.

Webb, Walter. *The Great Plains*. New York: Grosset and Dunlap, 1957.

Woolliams, Nina G. *Cattle Ranch: The Story of the Douglas Lake Cattle Company*. Vancouver: Douglas & McIntyre, 1979.

Articles

Baldwin, Alice Sharples. "The Sharples." *Alberta Historical Review* 5 (Spring 1957): 12.

Breen, David H. "The Canadian Prairie West and the Harmonious Settlement Interpretation." *Agricultural History* 47 (1973).

_____. "The Mounted Police and the Ranching Frontier." In *Men in Scarlet*, edited by Hugh A. Dempsey. Calgary: McClelland and Stewart, 1974.

_____. "Plain Talk from Plain Western Men." *Alberta Historical Review* 18 (Summer 1970): 1.

_____. "The Ranching Frontier in Canada, 1875–1905." In *The Prairie West to 1905: A Canadian Sourcebook*, edited by Lewis G. Thomas. Toronto: Oxford University Press, 1976.

_____. "The Turner Thesis and the Canadian West: A Closer Look at the Ranching Frontier." In *Essays on Western History*, edited by Lewis H. Thomas. Edmonton: University of Alberta Press, 1976.

Brown, Donald Edward. "The Cochrane Ranche." *Alberta Historical Review* 4 (Autumn 1956): 3.

Coppock, Kenneth R. "Another Western Pioneer Passes On [D.E. Riley]." *Canadian Cattlemen* 11 (June 1948): 6.

_____. "Early Ranching Days in the Canadian West." *Canadian Cattlemen* 1 (June 1938): 12.

Craig, Jack. "Old Ranches on the Red Deer." *Canadian Cattlemen* 21 (September 1958): 36.

Cross, Alfred Ernest. "The Roundup of 1887." *Alberta Historical Review* 13 (Spring 1965): 23.

Dempsey, Hugh A. "Calgary's First Stampede." *Alberta Historical Review* 3 (Summer 1955): 3.

_____. "Writing-On-Stone and the Boundary Patrol." In *Men in Scarlet*, edited by Hugh A. Dempsey. Calgary: McClelland and Stewart, 1974.

Eggleston, Wilfrid. "The Short Grass Prairies of Western Canada." *Canadian Geographical Journal* 50 (1955): 134.

Evans, Simon M. "American Cattlemen on the Canadian Range, 1874–1914." *Prairie Forum* 4 (Spring 1979): 121.

_____. "Spatial Aspects of the Cattle Kingdom: The First Decade, 1882–1892." In *Frontier Calgary*, edited by A. W. Rasporich and H. C. Klassen. Calgary, 1975.

Ference, E.A. "Alberta Ranching and Literature." In *Frontier Calgary*, edited by A.W. Rasporich and H. C. Klassen. Calgary, 1975.

Getty, I.A.L. "The Role of the Mounted Police Outposts in Southern Alberta." In *Men in Scarlet*, edited by Hugh A. Dempsey. Calgary: McClelland and Stewart, 1974.

Higginson, T.B. "Moira O'Neill in Alberta." *Alberta Historical Review* 5 (Spring 1957): 22.

Hughes, Katherine. "The Last Great Roundup." *Alberta Historical Review* 11 (Spring 1963): 1.

Inderwick, Mary E. "A Lady and Her Ranch." *Alberta Historical Review* 15 (Autumn 1967): 1.

Jacobs, Frank. "Rangeland Heraldry." *Canadian Cattlemen* 27 (May 1964): 12.

Jameson, Sheilagh S. "Era of the Big Ranches." *Alberta Historical Review* 18 (Winter 1970): 1.

_____. "The Quorn Ranch." *Canadian Cattlemen* 8 (September 1945): 68.

_____. "The Social Elite of the Ranch Community and Calgary." In *Frontier Calgary*, edited by A.W. Rasporich and H.C. Klassen. Calgary, 1975.

_____. "Women in the Southern Alberta Ranch Community, 1881–1914." In *The Canadian West: Social Change and Economic Development*, edited by H.C. Klassen. Calgary, 1977.

Jennings, John. "Policemen and Poachers—Indian Relations on the Ranching Frontier." In *Frontier Calgary*, edited by A.W. Rasporich and H.C. Klassen. Calgary, 1975.

Johnston, Alex. "A History of the Rangelands of Western Canada." *Journal of Range Management* 23 (1970): 3.

Kaye, Barry. "The Trade in Livestock Between the Red River Settlement and the American Frontier, 1812–1870." *Prairie Forum* 6 (Fall 1981): 163.

Laing, F.W. "Some Pioneers of the Cattle Industry." *British Columbia Historical Quarterly* 6 (October 1942): 257.

Lupton, A.A. "Cattle Ranching in Alberta, 1874–1910: Its Evolution and Migration." *Albertan Geographer* 3 (1967): 48.

MacEwan, J.W. Grant. "Background to Cattle in British Columbia." *Canadian Cattlemen* 15 (June 1952): 10.

_____. "The Matador Ranch." *Canadian Cattlemen* 2 (March 1940): 330.

_____. "The Town-Country Background at Calgary." In *Frontier Calgary*, edited by A.W. Rasporich and H.C. Klassen. Calgary, 1975.

Mathews, R.G. "The [Western Stock Growers'] Association in the Early Days." *Canadian Cattlemen* 9 (March 1947): 200.

McIntyre, William H., Jr. "A Brief History of the McIntyre Ranch." *Canadian Cattlemen* 10 (September 1947): 86.

McKay, W.H. "Early History of Medicine Hat." *Canadian Cattlemen* 13 (March 1950): 48.

McKinnon, Angus. "Bob Newbolt, Pioneer of 1884." *Canadian Cattlemen* 23 (February 1960): 10.

McLeod, D.M. "Liquor Control in the North-West Territories: The Permit System, 1870–1891." *Saskatchewan History* 16 (Autumn 1963): 81.

Mitchner, E.A. "William Pearce and Federal Government Activity in the West, 1874–1904." *Canadian Journal of Public Administration* 10 (1967): 235.

Naftel, William. "The Cochrane Ranche." In *Canadian Historic Sites* #6. Ottawa: Parks Canada, 1977.

O'Neill, Moira. "A Lady's Life on a Ranche." *Blackwood's Magazine* (January 1898).

Richardson, Ernest M. "Moreton Frewen: Cattle King with Monocle." In *Open Range Days in Old Montana and Wyoming*. Helena: Historical Society of Montana, n.d.

Riley, Dan E. "George Emerson: The Grand Old Man of the Southern Alberta Cattle Ranges." *Canadian Cattlemen* 1 (December 1938): 124.

_____. "I Remember." *Canadian Cattlemen* 1 (June 1938): 9.

Riley, Harold W. "The Growth and Development of the Western Canadian Ranching Industry." *Canadian Cattlemen* 3 (March 1941): 511.

_____. "Herbert William (Herb) Millar." *Canadian Cattlemen* 4 (March 1942): 140.

Ritchie, C.I. "Archie McLean—Pioneer Administrator: One of the 'Big Four'." *Canadian Cattlemen* 3 (March 1941): 504.

_____. "George Lane—One of the 'Big Four'." *Canadian Cattlemen* 3 (September 1940): 415.

Shepherd, George. "The Oxarat-Wylie Ranch." *Canadian Cattlemen* 5 (June 1942): 10.

Terrill, Mary. "Medicine Hat Pioneer William Mitchell, 1878–1946." *Canadian Cattlemen* 9 (December 1946): 150.

_____. " 'Uncle' Tony Day and the 'Turkey Track'." *Canadian Cattlemen* 6 (June 1943): 8.

Thomas, Lewis G. "The Rancher and the City: Calgary and the Cattlemen, 1883–1914." *Royal Society of Canada. Proceedings and Transactions.* 4th Series 6 (1968): 203.

Walker, James. "My Life in the North-West Mounted Police." *Alberta Historical Review* 8 (Winter 1964): 1.

Weadick, Guy. "Billy Henry of the Open Range." *Canadian Cattlemen* 12 (September 1949): 22.

———. "The 'Medicine Tree' Range." *Canadian Cattlemen* 14 (April 1951): 10.

———. "Range Men and Their Outfits." *Canadian Cattlemen* 12 (December 1943): 16.

Weinard, Phil. "Early High River and the Whiskey Traders." *Alberta Historical Review* 7 (Autumn 1964).

Wood, Edward J. "The Mormon Church and the Cochrane Ranche." *Canadian Cattlemen* 8 (December 1945): 128.

Local Histories

Carseland and Cheadle Historical Book Committee. *Trails to the Bow: Carseland and Cheadle Chronicles*. Carseland: Carseland and Cheadle Historical Book Committee, 1971.

Claresholm History Book Club. *Where the Wheatlands Meet the Range*. Claresholm: Claresholm History Book Club, 1974.

Cochrane and Area Historical Society. *Big Hill Country: Cochrane and Area*. Cochrane: Cochrane and Area Historical Society, 1977.

Dalemead Indus History Committee. *Tales from Two Townships: The Story of Dalemead, Indus and Shepard*. Dalemead: Dalemead Community Club, 1968.

Douglas, Helen Frances. *Echoes of Willow Creek*. Compiled by Helen Douglas and Vilda Ohler, assisted by Maud Ramage. Granum: Willow Creek Historical Society, 1965.

Finstad, Helen. *Prairie Footprints: A History of the Community in Southern Alberta Known as Pendant d'Oreille*. Pendant d'Oreille: Pendant d'Oreille Lutheran Church Women, 1970.

Fort Macleod History Book Committee. *Fort Macleod—Our Colourful Past: A History of the Town of Fort Macleod from 1874 to 1924*. Fort Macleod: Fort Macleod History Book Committee, 1977.

High River Pioneers' and Old Timers' Association. *Leaves from the Medicine Tree: A History of the Area Influenced by the Tree, and Biographies of Pioneers and Old Timers Who Came Under Its Spell Prior to 1900*. Lethbridge: High River Pioneers' and Old Timers' Association, 1960.

Hogg, Archie. *Tales and Trails, 1900–1972: A History of Longview and Surrounding Area*. Compiled and edited by East Longview Historical Society. Longview: Tales and Trails History Book Society, 1973.

Howe, Helen D. *Seventy-five Years Along the Red Deer River*. Calgary: D.W. Friesen, 1971.

Nanton and District Historical Society. *Mosquito Creek Roundup*. Nanton: Nanton and District Historical Society, 1976.

Pincher Creek Historical Society. *Prairie Grass to Mountain Pass: History of the Pioneers of Pincher Creek and District*. Pincher Creek: Pincher Creek Historical Society, 1974.

Newspapers

Brooks *Bulletin*; Calgary *Herald*; Edinburgh *Scotsman*; Macleod *Gazette*; Medicine Hat *News*; Medicine Hat *Times*; Montreal *Gazette*; Montreal *Herald*; Toronto *Globe*.